THE REBIRTH OF THE CHURCH

THE REBIRTH
OF THE CHURCH

Applying Paul's Vision for Ministry in Our Post-Christian World

EDDIE GIBBS

Baker Academic
a division of Baker Publishing Group
Grand Rapids, Michigan

Published by Baker Academic
a division of Baker Publishing Group
P.O. Box 6287, Grand Rapids, MI 49516-6287
www.bakeracademic.com

Printed in the United States of America

Library of Congress Cataloging-in-Publication Data is on file at the Library of Congress in Washington, DC.

ISBN 978-0-8010-3958-4 (pbk.)

13 14 15 16 17 18 19   7 6 5 4 3 2 1

*To my wife, Renee, who has supported me
far more than I deserve; our family; and the many
scholars and practitioners who have provided affirmation,
encouragement, and insights over many years.*

*I also thank Robert Hosack, senior acquisitions editor
at Baker Academic, for his constant support and
guidance during the past twenty years, and for the valiant work
of editor Lisa Ann Cockrel and her team of proofreaders—
Derek Keefe, Arika Theule-VanDam, and Barbara Dick.*

Contents

Introduction

In most places in the Western world, churches are declining in membership and in social influence. As they find themselves increasingly marginalized and unable to count on the support of the communities they are meant to serve, they are finding that long-established approaches to ministry—well-publicized, attractive services and a range of activities to meet the needs of individuals and families from the cradle to the grave—no longer have the broad appeal that they had for previous generations. Becoming increasingly nervous about the future, more and more church leaders are asking themselves, "Where do we go from here?"

But this is not the first time that this question has arisen. Throughout the centuries, the church has encountered times of crisis as it battled the storms of profound cultural and political upheavals. It must have been a question in the mind of the apostle Paul as he responded to God's call to take the gospel to non-Jewish peoples. He was himself a leading Jew with a reputation for zealous persecution of the new messianic movement that was causing alarm throughout the land of Israel and increasingly among the Jews of the Diaspora. How was he to translate Jesus the Jewish Messiah's message, focused on Jesus's inauguration of the reign of God, for a Greco-Roman world that was required to acknowledge Caesar as lord?

Much has been written on the need for Western churches to embrace a missional ecclesiology. But what will that look like in post-Christendom Western settings? This book outlines key responses to that question. As we endeavor to reimagine the church for the twenty-first century, we must look for models that are both biblically rooted and culturally engaged. There will be both continuity and discontinuity with the church's previous centuries of ministry and mission.

One of the serious issues concerning the church under the influence of Christendom, which has inhibited the vitality of churches throughout the Western world and beyond, has been the separation of ecclesiology from missiology. Mission became a department of the church that has often been marginalized and starved of human and financial resources. By contrast, a missional ecclesiology recognizes that mission is the heartbeat of the church precisely because the God that Christians worship is the God of mission. From Genesis to Revelation, God is the sending God, with all three persons of the Trinity engaged in that mission.

We begin by examining the cultural and political challenges facing the church today and comparing and contrasting them with those that faced churches birthed in the first century through the mission endeavors of Paul and his companions. We recognize the urban priority that characterized his missionary journeys as recorded in the Acts of the Apostles and affirm the same priority for today. At the same time, we recognize that the urban world of Paul's day was very different from urbanization in the twenty-first century. Having described the cities addressed by Paul in his letters, we identify the recurring issues he encountered in the pluralistic, neo-pagan, preindustrial cities in which he labored. These issues we then relate to the challenges facing churches today by asking to what extent they are relevant to contemporary contexts.

While we cannot reproduce pre-Christendom first-century models of church, we may have much to learn from them as we seek ways of birthing new faith communities in order to reach the 90 percent or more of the population who no longer darken the doorways of churches in most countries and in many regions within countries with higher average attendance rates.

I offer this volume with some hesitancy, in that I am neither a Pauline scholar nor a church planter. But I have been informed and inspired by a large number of biblical scholars, together with groundbreaking apostolic missionaries to the Western world. The number of these individuals and the networks they are developing are increasing significantly in our day. They are not content to simply ask the question, "Where do we go from here?" They are determined to embark on bold journeys of exploration. I pray that what I have written will serve to affirm them in many of the directions they are heading and perhaps provide a few course corrections along the way!

Eddie Gibbs

PART ONE

COMPARING CONTEXTS

1

Engaging Twenty-First-Century
Post-Christendom Contexts

There is an impressive, ever-growing body of literature highlighting that Western societies are in the midst of unprecedented cultural, economic, and political upheavals. This literature is not confined to one discipline but covers economics, political commentary, the business world, education, communication, entertainment, and religion.

In the midst of this seismic upheaval, the church cannot simply bury its head in the sand, hoping that the earthquakes and aftershocks will pass and that it will then be able to emerge and continue with business as usual. The changes taking place in Western societies have been described as all-pervasive, discontinuous, and irreversible. They are having a profound effect on churches of all traditions, including not only historic denominations but also diverse contemporary expressions of church. None is immune, although the changes are affecting different traditions in a variety of ways.

Defining *Christendom*

As the designations "pre-Christendom" and "post-Christendom" feature prominently in this book, it is appropriate to define *Christendom* at the outset. The term was developed from the Latin word referring to Christians collectively as the *corpus Christianum*, the "community of Christians."

3

With the conversion of the emperor Constantine and the Edict of Milan in AD 313, the church took on a more political aspect, reflecting the coming together of religion and the empire to present a united front against the external enemies that were threatening the Roman Empire. This relationship was further cemented with the First Council of Nicaea in 325. By 392, Christianity became the state religion of the empire, at which time pagan religions were prohibited. State recognition of Christianity had a profound impact on the significance of conversion for the bulk of the population. By the fourth century,

> Tertullian's primary concern as a leader was formation of a people around a specific set of habits and practices that came out of his engagement with Scripture. . . . This is a missional activity focused on formation of a people as God's new society. As church historian Alan Kreider points out, this focus on formation was lost in a Christendom that continued to shape the imagination of Christian life in late modernity. . . . As a result, the church entered the long period of Christendom and the focus of leadership shifted from formation of a people as an alternative society of God's future to oversight of orthodoxy, proper administration of the sacraments, and regulation of specialized and privatized ethical practices increasingly disconnected from any biblical or theological understanding of the *ecclesia* as the people of God.[1]

Christendom represents a dramatic shift in understanding, of both the church and its relationship to its broader cultural context, from that which prevailed during the first three centuries. The church shifted from a loose network of local faith communities to a much more institutional, bureaucratic, and centralized institution. *Christendom* named that amalgam of church and state bound by a common ideology in order to present a united front in the face of growing external threats.[2] Alan Hirsch identifies the following characteristics of Christendom:

1. Its mode of engagement is attractional as opposed to missional/sending. It assumes a certain centrality of the church in relation to its surrounding culture. (The missional church is a "going/sending one" and operates in the incarnational mode.)
2. A shift of focus to dedicated, sacred buildings/places of worship. . . . It became more static and institutional in form. (The early church had no recognized dedicated buildings other than houses, shops, etc.)

---

1. Roxburgh and Romanuk, *Missional Leader*, 119–20.
2. For a reassessment of the birth of Christendom, see Leithart, *Defending Constantine*, and the recent surprising change of mind of the Anabaptist scholar Craig Carter, under the influence of Augustine among others, which he reveals in his blog, *The Politics of the Cross Resurrected* (http://politicsofthecrossresurrected.blogspot.com).

3. The emergence of an institutionally recognized, professional clergy class acting primarily in a pastor-teacher mode. (In the New Testament church, people were commissioned into leadership by local churches or by an apostolic leader.)

4. The paradigm is also characterized by the institutionalization of grace in the form of sacraments administered by an institutionally authorized priesthood. (The New Testament church's form of communion was an actual [daily?] meal dedicated to Jesus in the context of everyday life and the home.)[3]

The Christendom model and its assumptions have shaped the church for the past fifteen hundred years. As a consequence, we have come to regard such churches as normative. Now that we are transitioning into a post-Christendom missional environment, we struggle to redefine church and to motivate and restructure church in order to function effectively in this changing environment.

Pre-Christendom Contexts

The biblical focus of this book is on the missionary strategy of the apostle Paul, which confines us to the first century. However, the pre-Christendom context lasted until the conversion of Emperor Constantine early in the fourth century and the eventual adoption of Christianity throughout the Roman Empire. During this period Christianity spread from the Eastern Mediterranean across North Africa and from Damascus east. Gradually it emerged from the margins of society and was no longer regarded with suspicion and hostility or even as a threat to established Roman order and the privileges that Jewish communities had established for themselves as a traditional religion. Jews existed in an ambivalent relationship with the new messianic movement. Some Hellenized Jews were, along with the Gentile "God-fearers" among them, attracted to the new movement, whereas other Jewish groups regarded the new movement as theologically heretical and socially disruptive.[4]

What is important for this study is to recognize from the outset that in our treatment of Paul we must not think we can return to that pre-Christendom period in looking for pioneering missionary strategies. Neither must we idealize

---

3. Hirsch, *Forgotten Ways*, 276–77. Bracketed question appeared in the original.

4. Scholars are divided in their assessment of the strength and duration of Christianity's appeal within the extensive Jewish population of the Diaspora. See Stark, *Rise of Christianity*, 57–59. He believes that the majority of the churches established by Paul were principally made up of Hellenized Jews.

the New Testament era by focusing on the impressive expansion of the church to the neglect of the challenges it had to face. Consequently, we will focus on lessons to be learned, not models to be reproduced.

Historical Development of Christendom

The church experienced a dramatic change in status and legitimacy following the Edict of Milan in AD 313, when embracing Christianity became a matter of birthright, instituted by infant baptism. Church became an obligatory weekly gathering at a specially designated building ruled by professional clergy. Theological orthodoxy was demanded. Moral values were made the norm, based largely on the Old Testament ethical demands and enforced by law. Within the Roman Empire, under increasing military pressure from beyond its porous borders, a sharp distinction was made between Christendom and "heathendom," with the latter regarded as ground to be conquered in order to bring about the conversion of its populace to Christianity. These measures radically changed the nature of Christianity as it had existed and spread during the previous centuries.

The primary focus of this book is on the first century, when the church expanded to non-Jewish communities, mainly around the Eastern Mediterranean, through the missionary initiatives of Paul and others. During the following two centuries, Christianity continued to expand at an exponential rate, and in the process the issue of control became a dominant concern. Darrell Guder draws attention to the expanding nature of this problem as cultural diversity became more emphatic in the wake of the disintegration of the Roman Empire.

> As Christianity became the established religion of expanding European culture, the problem of control constantly presented itself. Following the disintegration of the Roman Empire, as various cultures migrated and changed the cultural map of Europe, Christian mission was remarkably effective. These cultures rapidly became integrated into the Christian civilization over which the Latin pope exercised authority. Although originally Germanic, these various cultures (Franks, Saxons, Suevians, Allemanians, etc.) accepted (or had imposed on them) the Roman culture of established Christendom. Acknowledged as the spiritual authority in the western half of the empire, the Latin papacy claimed that it could define the doctrinal *and* cultural shape of faith as Christendom expanded its boundaries and absorbed more and more cultural groupings.[5]

5. Guder, *Continuing Conversion*, 85.

Christendom flourished throughout the medieval period and into the Renaissance with little questioning of the alliance of church and state. Each reinforced the other while at the same time creating tension between them. Church and politics were intertwined, with the assumption that Christian values undergirded society. Throughout Europe, church-state relationships remained close, with each reinforcing and seeking to gain advantage over the other, and reached their height in the medieval and early modern period when churches lived in a dynamic equilibrium with the culture.

Lesslie Newbigin points out that "Christianity had become almost the folk religion of Western Europe for almost a thousand years," during which the people of Western Europe, "hemmed in by the power of Islam to east and south, had the Gospel wrought into the very stuff of their social and personal life, so that the whole population could be conceived of as the *corpus Christianum*. That conception is the background of all the Reformation theologies" and the establishing of state churches.[6]

In subsequent centuries Christendom in the West faced new challenges when the legal basis of society became governed by canon law as decreed by the church. With power came cruelty and corruption, expressed in this period by the Crusades, to regain control of the Holy Lands; the Inquisition, to deal with religious heretics, who were regarded as a threat to the social order; and pogroms against Jews. Andy Crouch highlights the tragic cultural blind spots evident among Westerners with the Christendom mind-set: "Right in the midst of Christendom were firmly entrenched cultural practices—consider the Crusades and the relentless persecution of the Jews—that exhibited Christendom's failure to culturally embrace the gospel's key themes of peace and God's particular concern for his chosen people."[7] We might speculate, however, on what the subsequent history of Europe would have looked like without the cohesive response by Christendom to the military and religious challenge of Islam. Would it have succumbed, as did much of the Eastern Mediterranean and North Africa?

As corruption and greed became increasingly evident during the twelfth century so cracks began to appear in Christendom in the late Middle Ages, with the power struggle among three rival popes and increasing corruption and greed evident during the Renaissance. These conditions paved the way for the Reformation in the fifteenth century. These three centuries witnessed an unprecedented era of creativity, both technologically and in theological insights, many of which challenged the long-standing assumptions of the Catholic Church. This was the

6. Newbigin, extract from *The Household of God* (1953), in *Missionary Theologian*, 115.
7. Crouch, *Culture Making*, 176–77.

age of global exploration and of the dissemination of information made possible by the invention of printing. It brought about a transition from feudalism to capitalism and the rise of strong nation-states led by increasingly powerful and independent-minded monarchs. Alan Hirsch offers the following evaluation:

> For all its failings, the church, up till the time of the Enlightenment, played the overwhelmingly dominant role in the mediation of identity, meaning, purpose, and community for at least the preceding eleven centuries in the West. Its demise, or rather its forced removal, came about when two or three other major forces were on the rise. These were
> - The rise of capitalism and of the free market as the mediator of value
> - The rise of the nation-state as the mediator of protection and provision
> - The rise of science as the mediator of truth and understanding.[8]

Embedded in the Christendom cultural arrangement is an unresolved tension that surfaces in a variety of forms during the course of Christendom's long history.

> Within Christendom one is familiar with two contrasting attitudes: on the one hand there is the attitude, typical of a national Church, which accepts a certain responsibility for the whole life of the community, but fails to make it clear that the Church is a separate community marked off from the world in order to save the world; on the other hand, and in opposition to this, there is the attitude of the gathered community—the body which is very conscious of being called out from the world, and from a merely nominal Christianity, but which yet can wash its hands completely of any responsibility for those of its members who fail to fulfill its conditions for membership.[9]

Such inner tensions, plus the growing influence of secularization and pluralism in the 1960s, opened still wider the cracks within Christendom that eventually pushed the church to the margins and radically changed both the nature of Christian ministry within the church and the church's mission to the larger community. However, the Christendom cultural arrangement has proved to be amazingly resilient in the face of its weakening and fragmenting foundations. Alan Hirsch observes,

> It seems that the template of this highly institutional version of Christianity is so deeply embedded in our collective psyche that we have inadvertently put it

8. Hirsch, *Forgotten Ways*, 108.
9. Newbigin, extract from *The Household of God* (1953), in *Missionary Theologian*, 119.

beyond the pale of prophetic critique. We have so divinized this mode of church through centuries of theologizing about it that we have actually confused it with the kingdom of God, an error that seems to have plagued Catholic thinking in particular throughout the ages.[10]

In 2008, Phyllis Tickle drew attention to a continuing pattern of upheaval in her book *The Great Emergence: How Christianity Is Changing and Why*. She argues that we are currently experiencing another such dramatic upheaval and provides a historical overview identifying cultural upheavals of seismic proportions occurring approximately every 250 to 500 years. She describes the "Great Emergence" as a "monumental phenomenon." In my estimation, her description is no exaggeration, as such upheavals affect every aspect of our lives and permeate every dimension of our culture. In terms of the implication of the Great Emergence for the church, Tickle identifies at least three consistent results or corollary events.

First, a new, more vital form of Christianity does indeed emerge. Second, the organized expression of Christianity which up until then had been the dominant one is reconstituted into a more pure and less ossified expression of its former self. As a result of this usually energetic but rarely benign process, the Church actually ends up with two new creatures where once there had been only one. That is, in the course of birthing a brand-new expression of its faith and praxis, the Church also gains a grand refurbishment of the older one. The third result is of equal, if not greater, significance, though. That is, every time the incrustations of an overly established Christianity have been broken open, the faith has spread—and been spread—dramatically into new geographic and demographic areas, thereby increasing exponentially the range and depth of Christianity's reach as a result of its time of unease and distress.[11]

When one reflects on this statement in the light of the unrelenting decline of nearly every former mainline (now "old-line") denomination throughout the countries of the North Atlantic since the mid-1960s, the confidence Tickle expresses may be open to question.[12] Highly divisive theological and moral issues are tearing at the organizational fabric of many denominations—including those at the conservative end of the spectrum—by under-

10. Hirsch, *Forgotten Ways*, 51.
11. Tickle, *Great Emergence*, 17.
12. See Roozen, *Decade of Change*, for details of the FACT Survey of 28,789 randomly selected congregations, which reveals the continuation of the trend of fewer persons overall in the pews and decreasing spiritual vitality.

mining trust in leadership and eroding mutual respect and civility. Perhaps this is what Tickle had in mind when she spoke of an "energetic but rarely benign process"!

In an earlier book, *ChurchNext* (2000), I describe this comprehensive and deep-rooted cultural turbulence in terms of "discontinuous change," which has profound implications for church leadership.

> How do systems function, including church structures, in the midst of unpredict-able and discontinuous change? The quantum world is not the straightforward world of cause-and-effect relationships but of unanticipated consequences and previously unidentified potential and resources. Preparation for ministry [I would now add "and retraining in ministry"] in such a climate of uncertainty and surprise cannot best be accomplished in a highly structured environment or with predictable routines. Rather, the student [and experienced pastor] must be faced with the unexpected and the need for rapid response.[13]

Since I wrote those words at the dawn of a new millennium, we have so far witnessed three largely unanticipated upheavals that have played out on the global stage. The first is the 9/11 attacks on the World Trade Center and the Pentagon, the second is the economic meltdown that has caused the worst recession since the late 1920s and early 1930s, and the third is the social revolution impacting most of the Middle East with political, social, and economic repercussions that have left Western nations perplexed as to how to respond. And who knows how many more surprises await us just around the corner?

This is the unpredictable world in which we live. It requires renewed confi-dence in the Lord of history and being prepared to place our trust in God when earth-shaking events leave us feeling perplexed and powerless. Eschatology takes on fresh significance and urgency in such times.

Challenges Facing Churches in Post-Christendom Contexts

Across the theological spectrum, local churches and denominations are strug-gling to redefine the church in response to the new challenges they are facing. The debate and experimentation are taking place across a range of traditions, from Anabaptist to Anglican, embracing both long-standing congregations and recent church plants.

13. Gibbs, *ChurchNext*, 105.

Theological and Social Consequences of a Reductionist Gospel

As the church finds itself increasingly marginalized in post-Christendom contexts, and with the secular state moving into the spiritual vacuum that has been created, the question remains as to where society will now look for its values and vision. Traditionally these have arisen out of religious convictions shared throughout local communities and the nation as a whole. This challenge comes at a time when so much of the church in the West has succumbed to a reductionist gospel, narrowed to concern for personal piety and life after death. Darrell Guder, one of the founding members of the Gospel and Our Culture Network, expresses his concern regarding this restrictive understanding as it relates to the missional task.

> My thesis is that our particular Western reductionisms are the great challenge that the North Atlantic churches face when they seek to develop a theology of evangelistic ministry. We are not simply dealing with the need for continuing translation because of the inevitable reductions that occur in that process. *Our challenge is far broader. It is a question of the church's radical conversion from a deeply engrained reductionism whose result is a gospel that is far too small.*
>
> The reductionisms of Western Christianity are very deeply rooted in a long history. They are, by now, largely unconscious. They define the air we breathe as Western Christians. We have taken them with us into the modern missionary enterprise and left them as a dubious legacy with the churches we have founded. . . . *The reductionism we struggle with is related to our attempts to reduce the gospel, to bring it under control, to render it intellectually respectable, or to make it serve another agenda than God's purposes.*[14]

Reductionism has occurred on a number of fronts in Western Christianity. First, Christians in the West have taken the good news of the reign of God inaugurated by Christ and have individualized that message. It has been translated into personal benefits and a highly privatized form of religion, especially by people who consider self-reliance to be a high priority. Under the pervasive influence of secularization, churchgoers tend to divide the sacred from the secular and thus live in two separate worlds. The result for many is that they live by two standards: one set by the widely accepted norms of the marketplace and interpersonal relationships of today, and the other set by gospel values as presented in the New Testament. The problem is that the former prevails throughout most of their waking hours.

14. Guder, *Continuing Conversion*, 102. Italics added.

A further aspect of reductionism is to relate the good news primarily to the future life. It is the means by which individuals are forgiven for their sins and secure a place in heaven. In other words, the gospel has more to do with life after death than with how we should live as servants of Jesus here and now in preparation for his coming to reign on earth.[15]

Last, Western reductionism avoids too close an identification with Christ's suffering on the cross by placing most of its emphasis on the triumph of Christ's resurrection from the dead and ascension into heaven. Suffering is an essential part of being an apprentice of Jesus, according to his own teaching and the larger witness of the New Testament. Darrell Guder exposes the impact of reductionism on the mission of the church: "The benefits of salvation are separated from the reason for which we receive God's grace in Christ: to empower us as God's people to become Christ's witnesses."[16]

Reductionism can be understood in terms other than the establishing of no-go areas in which the gospel is not allowed by society to meddle. It can also be perceived as a diminution of influence. The radical nature of the gospel is progressively diluted to ensure the restriction of its impact on society to the point where it is simply ignored. But such a strategy fails to recognize that the churches remain one of the most viable institutions in many dysfunctional localities, with a numerical strength greater than any political party or interest group. The challenge for the churches remains one of motivation and their preparedness to set aside their internal agendas for the greater common good. We will return to this topic later in the chapter.

Again, Alan Hirsch provides trenchant comment: "Even America, for so long a bastion of a distinct and vigorous form of cultural Christendom, is now experiencing a society that is increasingly moving away from that church's sphere of influence and becoming genuinely neo-pagan." Hirsch laments: "So many of the problems in the world relate to the wrong use of power and authority—and in the history of Christendom it is to our great shame that the church has too often led the way. One has only to look at the Crusades, the Inquisition, the persecution of nonconformist Christians, and the treatment of Jews to see how we have so missed the mark in relation to authentic moral leadership."[17]

The woes afflicting Western societies in both Europe and North America give urgency to the task of reimagining the church in its post-Christendom contexts. The individualistic and consumerist churches that have arisen under

15. See Wright, *After You Believe*. For a summary, see http://trevinwax.com/2010/01/05/the-rebirth-of-virtue-an-interview-with-n-t-wright.
16. Guder, *Continuing Conversion*, 120.
17. Hirsch, *Forgotten Ways*, 118.

modernity will not prove either relevant or effective as agents of mission in the current climate—one in which society is becoming increasingly dysfunctional as communities crumble and the notion of civil society is eroded, with conflicting interest groups vying for power.

The Church's Role within Modern Dysfunctional Societies

There is growing concern in both the United States and the United Kingdom that society is fragmenting and trust in institutions of all kinds is eroding, resulting in growing dissatisfaction with leaders in every sphere: government, industry, financial institutions, and the church. Social issues have been exacerbated by the economic crisis of 2009, but they were present before this financial meltdown that spread across Europe and North America. Two influential books have drawn attention to the seriousness of the situation, one addressing the United Kingdom and the other addressing the United States.

In 2010, Phillip Blond, Anglican theologian and fellow of the National Endowment for Science, Technology and the Arts, attracted national attention with his analysis of the situation in Britain in his book *Red Tory: How Left and Right Have Broken Britain and How We Can Fix It*.[18] He highlights the failure of top-down, central-government approaches of both the Left and the Right to remedy the social and economic woes of society. He also attacks the monopolistic consumerism of those who depended on market forces to restore consumerist power to the people. Blond opens his book with a gloomy analysis of the woes of contemporary British society.

Something is seriously wrong with Britain. This is an intuition that everybody, whatever their politics, shares. But what is this malaise from which we suffer? We all know the symptoms: increasing fear, lack of trust and abundance of suspicion, long-term increase in violent crime, loneliness, recession, depression, private and public debt, family breakup, divorce, infidelity, bureaucratic and unresponsive public services, dirty hospitals, powerlessness, the rise of racism, excessive paperwork, longer and longer working hours, children who have no parent, concentrated and seemingly irremovable poverty, the permanence of inequality, teenagers with knives, teenagers being knifed, the decline of politeness, aggressive youths, the erosion of civil liberties and the increase of obsessive surveillance, public authoritarianism, private libertarianism, general pointlessness, political cynicism and pervading lack of daily joy.[19]

18. *Radical Republic*, a US edition of Blond's book, relates his analysis and argument to the United States and to US politics.
19. Blond, *Red Tory*, 1.

Blond underlines his concern by stating that his assessment "is not just a private opinion held by a disgruntled few but also a public discernment universally shared but seldom addressed."[20] He traces this social malaise back to the end of World War II, since which Britain has experienced two governing paradigms. The first, state-sponsored Keynesianism, extended from 1945 through the oil shocks of 1973 to its death in 1979. The second, neoliberalism, ran from 1979 until the global debt crisis of 2007–8. Blond argues that the consequence of these two approaches has been the creation of a bipolar nation—a bureaucratic, centralized state that presides dysfunctionally over an increasingly fragmented, disempowered, and isolated citizenry.[21]

The destruction of community from 1945 until the late 1950s left Britain financially bankrupt and with mounting social problems as hundreds of thousands of military personnel were demobilized; food and clothing shortages entailed severe rationing; and many homes, most concentrated in the deprived inner-city areas, needed to be rebuilt. ("Prefabs" that were manufactured from asbestos were regarded as a hard-to-come-by luxury.)[22] Squalid row housing was replaced by high-rise human filing cabinets, and other segments of the population were dispersed to new towns, which often lacked the most basic amenities. By contrast, older communities that—in spite of their squalor—provided mutual support and a sense of local identity were destroyed.

Phillip Blond was invited to the United States to lecture at the Tocqueville Forum at Georgetown University in March 2010.[23] That same month, political and cultural commentator David Brooks, a regular columnist for the *New York Times*, wrote an op-ed piece in which he argued that the United States is on a parallel track to becoming a broken and polarized society. "The public has contempt for the political class. Public debt is piling up at an astonishing and unrelenting pace. Middle-class wages have lagged. Unemployment will remain high. It will take years to fully recover from the financial crisis. This confluence of crises has produced a surge in vehement libertarianism. People are disgusted with Washington. The Tea Party movement rallies against big government, big business and the ruling class in general. Even beyond their ranks, there is a corrosive cynicism about public action." Aligning himself with Blond, Brooks expresses the conviction that "there is another way to respond to these problems that is more communitarian and less libertarian."[24]

20. Ibid.
21. Ibid., 9–24.
22. See Kynaston, *Austerity Britain, 1945–51* and *Family Britain, 1951–57*.
23. To access the video, see http://government.georgetown.edu/tocquevilleforum/90279.html.
24. Brooks, "Broken Society."

On both sides of the Atlantic, society has experienced a cultural revolution from the Left and a free-market revolution from the Right.

> These two revolutions talked the language of individual freedom, but they perversely ended up creating greater centralization. They created an atomized, segmented society and then the state had to come in and attempt to repair the damage.
>
> The free-market revolution didn't create the pluralistic decentralized economy. It created a centralized financial monoculture, which requires a gigantic government to audit its activities. The effort to liberate individuals from repressive social constraints didn't produce a flowering of freedom; it weakened families, increased out-of-wedlock births and turned neighbors into strangers. In Britain, you get a country with rising crime, and, as a result, four million security cameras.[25]

In his lecture, Blond argued that "the project of radical transformative conservatism is nothing less than the restoration and creation of human association, and the elevation of society and the people who form it to their proper central and sovereign station." His solution, as summarized by Brooks, is to "remoralize the market, relocalize the economy and recapitalize the poor."[26] In response to this polarization, there are moves on both sides of the Atlantic, from central government in the United Kingdom and state and city governments in the United States, to release financial resources into the hands of community leaders.[27] Such leaders are much closer to their local situations and are better able to prioritize needs in terms of financial institutions, the regeneration of local businesses, and support for local schools and community colleges. Central government must focus on the society-wide concerns it handles best, including social security and health care, national defense, upgrading the transportation infrastructure, regulating banks and financial institutions, and enhancing educational standards by allocating sufficient funding in a highly competitive

---

25. Ibid.

26. Ibid.

27. For example, see the autobiography of world-renowned business management guru Peter Drucker, *Adventures of a Bystander*, originally published in 1978. In his preface to the new edition in 1990, Drucker wrote,

> Where the prevailing doctrines preached control by big government or big business, I stressed decentralization, experimentation, and the need to create community. And where the prevailing approaches saw government and big business as the only institutions and as the "countervailing powers" of a modern society, I stressed the importance and central role of the non-profit, public-service institutions, the "third sector"—as the nurseries of independence and diversity; as guardians of values; as providers of community leadership and citizenship. . . . But I was swimming against a strong current. (vi–vii)

See also Professor Mark Mitchell of Matthew Henry College, who is also an enthusiastic advocate of localism: www.frontporchrepublic.com/about/who-we-are/contributors/mark-mitchell.

international environment and encouraging and monitoring the research and development of the next "big ideas" that will impact our global economies.

Fragmented Self

Blond writes as both a theologian and a social scientist. His analysis identifies the root causes of the woes of contemporary society, which have been widely recognized for some time. The first of these is the fragmented self. Blond's approach reflects his theological conviction that because humans are made in the image of God, their identity has more to do with their relationships than with their individual rationality. As relationship bonds are weakened and broken, so our very humanity comes under threat.

In *The Missional Church in Perspective*, Craig Van Gelder and Dwight Zscheile point out that Western societies have entered a vastly more complicated era of hybridity—signifying the mixing and fusing of cultures—especially within the context of globalization: "Locality today is rendered more complex because people live in both spatial and virtual neighborhoods."[28]

Both the fragmentation of self and the loss of neighborhood identity have weakened the position and influence of institutions that once provided neighborhood identity and cohesion. As Lesslie Newbigin discerned, writing in 1953, in such contexts, "the Churches tend to become loosely compacted fellowships within a wider semi-Christian culture, providing for only a small part of the total concerns of the members. Membership in a church may often involve only slight and relatively superficial contacts with other members, because the church is—for each member—only one among the many associations to which he belongs."[29]

In both the United Kingdom and the United States, we have witnessed the centralization of power. This has been easier to achieve in the United Kingdom due to there being no state legislatures to compete with central government. Also, the United Kingdom, being a much smaller country, brings the center closer to local contexts. It is too readily assumed that well-funded centralized projects are the best way to tackle urgent and widespread social and economic problems. But many of these government-initiated programs generate huge resource-devouring bureaucracies and spend money on the wrong priorities, because the people in charge are not sufficiently in touch with local realities.

The people on the ground are often in a much better position to direct the resources to achieve maximum impact. We have seen a recent example of this in the complaints of fishermen in the Gulf states following the catastrophic BP

28. Van Gelder and Zscheile, *Missional Church in Perspective*, 128.
29. Newbigin, extract from *Household of God* (1953), in *Missionary Theologian*, 118.

oil spill of 2010. The leaders of the shrimpers feel that they could have acted far more promptly and effectively to save their industry in the aftermath of the disaster, and they blame not only BP but also their own federal government for the slow and inadequate response.

More and more, significant change is taking place from the ground level up. As I write this chapter, two items have caught my attention on the national news. In one case, a seven-year-old named Joshua, who was just learning Braille, had the idea of putting Braille notices on all the produce at his local Trader Joe's grocery store so that he could share in the shopping experience with his parents. The store adopted his idea, which has now spread to the branches of Fresh and Easy (the US expansion of the United Kingdom's Tesco chain). In many other initiatives—for instance, in the provision of food and clothing for the homeless or in tree-planting projects—it is children who are leading the way. These are today's entrepreneurs who dramatically emphasize the need for imagination and creativity in education.

It is against this cultural backdrop that we see how so many of our inherited denominations are out of sync with the significant and, I believe, irreversible cultural trends of the twenty-first century. Van Gelder and Zscheile conclude, "Many denominations and judicatories still reflect the organizational assumptions of industrial bureaucracies in their (1) centralization of authority, communication, and resources; (2) regulatory approach to controlling and managing ministry; and (3) rigidity."[30]

If the Left believes that government programs will provide the answer, the Right has confidence in the power of market forces to turn around the economy, increase the standard of living, and thereby solve our urgent social problems. They believe that the very rich will pour their resources into the multinational companies to bring about a "trickle-down" benefit. The problem here is that it is more likely to be a "trickle" down than an inundation, human nature being what it is! As I write this chapter, we see this in the rise in gas prices, caused not by shortage of supply but by speculators taking advantage of the fear generated by an uncertain international situation.

We know that the big companies do not create most new jobs. Small companies with less than fifty employees in fact generate 80 percent of new jobs. Local banks need to provide financial backing and professional support to maximize these small companies' chances of success. Under current conditions, both the United Kingdom and the United States are experiencing increasing social inequality. The gap between the richest and the poorest continues to widen, with the vast majority of the profit remaining with the wealthiest.

30. Van Gelder and Zscheile, *Missional Church in Perspective*, 159.

Summarizing Phillip Blond's solution, David Brooks writes, "Essentially, Blond would take a political culture that has been oriented around individual choice and replace it with one oriented around relationships and associations." Brooks compares and contrasts the political cultures of the United Kingdom and the United States: "Britain is always going to be more hospitable to communitarian politics than the more libertarian United States. But people are social creatures here, too. American society has been atomized by the twin revolutions here, too. This country, too, needs a fresh political wind. America, too, is suffering a devastating crisis of authority. The only way to restore trust is from the local community on up."[31] I agree with Brooks that the challenges are greater here in the United States, owing to its tradition of rugged individualism in reaction to the controls of central government and to a number of space-related factors: the fact that the country is far larger, that family support structures are broken by distance, and that big cities have spread through the initiatives of property developers whose plans have shown little regard for providing community and "third-space" locations where neighbors can socialize and enjoy local amenities. (In fairness, it must be added that such property developers are only responding to the consumer demand for privacy and security.) Together, these factors will make it all the more difficult to change political structures in the United States.

Collapse of Culture and Erosion of Civil Society

According to Phillip Blond, the gradual erosion of a sense of place, where individuals feel that they belong and are known, is another root cause of the problems facing Western societies. Today's fragmented self travels from location to location and between networks of associates but belongs nowhere. The "nowhere person" lacks both accountability and support, with those who have contact with the individual knowing only a segment of that person's true self. The loss of place also fragments communities into competing groups, with a consequent loss of common vision, mutual concern and understanding, and civility toward one another.

Blond considers civil society to include "everything that ordinary citizens do that is not reducible to the imposed activities of the central state or the compulsion and determination of the marketplace."[32] Although groups abound at the local level, each has a narrow focus and insists on promoting its own rights over against the rights of groups with opposing views or different pri-

---

31. Brooks, "Broken Society."
32. Blond, *Red Tory*, 3.

orities. At the same time, however, "the culture of individual rights has also grown up at the expense of very important group rights or religious and other corporate bodies that preserve and encourage rights that may be at odds with the nihilistic culture of liberalism."[33] Western societies have been sliding toward a comprehensive relativism in which standards of good and bad, of right and wrong, are grounded in the opinions of individuals. Tolerance has become an absolute in a culture where anything goes. The exercise of discernment is frequently interpreted as an expression of judgmentalism.

The resulting erosion of social capital is having a devastating effect on our capacity to bring about significant social transformation at the local level, where the turnaround must begin. Before such a comprehensive change can take place, social capital must be restored. For Blond, *social capital* is "a term that tries to express the value, both in terms of money and quality of life, that we derive from our reciprocal social relationships through friendships, contacts, families, groups, neighborliness, political membership, sports teams and churches."[34] He draws attention to "the power and value that horizontal social relationships can have in reversing the symptoms of the erosion of social capital."[35]

The challenge facing Western societies consists in finding ways to recreate a geographical sense of community in a twenty-first-century world. The shattered "Humpty Dumpty" of Christendom cannot be pieced together and returned to its original vantage point on the wall, because the wall has itself crumbled. Western societies need radical restructuring if they are to return to the time when neighbors lived in close proximity, with their daily lives intertwined around local voluntary organizations and the shops that met their basic needs, whose owners and assistants were known by name by the customers and when they spontaneously rallied to the support of their sick and infirm neighbors, often without the need for government intervention.

Today's world, as we have noted, is far more complex—with increased mobility, long commutes to and from work, interest groups competing against each other, the breakup of the family, groups living alternative lifestyles, turf wars between rival gangs, and religious and ethnic pluralism—with some groups electing to colonize rather than assimilate. This is the overwhelmingly challenging environment in which local churches must carry out mission to their surrounding communities and beyond. And many of them are at a loss to know how to respond.

Every ministry situation is unique. In smaller, homogeneous, and stable communities, civil society still prevails. Neighbors readily come to one another's

33. Ibid., 156.
34. Ibid., 71.
35. Ibid., 81.

assistance, whether that consists of routine acts of kindness, coming together in response to a natural disaster, or raising funds for a person needing urgent lifesaving surgery. However, in the vast urban sprawl where so many of the multimillion inhabitants of a major metro area dwell, there is no sense of local identity or commitment. Faced with such daunting challenges, churches and other local voluntary organizations will need to be both creative and resilient to build a civil society, piece by piece.

The recent (2011) devastating earthquake and tsunami in northeastern Japan provides an impressive example of community support. With most government buildings having collapsed and many of the employees killed, the community came to realize that they could not rely on the central government to solve their pressing problems. But the survivors represented long-standing, tight-knit communities and began organizing to provide shelter and food and to develop cottage industries and farming cooperatives. There was no looting or civil disorder. One wonders what the social consequences of such a devastating experience would be like in a city such as Los Angeles.

In order to reconnect and reinforce civil society, we need to begin by learning about people who are very different from ourselves. Richard Mouw specifically addresses the need to show genuine curiosity in other persons as a basis for reestablishing common decency in our culture. He writes, "We ought to want to become familiar with the experiences of people who are different from us simply out of a desire to understand the length and breadth of what it means to be human."[36] Why should our curiosity be roused? In the words of Psalm 139:14, precisely because all of us are "fearfully and wonderfully made." According to Mouw, "All of this applies directly to our public lives. We ought to want to know what makes our fellow citizens tick, why they think and act the way they do, how they have formed their deepest loves and loyalties. To learn civility in the public square is one important way to satisfy a healthy curiosity about what is 'genuinely human.'"[37]

Challenge of Difference Experienced through Pluralism and Relativism

The churches in the West historically have had little exposure to pluralism, especially the kind in which they are in a minority position of relative powerlessness. Lesslie Newbigin reminds us that

36. Mouw, *Uncommon Decency*, 59.
37. Ibid., 60.

Western Christendom took its distinctive form during the long period in which it was the religion of a small region isolated from the religious worlds of Asia and sub-Saharan Africa by the massive power of Islam and from the religious world of the American peoples by the ocean. . . . But, such is the dominance of Western thought in the modern world, the idea that religious pluralism is something new is accepted as though it were true.[38]

The immigration flow into the Western world in the years following World War II has been from predominantly non-Christian cultures, by people seeking to escape poverty and avail themselves of work opportunities not only in low-skill sectors but increasingly in high-tech jobs, plus an ever-increasing tide of refugees, all of which has brought fresh challenges to local churches. Unfortunately, the majority of local church leaders had little preparation for such a change in their ministry priorities. They were effectively trained for the social reality of Christendom. Hence, the vast majority of churches were ill prepared to respond to the trauma of the 9/11 attacks on the World Trade Center and the Pentagon. Furthermore, they have struggled to make respectful and compassionate contacts with the influx of peoples from Southeast Asia, the Middle East, and the Muslim-majority areas of Africa, not to mention their failure to embrace the Christians from those areas. Many seminary-trained pastors came to the sudden realization that their education had not prepared them for the cultural and religious pluralism that now surrounded them. In particular they did not know how to enter into gracious, truth-honoring dialogue with devout followers of other monotheistic faiths, whether they be Jewish or Muslim.

How Will Churches Respond?

Here in the United States, working independently from Phillip Blond in the United Kingdom, James Davison Hunter has come to similar conclusions regarding the ills of society. More specifically, he has related his findings to the shortcomings of the three main Christian traditions, each of which have professed and pursued strong social agendas. He describes the approaches of the evangelical, the liberal, and the Anabaptist traditions as representing three paradigms of engagement. He labels the evangelical approach as "defense against" the culture, the liberal approach as "relevance to" the culture, and the Anabaptist approach as "purity from" the culture.[39] Each is engaged

38. Newbigin, extract from "Religious Pluralism: A Missiological Approach" (1993), in *Missionary Theologian*, 172.
39. Hunter, *To Change the World*, 213.

with the broader culture according to its own convictions and understanding of the gospel.

So many of these expressions of political and social concern have been largely confined to a war of words, with the result that when all is said and done, too much is said and too little is done. The problem is that words do not contain their meanings, especially across cultural divides. In other words, their distinctive cultural contexts and the baggage they carry convey different associations when people of different cultures hear them. Hunter explains: "When the objectified and shared meaning of words is undermined, when we no longer have confidence that words signify what we thought they signified, then it is possible to impute any meaning to words one desires. And if words can mean anything, then they have no intrinsic meaning or at least no possibility of a common meaning. They only mean what we say they mean."[40] People with opposing views talk about or past one another rather than to one another. Each is eager to score points over the other by means of well-honed sound bites. This dynamic contributes to an erosion of civility in public discourse. Despite the well-meaning efforts of a wide variety of groups, the benefits on the ground are meager in relation to the efforts exerted. Hunter proposes an alternative approach. "What has been missing is a leadership that comprehends the nature of these challenges and offers a vision of formation adequate to the task of discipling the church and its members for a time such as ours. By misreading the nature of the times and by focusing so much energy and resources on politics, those who have claimed the mantle of leadership have fixed attention on secondary and tertiary problems and false solutions."[41]

In other words, Hunter agrees with Blond that in order to set a different direction for society, the most hopeful course of action is to rebuild civil society from the ground up. The various local institutions that represent its constituent parts, engaging in dialogue and joint action, must gradually foster community. These include voluntary organizations, religious institutions, local businesses, and financial institutions. Neighborhoods must be planned to include a cross section of the population and to allow for natural interactions when shopping or engaging in social activities. "Nowhere" persons must feel that they belong "somewhere" and are making their distinctive contribution.

Reimagining Western Churches in Post-Christendom Contexts

Churches in the Western world have been shaped by the Christendom paradigm in which they occupied a privileged position as a central pillar of society

40. Ibid., 206.
41. Ibid., 226.

and guardian of its beliefs and values. But over the past two hundred years we have witnessed in Europe the gradual erosion of the alignment between church and state, leading to the collapse of this arrangement in the past century. Various dates have been suggested for its demise, which has been linked to the Enlightenment, the rise of scientific inquiry, two world wars, and, more recently, an aggressive atheism.

As European churches fragmented and were increasingly marginalized, it became apparent they were now facing a missional challenge as great as anywhere in the world. In some respects, their challenge may be greatest of all, in that churches throughout the Western world have a long and checkered history, leading to increasing cynicism regarding "institutional religion." Confusion and increasing conflict between religions add to the uncertainty, as Western societies become more pluralistic due to the immigration of peoples of other religions from around the world. For many of these migrants, their religion is a significant part of their identity, so that secularized Westerners find it difficult to appreciate how their faith convictions so comprehensively and powerfully influence their worldview. The majority of these immigrants do not buy into the individualism and privatization of faith so prevalent among Western Christians.

Churches today have to face questions that probe more deeply, comprehensively, and painfully than did questions in the past. These poignant questions of today are raised by Alan Hirsch: "Will more of the same do the trick? Do we have the inherited resources to deal with this situation? Can we simply rework the tried and true Christendom understanding of church that we so love and understand, and finally, in an ultimate tweak of the system, come up with the winning formula?"[42] Hirsch goes on to answer these questions in the negative: "The tools and techniques that fitted previous eras of Western history simply don't seem to work any longer. *What we need now is a new set of tools*. A new 'paradigm'—a new vision of reality: a fundamental change in our thoughts, perceptions, and values, especially as they relate to our view of the church and mission."[43]

In response to these challenges, the past twenty years in the United Kingdom and the United States have witnessed the beginning of a movement to reimagine the church, less as a static institution and more as a dynamic movement. The church's mission, rather than being envisaged as a program within the church, often "targeted" at peoples continents away, is now seen as defining the very nature of the church. Mission is rooted in the very being of

42. Hirsch, *Forgotten Ways*, 16.
43. Ibid., 17. Italics added.

God rather than developed as the initiative of enthusiasts within the church. In order to express this new understanding and commitment, the term *missional* was coined.

The term rapidly gained popularity and began to replace *church growth* and then *church health*, which were on the lips of church leaders in the 1970s and 1980s and were promoted by many programs and much literature. Unfortunately, as the term has become popular, so has it lost coherence. When everything becomes missional, then nothing is missional. Lutheran theologian Craig Van Gelder has provided a timely identification of the main themes defining an authentically missional church.

1. *God is a missionary God who sends the church into the world.* This understanding shifts the agency of mission from the church to God. It is God's mission that has a church rather than a church that has a mission.

2. *God's mission in the world is related to the reign (kingdom) of God.* This understanding makes the work of God in the world larger than the mission of the church, although the church is directly involved in the reign (kingdom) of God.

3. *The missional church is an incarnational (versus an attractional) ministry sent to engage a postmodern, post-Christendom, globalized context.* This understanding requires every congregation to take on a missionary posture for engaging its local context, with this missionary engagement shaping everything a congregation does.

4. *The internal life of the missional church focuses on every believer living as a disciple engaging in mission.* This understanding makes every member a minister, with the spiritual growth of every disciple becoming the primary focus as the body is built up to participate more fully in God's mission in the world.[44]

These four foundational intentions emphasize that missional church cannot be reduced to an add-on program, because it is comprehensive in scope and examines the self-understanding of the church. In addition, no congregation can claim to be a missional church as a point of arrival. Rather, this identification expresses a direction and lifelong pilgrimage as the church endeavors to embody these convictions. Each member will have to be encouraged to buy into this understanding of church, which is no easy achievement for the vast majority of churches that have largely attracted numbers through consumer-driven programs.

44. Van Gelder and Zscheile, *Missional Church in Perspective*, 4.

Under the influence of Christendom, ecclesiology became separated from missiology, to their mutual impoverishment. The urgent task now facing the churches in the West is to develop a reconnected ecclesiology and missiology and to demonstrate what a missional ecclesiology will look like within Western contexts. As they undertake this daunting task, they must also avoid the mistake of making the institutional church central to the enterprise, resulting in a survival strategy for institutional churches under threat. Rather, the missional church's witness is not so much attraction, with the goal of increasing church attendance and membership, but to bear witness to the mission of God throughout every segment of society. The Christendom church, and especially the state churches, largely focused on *attraction*, whereas the missional church is even more concerned and structured on the *dispersion* of the people of God to undertake their God-given mission in the world.

An understanding of the church as essentially missional in nature must not be regarded as an elitist concept but rather as something that is embraced by entire congregations. Alan Hirsch and Lance Ford express this conviction: "We believe it [the concept of *missional*] belongs to the whole church and must somehow be factored into the equation of discipleship, spirituality, and church at every level of our experience if we are going to be the people God has made us to be."[45]

Connecting the Twenty-First Century to the First Century

As churches in the West emerge from centuries of Christendom existence, they have much to learn from the early church's life prior to the introduction of Christendom. However, this does not signify that we can return to that era, which in many ways is so very different from our own. This is not an exercise in what is known as "restorationism," as though the New Testament church existed in some ideal form to which we need to return. Rather, we will revisit the early church from the perspective of our post-Christendom awareness to see what we might have missed in our previous reading because of our Christendom-bound cultural bias or blindness. We may find that we have much to learn from the early church, operating from the margins in its pre-Christendom, highly pluralistic, and pagan contexts.

In the account of the expansion of the church in Acts and from the letters Paul addressed to the recently formed faith communities, we will discover that the first missionaries had to translate the message of Jesus and his discipling

45. Hirsch and Ford, *Right Here, Right Now*, 22.

methods—originally developed within a Jewish and largely rural context—into the urban Greco-Roman world. Jesus's model had to be adapted and contextualized. In other words, the early missionaries were making it up was they went along. Paul's letters are especially helpful in that they deal with a wide spectrum of specific issues arising in those faith communities.

This study seeks to make the connection between the first-century and twenty-first-century mission of the church, with due regard to their very different cultural settings. Despite the two millennia that separate them, both missions continue as expressions of the ongoing mission of the ascended Christ. The challenge faced by Paul and his colleagues in his pioneering missionary journeys in a pre-Christendom environment, and that faced by churches in post-Christendom contexts today, is how to translate the message of Jesus, originally proclaimed in a Jewish, rural, Galilean context, into the pagan and pluralistic world of either the Roman Empire or contemporary secular society.

How can the message and ministry model of Jesus, with its all-embracing concerns relating to every area of life, be expressed incarnationally and make a transformative impact on society? How can churches be truly relational in order to impact the lives of members as lifelong followers of Jesus? How can they operate from the margins to the center of the wider culture with a bottom-up approach? And to what extent are they prepared to pay the price of following in the footsteps of the Suffering Servant role of Jesus, the crucified Messiah?

The Importance of Imagination and Creativity for Post-Christendom Churches

As church leaders agonize over the future of the church in the wake of so many failed turnaround strategies and attempts at new growth, they repeatedly ask, "Where do we go from here?" The latest programs promising growth and renewal have proved no more effective than the programs of their predecessors. In this opening chapter, we have argued that the answers do not arise from our past experience. The issues are too deeply rooted and comprehensive to be addressed with any add-on program.

Doug Pagitt, pastor of Solomon's Porch community in Minneapolis, traces the significant changes that have taken place in Western societies from the "Agrarian Age," through the "Industrial Age," to the "Information Age," and now into the "Inventive Age." Each of these eras has made a profound impact on the church. The church has been sluggish in its response and has suffered the negative consequences. His brief book *Church in the Inventive Age* is a tract for the times, alerting church leaders to the significance of the changes taking place around them. Of our current age, he writes, "The Inventive Age is one in which inclusion, participation, collaboration, and beauty are essential values."[46] Influence and authority arise not in any hierarchical, top-down way but through the establishing of networks of relations around a creative concept. This cultural shift has enormous implications for the church.

The term *paradigm shift* is often used in a loose and even trivial sense, whereas its true meaning identifies a period when everything is changing around us and there is no going back to the previous state of affairs. There is widespread agreement politically, economically, socially, and at every level of society that we are in such a period. Institutions that prospered under the previous paradigm but now ignore the significance of the changes taking place put themselves in peril. Institutions of all kinds fail to survive, and that includes churches and the seminaries that serve them.

Returning to the issue of the Inventive Age, both the educational and business worlds generally recognize that entrepreneurship must be encouraged if companies and nations are to maintain their influence, both locally and globally, in the twenty-first century. They must encourage imagination and creativity at every opportunity. Sir Ken Robinson has undertaken some of the pioneering research on this important issue and has come up with some disturbing findings. Whereas young children demonstrate high levels of creativity, this capacity dramatically diminishes as they grow older. Robinson claims that "we are educating people out of their creativity."[47] He elaborates on the inadequacy of prevailing approaches to education: "One of the essential tasks of education is to develop academic ability to the best standards possible for everyone. But there's much more to intelligence than academic ability and much more for education than developing it. If there were no more to intelligence than this, most of human culture with its complex fabric of scientific, technological, artistic, economic and social enterprises would never have happened."[48]

The formal educational process focuses on memory and logical reasoning but instills a fear of being wrong. Under the influence of the Enlightenment rational tradition, it has driven a wedge between the arts and the sciences and has sidelined the former. But creativity requires imagination, interdisciplinary cooperation, exploring possibilities, and the freedom to fail with dignity—as well as making all of this a valued part of the learning curve. Robinson provides

46. Pagitt, *Church in the Inventive Age*, 30.
47. Robinson, "Schools Kill Our Creativity."
48. Robinson, *Out of Our Minds*, 7.

a list of insights about the nature of creativity that could help churches and seminaries develop a culture that fosters creativity.

- *Creativity is not a purely personal process.* Many creative processes draw from the ideas and stimulation of other people. Creativity flourishes in an atmosphere where original thinking and innovation are encouraged and stimulated.
- *Creativity is a dynamic process and can involve many different areas of expertise.* The exponential growth of knowledge has led to increasing levels of specialization.
- *Creativity is incremental.* New ideas do not necessarily come from nowhere. They draw from the ideas and achievements of those that have gone before us or are working in different fields.
- *Cultural change is not linear and smooth.* It can be tumultuous, complex and drawn out. New ways of thinking do not simply replace the old at clear points in history. They often overlap and coexist with established ways of thinking for long periods of time.
- *Cultural change is not strictly logical.* Creativity and innovations should be seen as functions of all areas of activity and not only as confined to particular people or processes.[49]

The question arises as to which model of church corresponds most closely with the faith communities birthed by Paul and his missionary team in the first century. Were they characterized by consumerism or participation?

Looking Ahead

Throughout the following chapters we will intersperse biblical exposition with contemporary issues in order to link the first century with the contemporary challenges facing the churches. This will not simply represent an attempt to reproduce ancient issues. Social and economic circumstances have changed—sometimes dramatically. Furthermore, the churches living after nearly two thousand years of checkered history are in a position different from that of a new and dynamic movement that was often misunderstood and misrepresented.

In today's world many churches in the West face the opposite challenge, in that society at large claims to know too much about the institutional church. Many have had painful personal experiences, and many more have been exposed to media biases and caricatures. Therefore, we must mine the past with discernment.

49. Ibid., 182.

But the effort is worth it, for we Western Christians have often read the New Testament with our understanding limited and skewed by the assumption of Christendom that the church is a central pillar of society and guardian of its moral norms. In chapters 3 to 9, we will endeavor to reread Paul's letters to the young churches from a missional perspective, which I believe was the original intention of the author. Rather than providing strings of references on given topics, I have opted to quote Paul in full so that we listen to his voice rather than focus on the accompanying commentary. The faith communities birthed in cities around the Roman world may provide some valuable insights for churches today to contribute to the rebuilding of a civil society and the reestablishing of communities that provide a sense of belonging, fulfillment, and self-worth.

2

Engaging First-Century Contexts

As we move back from modern times to the first century, a cautionary word must be given at the outset. There is a tendency among some ardent Bible students to idealize the churches of the New Testament period. So impressed are they by these churches' spiritual vitality and rapid expansion that they overlook the frequent warnings and admonitions to the young churches throughout the letters of Paul.

Letters provide a highly personal form of communication, and in Paul's case deal with specific issues arising within individual congregations. But many of the matters that he addresses are not confined to a single church. As we will see in the following chapters, there are a number of issues that continue to emerge in the majority of churches.

Although letters provide an intimate picture, from time to time they also present difficulties in interpretation. We may not have knowledge of the specific questions his letters are answering, nor of the details of the situation that require his attention. Despite these limitations, the letters of the New Testament provide us with informative glimpses into the first-century contexts in which Paul and his missionary associates operated.

The Greco-Roman Empire

Before we focus on the cities specifically addressed by Paul, it is important to take in the broader picture of the Greco-Roman world of the period. We are dealing with a time of significant transition arising from the reign of Caesar Augustus (27 BC–AD 14) and the Pax Romana he introduced.

The main threat to Pax Romana was the deplorable state of the government. Its failure to govern effectively resulted in the enemies of the empire along the frontiers rebelling against Rome's control and refusing to pay the taxes, which were becoming increasingly burdensome. Having lost literally hundreds of senators who had died in the course of the wars, Caesar Augustus needed to replace them with alternative leaders, which he wisely drew from other Italian cities outside of Rome, thus widening his power base. His top priority was to reorganize both the government and the military. In addition, he recognized that in order to govern such a far-flung empire he would need a network of roads to link together the strategic centers and thereby ensure that all roads led to Rome. As a result of his efforts, "the people of the Roman world traveled more extensively and more easily than anyone before them—or would again until the nineteenth century."[1]

Caesar Augustus's other accomplishments included changes in the way finances were handled and in the issuing of suitably inscribed new gold and silver coins. He gave free food to the poor. He built the Forum of Augustus and decorated it with statues of his ancestors. Boasting of his accomplishments in the beautified city, he is quoted by Mellor and McGee as having said, "I found a city made of brick and left it a city of marble." In spite of poor health, Augustus lived to be seventy-six years old and reigned for forty-one years as emperor.[2]

Cities in Paul's Day

The cities of the first century were different in many respects from cities we know today. Cities then, as now, were of strategic importance. People flocked to them from every corner of the empire for the amenities they provided, the carnal pleasures they offered, as well as the protection, legal redress, trading opportunities, and rich pickings through theft and exploitation. But ancient cities did not sprawl as today's do.

> The cities where Pauline Christianity took shape were very small compared with our postindustrial and post-population-explosion megalopolises. Antioch-on-the-Orontes, for example, was one of the giants of the first century, yet a person could easily walk the circumference in an afternoon. The modern town Antakya

1. Meeks, *First Urban Christians*, 17.
2. Mellor and McGee, *Ancient Roman World*, 90–92.

is somewhat less than half the area of the ancient city. A generous estimate of the modern population would be 75,000, and the town seems, to Western eyes, fairly crowded. Yet estimates of the ancient city at its peak, based on guesses of ancient writers, range as high as six times that number. Even a more modest estimate, perhaps a quarter of a million, yields a high density in a relatively small area. The scale of a Philippi or a Beroea or even a Corinth would be a good bit smaller, but the density probably as high.[3]

These distinctions must be kept in mind as we read the account in Acts of the missionary strategy of Paul and his companions, as well as the letters he addressed to the young churches birthed through his evangelistic endeavors.

For the previous four to five hundred years, the Greeks had regarded living in the *polis* as the only form of truly civilized life.[4] The Romans, sharing the Greeks' low opinion of those who lived in the countryside, built upon this ancient Greek concept. Reading the destinations of Paul's journeys around Galatia, Macedonia, Achaia, and Asia Minor, we must remember that first-century cities were as diverse as cities in the twenty-first century, thus avoiding misleading generalizations. Oswyn Murray emphasizes this point in his observation that

> many aspects of their [classical Greek cities'] social and economic life were different: some cities possessed large agricultural territories or serf populations, others were heavily engaged in trade in raw materials such as corn, olive oil, dried fish, wine, metals, timber, slaves, or in manufactured goods, whether made on the spot or imported from eastern and other cultures; there was also a huge outflow of Greek goods in certain areas, and of skilled labour such as doctors, stonemasons, and professional mercenaries. The economy of the cities varied enormously, and so did their functions: some were essentially fortresses, others based on a religious shrine; but most had ports, and all had some land and constituted an administrative centre.[5]

Although these comments refer to an era that predates the brief period covered in this chapter and the following chapters, because cultural change came slowly in the ancient Mediterranean these observations still provide a fairly accurate picture. The one significant difference is that by the first century AD the trade in slaves had shrunk considerably. By then most slaves were the children of slaves within existing households.

3. Meeks, *First Urban Christians*, 28.
4. Murray, "Life and Society in Classical Greece," 204.
5. Ibid.

Population estimates of the cities visited by Paul vary enormously between experts. Sociologist Rodney Stark provides the following estimates for the cities mentioned in the New Testament:

Rome	650,000
Alexandria	400,000
Ephesus	400,000
Antioch	200,000
Pergamum	120,000
Sardis	100,000
Corinth	100,000
Smyrna	75,000
Damascus	45,000
Athens	30,000[6]

As we look more closely at the various strategic centers of Paul's missionary activities, we will explore a variety of approaches he adopted in each location. Although he, as a prominent Jew, began his mission with existing synagogues, he did not have a step-by-step plan of action. Rather, he followed where the Holy Spirit was leading. This is an important consideration for those who want a surefire formula that can be applied wherever and whenever.

Neighborhoods

Despite the compact nature of first-century Greco-Roman cities, a strong sense of neighborliness animated each district. People knew one another, shopped locally, and consumed their stew, pastries, and wine at the corner eatery. "Kindred crafts and trades also tended to gather in the same areas, which often took their names from the fact: Linen weavers' Quarter, Leatherworkers' Street, Portico of the Perfumers."[7] Many districts also had their own security guards (*vigiles*), who were often retired soldiers. Within such a tight-knit community an outsider could be readily identified.

For a twenty-first-century city dweller, daily life in a first-century city is difficult to imagine. In the first place, cities were compact, as many were confined within protective walls, with gateways to monitor comings and goings. At night,

6. Stark, *Rise of Christianity*, 131–32.
7. Meeks, *First Urban Christians*, 29.

city streets and alleys were dangerous places, with robbers ready to pounce on the vulnerable. They were also smelly, owing to the open sewers that ran through the middle of many streets. Until the Middle Ages, such was the basic sanitation in many of Europe's poorer districts, known as *middens*. It was common practice for residents to throw out their slops and empty their chamber pots from their windows at night, which would keep unwelcome visitors at bay! The mystery novels of Lindsey Davis provide one of the most engaging accounts of everyday life in Rome during this period. Her scholarly research allows her to paint an accurate picture as well as tell entertaining whodunits![8]

In order to keep out the noise and unpleasant aromas of the city, the ground floors of middle-class homes were entirely inward looking. "Apart from a few slit windows at a high level, its exterior walls presented a blind face to the surrounding world—as much to ensure against burglary, one imagines, as to shut out the noise and bustle of the streets."[9]

Types of Housing

First-century cities included a wide range of housing, which varied according to the owners' economic status, whether they lived within the city or on its perimeter, and their social role within society. Unfortunately, details about types of housing are often scant due to the state of ruin, and we find little evidence in the New Testament of the types of accommodation that housed the early faith communities resulting from Paul's missionary endeavors. In what follows we examine the primary housing forms and their known characteristics.[10]

Villa

The social elite lived in an atrium house or villa. Many of these were located in the suburbs, where more space was available and where families could enjoy rural tranquility. Roger Gehring provides the following description of a villa in Anaploga, near Corinth:

> An atrium house contained a series of rooms surrounding a courtyard (*atrium*;
> 35 square meters) with a small pool (*impluvium*), a living room (*triclinium*)

8. *The Silver Pigs* is her first novel in a continuing series of mysteries featuring Marcus Didius Falco.
9. Ling, "Arts of Living," 719.
10. It is important to keep these descriptions of the various types of housing in mind as we discuss the variety of possible locations of faith communities birthed in mission in the next chapter.

measuring 41.25 square meters. Such a living room would have accommodated nine people on the couches placed along the walls, and in the courtyard there would have been room for several more. If all of the couches were removed, there would have been room for about twenty people total. If the courtyard were used for extra space, the capacity could have been expanded to about forty or fifty. This can serve as a helpful guideline for determining the hypothetical size of Pauline house churches at least in Corinth.[11]

We must not assume, however, that villas constituted the typical venues for Paul's churches. Because this type of housing features so prominently in the depictions of contemporary films and novels, it has skewed popular conceptions of the Roman city.

Domus

The middle and upper classes occupied the typical townhouse (*domus*). Fortunately, we have well-preserved structures from Pompei that enable archaeologists to gain a more accurate picture of urban dwellings in Italy. It is likely, although by no means certain, that similar structures existed in other urban centers, especially those rebuilt in Roman times.

Roger Ling describes the *domus* as "a spreading mansion focused on two inner light-sources, the *atrium* at the front and a colonnaded garden or peristyle at the rear. The *atrium* provided the first open space to confront the visitor as he entered from the street, serving as the social and religious centre of the house. It was fittingly endowed in most cases with majestic height, and sometimes with lofty columns framing the shallow rectangular catchwater basin (*impluvium*) in the centre of the floor."[12]

Chambers were located around the atrium, consisting of bedrooms, offices, storerooms, small dining rooms, and often a pair of broad and deep recesses (*alae*) used to display masks or busts of the family's ancestors. At the back of the house was the peristyle, which was also surrounded by open-fronted rooms and banqueting halls.

It is important to bear in mind that first-century urban societies had, by modern standards, a very small elite or middle class. Whereas public buildings and the homes of the more prosperous occupied a disproportionate amount of space, the poor lived in crowded accommodations consisting of no more than one or two rooms, or at the back of a stall or workroom.

11. Gehring, *House Church and Mission*, 141.
12. Ling, "Arts of Living," 718. See also Everett Ferguson, *Backgrounds of Early Christianity*, 140.

Given the cramped nature of first-century cities, many homes were narrow and tall rather than expansive. Everett Ferguson writes, "Private houses in the eastern provinces were one-family dwellings up to four stories high. The dining room on the top floor was the only large room and often opened on a terrace."[13]

Insula

A further development seen in Rome, and then spreading to Corinth and perhaps to other cities, was the "high-rise" (*insulae*), which made room for the rapidly growing population within the city's walls. It was not until late into the second century that these high-rises became popular in many large cities. In Rome the tallest of the *insula* may have had as many as six floors, with the cheapest accommodation located on the top floors, as this was the most dangerous place to be in case of fire. According to Ling, "By the late first century BC the architectural writer Vitrius was able to refer to tower blocks with fine views, and Augustus was obliged, for safety reasons, to limit their height to 70 feet. . . . By AD 79 Herculaneum had at least two new-style shop-and-apartment blocks, one of which has survived to a height of three storeys."[14] Everett Ferguson offers the following description: "The masses lived in tenement houses of five or six stories (tall tenement buildings are mainly after Nero), either towerlike with apartments on top of each other as in Alexandria (or modern-day Athens) or forming large blocks (*insulae*) as in Rome and Ostia with shops or warehouses at street level and numerous apartments on each of the upper floors."[15]

An entire family typically would occupy a single room. Usually shops and stalls, with direct access to the street, occupied the first floor. Sometimes stall owners would make their beds under their counters to spend the night. Cooking and heating arrangements consisted of open fires, so that the danger of buildings catching fire was always present—hence the urgent need to organize fire brigades. Once a fire took hold, it spread rapidly through the wooden structure and jumped across the narrow streets. Great fires could consume a third of a city. In addition to fires, plagues periodically devastated cities as a result of overcrowding and unsanitary conditions.[16]

13. Ferguson, *Backgrounds of Early Christianity*, 139.
14. Ling, "Arts of Living," 721–22.
15. Ferguson, *Backgrounds of Early Christianity*, 140.
16. See Stark, *Rise of Christianity*, chap. 4, for his assessment of the significance of epidemics in the growth of the church. (In brief, he argues that the church grew because Christians took care of their afflicted pagan neighbors.) And for a vivid description of the physical and social chaos that resulted in chronic urban misery, see 149–62.

Privacy was a luxury few enjoyed. Residents shopped at the street-level stalls and climbed the stairs to their rooms. By the stairwell, a laundry might be conveniently located, so that the residents could drop off their laundry as they passed by, but also so that they could use the chamber pot, to augment the supply of bleach! (At the time, the most common means to make dyes fast was to soak wool cloth in urine or vinegar.)

The vast majority of the urban population lived in the *insulae*. These people worked in construction or warehousing or as casual laborers or domestic servants, or they were fringe members of households. It is likely that only a small percentage of Christians lived in their own houses. Most lived in cramped and squalid conditions. Consequently, urban living was very public.

Taberna

The *taberna* is a street-level workshop, with accommodation attached for the owner consisting of either a single room at the back of the business or a loft. In Corinth a row of fourteen *tabernae* have so far been excavated. The workspace in these examples would provide seating for about twenty people. Robert Gehring provides the following details:

> In a row of small workshops north of the southern stoa there are fourteen *tabernae*, altogether about 44 meters long. This results in a width of 3 meters per workshop. Their length was just below 4 meters. In the row of workshops on the western side of the forum there is a series of larger workshops, which are approximately 4.5 to 6 meters in size. This results in a shop area of 27 square meters. The work was done in the lower level of the shop. The living, dining, and bedroom [*sic*] was either in the back of the shop or in a loft above it, lit by an unglazed window centered above the shop entrance. The loft was accessible by a series of steps in stone or brick, continued by a wooden ladder located in one of the back corners of the shop. In such a room or in the shop itself, about twenty believers could have assembled in a house church meeting.[17]

In addition to the *taberna*, many private houses also functioned as centers of business and manufacture.

In summary, cities were crowded, cosmopolitan, smelly, and violent. They were prone to epidemics that swept through their crowded quarters and resulted in the death of a quarter to a third of their populations. Building fires and collapses due to poor construction were a common occurrence.

17. Gehring, *House Church and Mission*, 135.

Urban Authorities and Social Structures

In order for it to function, every city has recognized authorities that allocate resources, provide basic services, and maintain order. Nicholas Purcell identifies the three principal authority figures who served these functions in Roman society: "magistrate, soldier, and master of a household; and all governmental activity in the Roman Empire can be aligned to one of these."[18]

In addition, the trade guilds were growing in economic influence, especially in Rome. As Wayne Meeks observes, "Trade and professional associations were especially important in Rome. . . . Although it is now common to call these groups guilds, their purpose is not to be confused with those of medieval guilds, much less with those of modern trade unions. 'So far as the evidence of the inscriptions goes the guilds seem to have been purely social bodies, unconcerned with the business activities of their members.'"[19] He concludes from this observation that "the *ekklesia* that gathered with the tentmakers Prisca, Aquila, and Paul in Corinth or Ephesus might well have seemed to the neighbors a club of the same sort."[20] But he adds this caution: "That the Christian groups did not consciously model themselves on the associations is apparent from the almost complete absence of common terminology for the groups themselves or for their leaders."[21] Roman cities, as with earlier Greek cities, consisted of a complex network of such associations, each of which brought commitments and obligations. Oswyn Murray writes, "The conception of the autonomy of the individual apart from community is absent from Greek thought: the freedom of the Greeks is public, externalized in speech and action."[22]

As will be immediately apparent, these many obligations to diverse groups could easily lead to conflicting allegiances and entanglements, with individuals having to play one off against another. This complex matrix of relations inevitably led to divided loyalties and mutual suspicion. Any reconfiguring of allegiances, not to mention one community claiming priority over all other relationships, would cause social tension for any person in the groups who had identified with other social networks. Society was stratified and stable, with little social movement or expectation of any. "As Aristotle saw, it was such associations that created the sense of community, of belonging, which was an essential feature of the *polis*."[23]

18. Purcell, "Arts of Government," 565.
19. Meeks, *First Urban Christians*, 31.
20. Ibid., 32.
21. Ibid., 79.
22. Murray, "Life and Society in Classical Greece," 210.
23. Ibid., 209.

We need to constantly bear in mind the presence of, and pressures exerted by, this complex social context when we read the accounts of the birth of new faith communities and the issues that Paul had to address in writing to new Christians. Unlike individuals in many modern cities, these ancient city dwellers lived within a matrix of social entanglements, and economic dependence and reliance on patronage were basic realities.

Status of Women

A woman's main sphere of influence in Greek society was the home, where she looked after the domestic arrangements and cared for the children she bore. The women's quarters were off-limits to others. Women were expected to provide entertainment for the men but were not to eat with them. However, in Macedonian society women "had greater independence and importance in public affairs. This coincides with the greater prominence women held in the Macedonian churches, which we find hinted at in Paul's reference to women associated with the Philippian church (see Acts 16:14–15; Phil. 4:2–3)."[24]

Within Roman society women came to achieve a higher legal status, and some within the household structure took leadership in running a business from the premises. They frequently held civic offices. In addition, "they are found as physicians, musicians, artists, winners of athletic events, selling groceries, and in all sorts of manufacturing and commercial activities."[25] In the sphere of religion, women also came to positions of influence as priestesses, especially in the newer cults.

While a Jewish woman in Roman and Hellenistic society enjoyed a measure of freedom outside of the home, she "was not qualified to appear as a witness in court and was exempt from fulfilling religious duties that had to be performed at stated times (because her first duties were to her children and the home and she might not be in the required state of ritual purity)."[26]

Attention is frequently drawn to evidence of a negative attitude among Jewish males toward women, as seen in the prayer in the Jewish prayer book, "Blessed art thou, O Lord our God, who has not made me a woman." But, as Ferguson explains, this sentiment "must be understood in this context as referring to women's inability to fulfill all the demands of the law, which was the highest privilege recognized by rabbinic Judaism. It must be balanced by many statements in rabbinic literature giving a positive estimate of women."[27]

---

24. See Ferguson, *Backgrounds of Early Christianity*, 78.
25. Ibid., 79. See also Meeks, *First Urban Christians*, 24.
26. Ibid., 78.
27. Ibid.

In the following chapter, we will draw attention to the significant role played by women in the ministry of churches in Macedonia.

Status of Slaves and Freedmen

The modern reader is overly influenced by the model of slavery associated with the sugar and tobacco plantations of the American South and the Caribbean. In the Roman world of the first century, slaves had a different social standing. It is estimated that 80 percent of workers were indentured. John Matthews emphasizes the mingling within society of slaves, freedmen, and free citizens.

> One of the most important facets of the social and economic history of the Empire as opposed to the Republic is the declining rate of slave importation, the servile population being now to a far greater extent (one would not say entirely, in view of the evidence for the continuance of the slave trade under the Empire) maintained by reproduction among those who were already of this status, through what were in effect recognized as slave marriages. The effect of this is that the function of slavery in the Empire evolved within a wider social and economic pattern and was not imposed upon it. In whatever occupational milieu we find ourselves—among shopkeepers, building workers, members of *collegia*—we encounter a mixed population of slave, freedmen, and free citizen.[28]

However, a slave was still the property of his or her master and subject to abuse and cruel treatment without redress. Hence, "the most fundamental change of status for a person of the lower class was that from slavery to freedom—or vice versa. This does not mean that all free persons were better off than all slaves; far from it."[29] Much would depend on the character and integrity of the head of the household and the reputation and status of the family. In some families, slaves would be treated with respect; in others, they would be exploited and humiliated. Those slaves who belonged and labored in a household of influence with a beneficent patron could not only experience security and well-being but also be entrusted with considerable responsibility and build prestige.

Another significant difference between first-century slavery and that of the eighteenth and nineteenth centuries was the degree of social mobility that was possible in Roman times. Slaves could rise to positions of responsibility

28. Matthews, "Roman Life and Society," 768.
29. Meeks, *First Urban Christians*, 20.

within the family business, mentor and discipline children of the household, and, within the Roman administration, occupy high positions in Caesar's household. The latter depended heavily on slave labor, because slaves guaranteed loyalty and did not pose a threat as possible rivals grasping for power. Meeks affirms the possibility of such significant social mobility, especially among "Caesar's family," extending to many parts of the empire: "The *familia caesaris* was virtually the civil service of the empire, in the provinces no less than in Rome."[30]

Slaves in Roman times could be awarded their freedom, something that was not possible in the American South until after the Civil War. "The freed person occupied a peculiar niche in society, a transitional category between slave and free. The *libertus* or *liberta* was clearly superior to the slave but still obliged to the former owner, now patron, in numerous ways both legal and informal, and carried to the grave the more general stigma of servile origin."[31]

Within the early church, as we will see in the following chapter, there is evidence of the valued presence of slaves and freedmen. Even those who were freed often continued to serve within the household out of gratitude and in order to continue to benefit from the employment and social support provided by the extended family in which they continued to be regarded as members.

Significance of the Household in a Preindustrial Society

The *oikos* or "household" was not just a domestic arrangement but the basic economic structure of preindustrial societies. It was where most manufacture took place and business was transacted. A household might be a banking house, a medical practice, an artist studio, or a scriptorium where legal documents were copied or as many as thirty scribes produced parchment copies of poetry, plays, or history or philosophy texts for sale. As businesses expanded, so additions were made to the original house.[32] Located alongside the scriptorium was the "retail outlet" for the sale of the parchment scrolls. These would differ in quality according to the fame of the author and the economic means of the purchaser.

A typical household represented an extended family. In addition to the immediate family members were slaves and freedmen, apprentices, the *amici*

30. Ibid., 21.
31. Ibid., 121.
32. While writing this chapter I was also reading a Lindsey Davis whodunit, *Ode to the Banker*, set in Rome, which alerted me to the enormous labor entailed in producing multiple copies in the pre-Gutenberg era.

(friends of the family), and the *clientela*, made up of the people who traded with these others. Consequently, membership in a household provided a sense of identity and security. The conversion of someone "with all his house" involves many more than are numbered in nuclear families of the modern West. It is instead much closer to the extended family that is found throughout the Middle East and Africa today, with obligations to scores of relatives. In addition, the household of the first century was based not on family obligations alone but also on a broader web of social identity and economic dependence. "'Family' is defined not first by kinship but by the relationship of dependence and subordination. The head of a substantial household was thus responsible for—and expected a degree of obedience from—not only his immediate family but also his slaves, former slaves who were now clients, hired laborers, and sometimes business associates or tenants."[33]

Dirk Jongkind challenges the assertion that Corinthian society, in line with Roman society in general, consisted of two essential groups: the elite and nonelite, with the latter leading a life just above starvation level. He does so in response to the comprehensive study by Justin Meggitt in *Paul, Poverty and Survival*,[34] which concluded that the nonelite group comprised more than 99 percent of the Greco-Roman society. After describing the range of housing found in Corinth, Jongkind concludes, "The housing evidenced in Corinth betrays the existence of distinctions in Meggitt's 'non-élite class' that go beyond his distinction between 'the poorest' and the 'marginally economically more successful.' The range of housing seems to indicate the existence of a 'middle class' whose absolute wealth cannot be ascertained but who could afford themselves some kind of luxury and have to be distinguished from the very poor."[35]

Applying the *Oikos* Concept Today

Rather naively, beginning in the 1960s, the *oikos* concept was made the basis for church growth through home-based meetings. As is now apparent, one cannot simply take a term and transpose it from the first century to the twentieth century without taking into account the broader social context. In the ancient world, the household was the very building block of social structure. Meeks writes, "Our sources give us good reason to think that it [the individual

33. Meeks, *First Urban Christians*, 30.
34. See Jongkind, "Corinth in the First Century AD," 139–48. See also Meggitt, *Paul, Poverty and Survival*, 66–67.
35. Jongkind, "Corinth in the First Century AD," 147–48.

household] was the basic unit in the establishment of Christianity in the city, as it was, indeed, the basic unit of the city itself."[36] He goes on to explain,

> to be part of a household was thus to be part of a larger network of relationships, of two sorts. Within the household, a vertical but not quite unilinear chain connected unequal roles, from slave to paterfamilias, in the most intimate strand, but also included bonds between client and patron and a number of analogous but less formal relations of protection and subordination. Between this household and others there were links of kinship and of friendship, which also often entailed obligations and expectations. . . . It was ordinarily assumed that the subordinate members of a household, particularly the servile ones, would share the religion(s) of their master.[37]

This description reveals the great difference between the ancient *oikos* and privatized huddles of contemporary Christians, who meet occasionally as a "home group" but live their lives largely independent of one another in their nuclear families and diverse places of employment.

When engaging in urban mission, it is important to know where authority lies. Who are the movers and shakers within the city? Who is beholden to whom? Who makes the significant decisions that affect most or all in the city? Who holds the purse strings? What major businesses, educational institutions, and industries determine the economic well-being of the city? What positions do the local and regional media take on important issues? Are they friendly to the churches or hostile? Are social services responding sensitively and adequately to the most vulnerable in society? To what extent do voluntary organizations endeavor to meet their needs, and do the churches work together in cooperation with these agencies? Who are the most vulnerable within society? Are they the single mothers trying to raise children and keep a full-time job? What are the employment opportunities for these women, and are local businesses sensitive to their needs and able to provide child care and maternity leave? Is there evidence of human trafficking in your area? Such forced labor is a widespread problem in many large cities. Are there local organizations to which those trapped in this shameful trade can turn for help in obtaining legal citizenship and alternative employment? The Christian church must help these people work through their shame and gain a sense of human dignity as persons made in the image of God.

For many vulnerable people in society, the *oikos* will consist of a safe refuge where they can rebuild their lives and learn skills to enable them to find employment.

36. Meeks, *First Urban Christians*, 29.
37. Ibid., 30.

Locations Addressed by Paul

In order to provide a picture of various contexts for mission, we move now to a consideration of the principal locations visited by Paul and his missionary team. Unfortunately, the New Testament itself does not provide geographical, economic, or cultural context. We have to read more widely to gain the broader picture. Luke does not offer a description of the locations because he writes as a biographer. Also, it is likely that he is a native of Macedonia, so perhaps he assumed his contemporary readers would be familiar with dates and places. And the recipients of Paul's letters knew far more about their local contexts than he did as a visitor.

In the course of Paul's letters, a range of issues emerges, which can best be understood in light of the broader social context. We will explore these during the course of the following chapters. All of the letters we will be considering were addressed to specific locations, with two exceptions: one was addressed to a group of churches in the province of Galatia, and the other (Ephesians) may have been distributed to the various churches in the Lycus Valley of Asia Minor.

Galatia

The Romans established the province of Galatia in 25 BC. However, there is some confusion regarding the area designated, as G. Walter Hansen notes. "In Paul's time Galatia was the name for the entire Roman province stretching from Pontus in the north to Pamphilia in the south. All the residents of this province were properly called Galatians, whatever their ethnic origin. By the third century AD, the province of Galatia was reduced to approximately its ancient ethnological dimensions, the original northern territory of the Celtic invaders."[38]

Pamphilia, located to the south, in pre-Roman times consisted of a small region in southern Asia Minor between Lycia and Cilicia, with Perga as its capital. Pisidia provided the northern boundary until Roman times, when Pamphilia and Pisidia were consolidated as an administrative convenience. During the reign of Augustus, eight colonies were established in Pisidia, with Antioch eventually rising to the position of the regional capital. In modern Turkey, Antioch is the province of Antalya.

In the course of his first missionary journey (AD 47–48), Paul traveled through the region of Pisidia in southern Galatia, visiting the towns of Perga, Lystra, Pisidian Antioch (not to be confused with Syrian Antioch), Iconium,

38. Hansen, *Galatians*, 17.

and Derbe. These were located in the former Seleucid territory, which was replaced by the Attalid kingdom of Pergamum—with its strong cultural identification with Hellenism—during the third and second centuries BC. Ferguson informs us that "the warlike Galatians remained largely untouched by Hellenism until the Roman period."[39]

During the Roman era, Pisidia was colonized by veterans as a means of control and to buttress weak local administrators. It was a popular area in that it enjoyed a cooler climate than the Mediterranean shoreline because of its elevation and the presence of the Taurus Mountains. Its abundant rain and rivers ensured the fertility of the soil and plenty of fruit and grazing pasture. Several key trade routes passed through the area, with Iconium as a strategic center. Lystra was located twenty-five miles southwest of Iconium, and Derbe a farther fifty-five miles to the east of Lystra. All of these towns visited by Paul were located on the busy road that led through the Cilician Gate to Tarsus, the capital of Cilicia.

Before we consider Paul's urban missionary strategies and his various experiences in the cities he addresses in his letters, it is important to take a broader look at each of the cities in order to appreciate their distinctive features. Each presented unique challenges. The accounts of the founding of each of the churches as recorded in Acts are frustratingly brief. During the course of Paul's third missionary journey, he continued west under the guidance of the Holy Spirit through Galatia and Asia Minor, eventually arriving at Troas, at which point he responded to the "Macedonian call" to cross the Aegean Sea into Macedonia and travel south to Achaia, the two Roman provinces that today constitute Greece.

Philippi

Paul's first destination on landing in Macedonia was Philippi, where he began his missionary labors in Europe. Philippi is located 10 miles inland from Neapolis and 115 miles north of Thessalonica. Although a small Roman colony, Philippi was nevertheless a leading city of Macedonia because of both its strategic location on the Egnatian Way and its function as a garrison station for the "eastern gate" from Europe to the Persian cities. It was a town in which military veterans were settled (as was Corinth, Antioch of Pisidia, Iconium, Lystra, and Troas). This strategy not only represented the emperor's expression of gratitude for service rendered but also provided a base of loyalty and the manpower to maintain order. Octavian endowed the populace of Philippi with Roman citizenship in 42 BC.

39. Ferguson, *Backgrounds of Early Christianity*, 20.

Philippi's population was both Roman and Greek, but the city also attracted immigrants from Thrace, Egypt, Anatolia, and elsewhere.[40] Although Latin was the official language, Greek was dominant in commerce and everyday life. Lydia, Euodia, and Syntyche are all Greek names. Unlike the other cities Paul visited, Philippi was a center of agriculture rather than trade, being located on a plain that had a large swampy valley. Nearby were located the great gold and silver mines at Mount Pangeo, largely mined by slave labor. These valuable minerals added to the prosperity of the city.

Thessalonica

Thessalonica is located at the intersection of two major Roman roads, one leading from Italy eastward (Egnatian Way) and the other from the Danube to the Aegean. Its strategically located port made it a prominent city. In 168 BC it became the capital of the second district of Macedonia, and later (146 BC) it was made the capital and major port of the whole Roman province of Macedonia.

Very little has been uncovered at ancient Thessalonica because the modern city sits atop the archaeological remains, severely limiting excavation of promising sites. When the bus station was removed in 1962, a first- or second-century forum was revealed. Excavators found a bathhouse and mint dating to the first century. An inscription (dating between 30 BC and AD 143) from the Vardar Gate bears the word *politarches*, which Luke uses for the city officials before whom the mob brought Jason (Acts 17:6). The word does not appear in any other Greek literature but does match the archaeology of the site.

This major city of Macedonia enjoyed the goodwill of Rome and was not subject to Roman taxation. It prospered as a political and commercial center, benefiting from its strategic location at the midpoint of the Egnatian Way and its possession of an excellent harbor. It was rivaled only by Corinth as a center of trade in Roman Greece, and as a mark of its commercial importance it was given permission to mint its own coins. Unlike many other Roman cities, it was not obliged to garrison Roman troops within the city walls. The population of Thessalonica was mixed, consisting of Romans and Macedonians, with a Jewish contingent large enough to warrant its having a synagogue (Acts 17:1).

Corinth

Moving southwest from Thessalonica, we come to the city of Corinth, located at the southernmost tip of Greece. It was the senatorial capital of

40. Meeks, *First Urban Christians*, 46.

the province of Achaia, which included all of southern Greece. Strategically located on a four-mile-wide isthmus, Corinth had access to two ports, one on the Asian side of the isthmus and the other on the Italian side, making the city a convenient stopping point on a major Mediterranean trade route. Corinth was destroyed by the Romans in 146 BC and then populated in large part by Roman slaves. By Paul's time it was a cosmopolitan city consisting of Romans, Greeks, Jews, and other ethnic groups.

In addition to its maritime trade, Corinth was known for its handicrafts. The surrounding land was of poor quality, so agriculture did not assume much importance there. It profited from travelers crossing the isthmus, and as a transit stopover for so many people without local connections, it gained the reputation for vice that found expression in the term *korinthiazomai*, which simply meant to act like a sexually promiscuous Corinthian (1 Cor. 5:1–13; 6:12–20). This term was coined by the Greek poet Aristophanes in the fourth century BC.

Corinth was a walled city, twice the size of Athens, with an estimated population of about 75,000, plus a considerable overspill population consisting largely of traders. Within the small land area of the isthmus were some flat areas, fertile and well watered from the surrounding hills and mountains. The city prospered both commercially and administratively, with a diversified economy covering manufacturing, agriculture, and tourism. The tourists were attracted by the Isthmian Games, held every other year in honor of the Greek god Poseidon. Women competed as well as men, and the games combined artistic and athletic events. In large part due to Corinth's vibrant economy, slaves as well as elite families prospered and achieved social status through the accumulation of wealth.

In keeping with other cities of the period, religious pluralism held sway in Corinth. The many cults to be found there included worship of traditional Roman or Greek gods and goddesses. The most renowned goddess was Aphrodite, whose temple housed cult prostitutes who provided a potent mix of religion and sex. Other deities included Dionysus and Isis. Pagan worship permeated Corinthian society. Eating out often involved offering gifts to placate the gods, with the offered meat consumed at the close of the meal or later sold in the marketplace. Because they offered intense emotional experiences, the mystery religions were also popular. Mithraism induced such experiences through its initiation rites involving the blood of a bull.

The Roman authorities were tolerant toward this array of cults, provided they did not disturb the peace, because none required exclusive devotion. But the cult of the emperor demanded that everyone bow to Caesar as a civic duty. This requirement presented a particular difficulty to both Jews and Christians because of the monotheistic nature of their faith, and it became a pressing issue with the emperor Domitian toward the close of the first century.

Ephesus

We now journey back east across the Aegean Sea, to the province of Asia Minor and its principal city and center of government, Ephesus. In the first century it was the second-largest city in the Roman Empire, with a population estimated at a quarter million. In Roman times it possessed a significant harbor on the Cayster River. But in subsequent centuries, due to the silting of the estuary, two outer harbors had to be built, leaving the city farther inland. Modern Ephesus is now located about five miles from the coast. The city was acclaimed for its magnificent temple dedicated to Artemis, which was regarded as one of the seven wonders of the ancient world.

Ephesus had close links with a cluster of cities in the Lycus Valley due to its strategic location at the heart of two trading routes: north-south between Lydia and Pamphylia, and east-west between the Euphrates and the Aegean Sea. Paul mentions Colossae, Laodicea, and Hierapolis, all of which were centers of the wool trade, with craftspeople trading between them. "These included not only those directly connected with the wool trade, like the most august guild of the wool washers, the fullers, dyers, and so on, but also smiths, nailmakers, gardeners, and others."[41] Ephesus was home to a very wealthy elite, as is evidenced in the luxurious homes that have been excavated.

Several ruins are of particular interest. One is the second temple of Artemis (or Diana), which was also recognized as one of the seven wonders of the ancient world. It was built to impress, being 377 feet by 180 feet in area and supported by 117 columns 60 feet in height. Such temples were not intended to accommodate a congregation but rather to house the statues of the god or goddess and for the priests to fulfill their ceremonial functions. The temple was regarded as a particularly sacred place, as it housed the great statue of Artemis that was popularly believed to have fallen from heaven. Her statue has survived, depicting her with three rows of breasts, or eggs, symbolizing fertility. Another ruin worth noting is the theater in Ephesus, which is still intact and is an impressive structure built to seat 25,000 people. It was here that Paul wanted to make his defense but was persuaded that this would not be a wise move.[42]

41. Ibid., 44.
42. Although Christians today are unlikely to be opposed by silversmiths manufacturing idols, whenever commercial interests are threatened, opposition is likely to arise from local businesses

Colossae

Colossae was an insignificant town located on the northern edge of the Lycus Valley. Since Roman times it has remained a popular center for recreation and healing because of its warm mineral springs. The city has yet to be excavated. All that is visible aboveground is a huge mound under which the city is buried. In previous centuries more remains could be seen, including a theater, a necropolis, and several pillars that indicated a ceremonial processional way. Unfortunately, over the centuries local inhabitants have removed these remains for building purposes or taken them as souvenirs.

Rome

All roads led to Rome from across the empire, so it is not surprising that the imperial city was Paul's ultimate destination. When he wrote his letter to the Christians in Rome, Paul had not had opportunity to fulfill his ambition, but when he eventually arrived, what kind of city did he encounter? David Stockton provides the following information: "Rome itself was organized into fourteen 'regions,' subdivided in turn into 'districts' (*uici*) with their own local officers (*uicomagistri*)." Through the initiative of Augustus, Rome underwent considerable expansion. The construction of many new buildings and the introduction of "traffic regulations, a new board of Public Works, the creation of a Metropolitan Police Force and Fire Brigade, a Water Board to ensure the needs of a city now approaching a million inhabitants, a Tiber Conservancy Board to dredge and embank the river, and proper provision and supervision of the corn supply are only the most noticeable of the benefits which could come from a stable and effective government."[43]

Most modern capital cities tend to have a population that is more cosmopolitan than the rest of the country. This was especially true of Rome, which acted as a magnet attracting people from all corners of the empire.

> At Rome itself, the growth of the Empire had brought about indirectly an ever-growing population of slaves, freedmen, foreigners, and Italians, the ambitious, the curious, the needy and the desperate. Quite apart from the very serious problem of keeping the peace, the nourishment of scores of thousands of people and the keeping of the city wholesome and habitable posed very serious

---

or town hall officials who are concerned that their tax base is being eroded. Planning permissions for churches in new developments are increasingly difficult to obtain.

43. Stockton, "Founding of the Empire," 547.

difficulties. Fortunately proceeds of empire could be diverted to the building of projects, above all aqueducts, which alone made it possible for so large a population to survive.[44]

The period we are considering, from Pentecost in AD 30/33 until Paul's imprisonment in Rome, covered the reigns of four Caesars: Tiberius (AD 14–17), Gaius Caligula (37–41), Claudius (41–54), and Nero (54–68). During that period, the imperial city continued to grow in both size and influence. Caesar Augustus had boasted that he had found a city of sun-dried brick and left a city of marble. In reality this was something of an exaggeration, in that it applied only to the principal buildings. The rapidly expanding population necessitated the building of tenement blocks on a large scale, which were built either of brick or of concrete covered in plaster. For the larger buildings, fire-baked brick replaced dried brick.

The growth of an ancient city depended on adequate supplies of local produce. Fortunately, Rome was surrounded by fertile farmland that provided good quality grain and all manner of vegetables and fruit. However, despite the fertility of the region, Rome had to look to the southern shore of the Mediterranean to find additional supplies to feed its growing population. Emperor Claudius constructed a new harbor beside the old colony of Ostia in the marshy plain at the mouth of the Tiber River. This harbor enabled Rome to expand imports of grain and other stable foods, slaves, and luxury items such as linen, furs, ivory, silk, and jewels, and to export wine and glass, woolen and linen goods.[45] Warehousing became a major industry both in Ostia and in Rome itself.

The Egyptian port of Alexandria was Rome's main source of essential food supplies for four months of the year. Fortunately, during this period shipbuilding had been improving in both design and cargo-carrying capacity. Michael Grant writes, "Corn-ships attained sizes that had never been seen in the Mediterranean before, carrying up to six hundred passengers and three hundred and forty tons of cargo."[46] Propelled by sail and oars, the journey from Alexandria to Rome could be made in ten to fourteen days. However, despite improvements in ship design, shippers and their insurers would not accept cargoes between October 10 and March 31. This closed season was due to the many winter storms. Paul himself experienced three shipwrecks. His journey to Rome came at the very end of the seagoing season, which explains

44. Purcell, "Arts of Government," 569.
45. Grant, *Ancient Mediterranean*, 290–91.
46. Ibid.

the ship captain's eagerness to reach his destination ahead of the storms and before his insurance coverage ran out!

Rome was the destination for returning soldiers, provincial governors, traders, and bankers, as well as philosophers, historians, poets, and playwrights who wanted to gain recognition. During this time, Rome was beautified with many gardens. Throughout the city the population was reminded of their benefactor Caesar Augustus by "the distribution of his own sculptured portraits far and wide."[47]

Significance of Paul's Urban Strategy for Today

In the contemporary Western world, a far greater proportion of the population lives in urban locations than in Paul's day. Modern cities represent even greater diversity, which also poses challenges and has strategic implications for mission. One cannot simply transfer an apparently effective model of urban mission from one context to another. The social and economic contexts must be taken into consideration. Church growth, for example, may be due to new industrial and commercial development resulting in an influx of new residents, a significant proportion of whom may simply be transferring their church allegiance. Alternatively, the new arrivals may be transitioning from a conservative cultural context to a context that is more liberal, or vice versa. Such a transition may result in their being selective as to the churches they decide to join.

The growth of a church may also have something to do with its strategic location and the availability of transportation, whether private or public. Yet another explanation for a church's growth may relate to the popularity and high public profile of the preacher or to the attractiveness of the venue and the range of its programs. Both institutional and external contextual factors have to be taken into careful consideration.

Today's World-Class Cities

The church today must recognize the strategic importance of world-class cities. These are the cities where political and economic power and cultural influence reside. These cities also make a global impact in shaping culture. Here in the United States, for example, we think of New York, Chicago, Nashville, Los Angeles, and San Francisco. Notice that a world-class city

47. Ibid., 282.

is not necessarily the capital of the country. At the same time, we must not overlook the fact that new world-class cities are emerging in the East: Beijing, Shanghai, Singapore, Tokyo, Mumbai, and so forth. World-class cities differ in terms of their major spheres of influence. Some, such as Tokyo, are renowned for their technological innovation, while others are known for their global financial influence, artistic expression in movies or theater, or political and military power.

As the example of first-century Rome clearly warns, power that is centered within a given city, then as now, can be misused to impose cultural imperialism. The imperial city became the dominant center of Western Christianity in the second century, but by the fourth century it had begun to impose its culture throughout the empire. Bishops, more concerned with order than with mission, increasingly assumed the authority of Roman administrators. Clergy adopted Roman dress. Church buildings were influenced by Roman styles of architecture. And Roman Christianity drove to the western extremities of Britain the vibrant Celtic expressions of the Christian faith.

In the past two centuries we have seen the dominant cultural influence of the church in North America exported to Europe and other parts of the world, as happened with European colonial expansion in the eighteenth and nineteenth centuries. The challenge remains to distinguish between the treasure of the gospel, the baggage of our culture, and the economic and political power that world-class cities exert.

Erosion of Neighborhood Communities in Modern Cities

Modern industrial society did much to undermine the concept of the neighborhood. Manufacture moved from being primarily a cottage industry located in the home to being a factory-based production line. Initially, factories were located close to housing so that most workers could either walk to work or, later, ride bicycles or take public transportation. Lance Ford recalls his visits to his grandparents' house in the small town of Era, Texas. It was a place where everyone knew everyone else, watched out for one another's kids, shared tools and kitchen goods, and offered a helping hand, especially in times of crisis.[48] Life in the communities of today is, by contrast, much different. "Social disintegration dominates American culture and suburbs have aided in spawning it. This social pattern of *disintegration* fosters our lifestyle, which means that it is very difficult to bring the differing 'parts' of our lives together. It's hard to integrate such a wide variety of relationships from so many different

---

48. Hirsch and Ford, *Right Here, Right Now*, 167.

compartments. Life becomes a churning machine, made up of many parts, rather than an organic and holistic body of life."[49]

In Britain, where cities are much more compact than in the United States, these conditions prevailed until the mid-1950s. After leaving school I worked for two years in a chemical and warehousing factory that had no parking lot for employees, just sheds for bicycles. I can remember the lineup of hundreds of bicycles as workers awaited the factory whistle to sound for the start of their journey home.

The advent of the affordable family car resulted in a workplace even farther from home. This development came sooner to the United States than to Britain. Although I grew up in inner-city Nottingham, with a population at that time of more than 250,000, we still had that sense of intimate community due to the austerity conditions that prevailed for the decade following the end of World War II.[50] No one owned a car on our street, apart from the family that operated a taxi service. Our play in the cobblestone street was only occasionally interrupted by someone calling, "Car coming!" We shopped locally, and every store was referred to by the name of the owner rather than whether it was the butcher's, grocer's, or newsagent's. Neighbors and their kids shopped for the elderly and shut-ins.

During the week, we walked everywhere: to school, the shops, the library, the pub, the movies, and church. Wherever you went, you encountered familiar faces and would often stop for a chat. On a Saturday morning, you might take the bus into town for specific purposes or simply to window-shop. And that was a special event for which you dressed in your best! Shops closed at midday, and after lunch the men mounted their bicycles for the football (soccer) match. So, in just my lifetime, the culture of the city has changed significantly, and the traditional neighborhood has collapsed.

Suburban sprawl is much more pervasive in North America and Australia, for the simple reason that there is much more space for new housing development. This results in lifestyles that are even more fragmented than those in European contexts. Although millions of Europeans commute into city centers, they return to smaller communities, many of which retain something of the small town or village environment. This is especially the case in much of Scandinavia. "It is not enough merely to focus on an immediate geographic neighborhood. If one does, one will likely discover that the neighbors' tightest relationship networks may span hundreds or thousands of miles. Building

49. Ibid., 165.
50. In *Austerity Britain, 1945–51*, Kynaston employs contemporary diaries and newspaper correspondence to graphically describe austerity conditions.

relationships with neighbors and participating in their lives and living spaces must engage virtual, as well as physical, forms of community."[51]

The issue of relational community versus virtual community should not be made mutually exclusive. In order to be truly human, persons need both forms of community in the context of the twenty-first century. When churches and other local institutions focus exclusively on their geographical turf, they fail to connect with those whose social network reaches far beyond those boundaries. Indeed, their sense of identity may have little connection with where they sleep at night. They are strangers to their own neighborhoods. If, however, they define themselves primarily, or even exclusively, in terms of their virtual community, they may enjoy a measure of privatized intimacy as they relate to their social networks, yet this is an intimacy with severe limitations. They may make themselves more vulnerable than they would in face-to-face communication, because they feel safe. Yet there is no sense of mutual accountability. Individuals can misrepresent themselves online or even invent a persona. They can also terminate a conversation or break off a contact with the tap of a key. Those who depend on virtual community for their social interaction often display poor face-to-face relational skills.

The disintegration of local communities has been accompanied by a proliferation of special-interest groups, each providing a sense of identity and personal fulfillment. But these groups are the result of self-selection around sporting, recreational, fitness, hobby, occupational, and other interests. Furthermore, some people socialize more readily than others. Those most at risk of isolation are the social misfits, the housebound sick, and the elderly. These are the lonely individuals in society, who are prone to be overlooked by overstretched social agencies or neighbors who no longer have discretionary time to look out for those in need.

Prioritizing the City

The many challenges presented by urban society mean that the churches must not take the easier course and abandon the city for the suburbs. Cities are complex sociological phenomena, and church leaders trained in interpreting the Scriptures also need a high level of skill in exegeting the city. How many seminaries have religious sociologists on faculty to provide this level of expertise? Also, field research has to be given a much higher priority if students are to understand the unique culture of each city, appreciate its history and

51. Van Gelder and Zscheile, *Missional Church in Perspective*, 130.

the economic and sociological influences shaping its future, and evaluate the impact the churches are making.

As church leaders embark on mission within a city, they need to tap into the information and expertise already available through the sociology departments of the university and community college, the local chamber of commerce, the school district, editors of local newspapers, and law enforcement agencies. I heard Donald McGavran comment many years ago, "There is nothing spiritual in undertaking a work of God in ignorance of obtainable facts!"

Different approaches are needed to reach people in different types of housing. Those who live in high-rises or gated communities cannot be reached through door-to-door visitation. Public places where neighbors socialize might provide a more accessible and socially congenial place to meet. I am amazed at the frequency with which Starbucks is mentioned as providing such opportunities. But coffeehouses cater to only a thin slice of the population. Imaginative alternatives need to be developed if we hope to mingle with the majority of the urban population, who do not frequent such places.

Looking Ahead

In the following chapters, we will examine the Pauline letters to the region of Galatia and the various cities of the Greco-Roman world: Philippi, Thessalonica, Corinth, Ephesus, Colossae, and Rome. This study is inductive in nature, allowing the letters to speak for themselves and seeking to identify the dominant themes and issues that Paul and his mission team had to address. I am particularly impressed by the recurring nature of many of the issues. The following are the questions we will explore:

- How were new faith communities (churches) born in each urban setting?
- What steps were taken to nurture these communities of new believers, and how were they networked?
- How were new believers—whether from a Jewish background or, to an increasing extent, from pagan backgrounds—taught and formed into becoming lifelong followers of Jesus?
- What core beliefs were proclaimed, applied, and defended against detractors?
- How were relationships among members of the faith community forged to their mutual benefit, and how did they relate to the wider society, which was often suspicious if not openly hostile?

- How did mutual ministry and leadership emerge within these communities, and what challenges did they face both from within the membership and from without?

One final word before launching into the main body of our study: My intention is not to return to the first century in a misguided attempt to reproduce a twenty-first-century version of the first-century church. As we have already indicated, and will further emphasize in the following pages, the social conditions have changed radically since that time. Furthermore, we cannot ignore or undo two thousand years of church history. I believe that it was C. S. Lewis who commented, "It is one thing to court a virgin, but quite another to court a divorcée!" Here in the West, churches have established long-standing reputations for good or ill. Hence, our purpose is more modest. We will employ a missional hermeneutic in examining the early church, to see what lessons we can learn and to what extent they relate to our current situation in post-Christendom late modernity.

PART TWO

ISSUES AND INSIGHTS

3

Urban Engagement

It is easy to overlook the tremendous challenges that the disciples of Jesus faced in responding to his commission to become apostles and to make disciples among all peoples everywhere. Up to that point, these followers of "the Way," as the early followers of Jesus were described, represented an exclusively Jewish movement confined to the land of Israel. It is one thing to receive a commission but quite another to heed it and respond to the challenge.

Despite the apostles' commissioning and the subsequent outpouring of the Holy Spirit on the disciples on the day of Pentecost, the movement remained Jerusalem based, with mission outreach confined to Judea and Samaria. Apparently, the focus was still nationalistic, missing the significance of Jesus's opening declaration, "All authority in heaven and on earth has been given to me. Therefore go . . ." (Matt. 28:18–19 NIV), which challenged any restrictive ethnic view of his mission.

It was on the unassailable authority of the ascended Lord of the cosmos that these disciples were given both the authorization and the confidence to embark on their mission. The Great Commission also represents the witnesses' realization that the actualization of the reign of God, even in its provisional form, is not something they can bring about through their own ingenuity, but is utterly dependent on the will and power of their heavenly Lord.

The disciples' entrenched nationalistic mind-set prevailed, as is evident from the question posed to Christ just before his ascension: "Lord, is this the time when you will restore the kingdom to Israel?" (Acts 1:6). In response, Jesus redirects their attention to what he will do through them. "It is not for you to know the times or periods that the Father has set by his own authority. But you will receive power when the Holy Spirit has come upon you; and you will be my witnesses in Jerusalem, in all Judea and Samaria, and to the ends of the earth" (Acts 1:7–8). A similar self-focused and shortsighted attitude prevails today in churches that have suffered sustained numerical decline and fear for the future, not knowing where or how to take the next step. In coming to the Lord in our distress, we are likely to begin where the original disciples began, with a plea for restoration to some golden age in the past. In response, the Lord will point us to the future and give us purpose and courage by assuring us of the presence of the Holy Spirit in our midst to empower and guide us. The path ahead is one of renewal, not of restoration, and it begins right where we are, in our "Jerusalem," and moves out in ever-widening circles.

Continuity and Discontinuity in Mission

The extension of the Way beyond the confines of Palestine was not the result of strategic planning by the leaders of the Jerusalem church in response to the Great Commission and Jesus's ascension-day assurance. Rather, it came about through the persecution of the movement by the Jewish religious authorities. When a severe persecution broke out in Jerusalem, it was directed at the entire Christian community "except the apostles" (Acts 8:1). We are left to conjecture why they were exempt. Arthur Patzia offers the most likely suggestion. "Could it be that the local Jewish authorities (the Sanhedrin) and Hellenistic conservatives saw the apostles as representing a segment of the early church that could coexist peaceably with Judaism? . . . The apostles avoided persecution at this time because they were not perceived as a threat to the status quo and because the Jerusalem church continued to be quite Jewish in nature and practice."[1] Paul McKechnie provides further insight when he suggests, "The authorities may have calculated that expelling could cause a backlash. They may have hoped to reduce their influence by removing their followers. As it was, the expulsion gave a fillip to the spread of Christianity."[2] Alternatively, authorities may have been putting pressure on the apostles by going after their followers. If you know that the leaders care for their followers, you can hurt the followers in order to get the leaders to stop what they're doing.

It seems that the Jerusalem church remained preoccupied with its witness to the predominantly Jewish communities of Judea. On Paul's return to

1. Patzia, *Emergence of the Church*, 85.
2. McKechnie, *First Christian Centuries*, 44.

Jerusalem at the conclusion of his third missionary journey, he "reported in detail what God had done among the Gentiles through his ministry" (Acts 21:19 NIV). The leaders in Jerusalem praised God for Paul's news but at the same time were determined not to be upstaged! They immediately responded, "You see, brother, how many thousands of Jews have believed, and all of them are zealous for the law" (v. 20 NIV). We might add, "So there!"

This tension between the two expressions of the Christian faith—one within a monocultural Jewish context and the other within the pluralistic Greco-Roman environment in which Paul conducted his mission—is not confined to the first century. Brian McLaren, in his foreword to Ray Anderson's *An Emergent Theology for Emerging Churches*, presents the challenge in contemporary terms by asking the following questions: "Are we going to follow a Jerusalem-based faith, where our message is tamed and contained by a dominant culture from the past? Or are we going to follow an Antioch-based faith, where our message never loses its wild, untamed essence (flames of fire, rushing wind), but like a spring of living water or vibrant new wine, it always flows and is never contained by old forms?"[3]

As we ponder Paul's letters to the predominantly Gentile churches that were the fruit of his groundbreaking apostolic mission, we are aware that he is grappling with many issues that arise from the intersection and interaction of theology and mission. Ray Anderson comments, "Paul's letters to these churches during his own travels produced a narrative theology that to this day constitutes the theological core of the New Testament."[4] He goes on to state, "The nature of the church, argued Paul, could not rest solely upon a historical link with Jesus and the Twelve but upon the Spirit of the resurrected Christ who has 'broken down the dividing wall . . . [of] hostility,' and created in himself 'one new humanity in place of the two' (Ephesians 2:14–15)."[5]

The bias in our Christendom-bound theologizing has been to look to the past, from which we can certainly learn some valuable lessons and which we ignore to our peril. But while our theology must be informed by the past, it cannot be bound to it. Ray Anderson's concern is "to tease out an emergent theology that is truthful only because it is discovered along the journey (revelational), contextual only because it is currently being lived out (incarnational), and contemporary only because it viably takes us into the future (eschatological)."[6] The church today must combine Pentecostal experience with orthodox Christology. Anderson provides a helpful contrast:

3. McLaren, foreword to *Emergent Theology*, 5.
4. Anderson, *Emergent Theology*, 32.
5. Ibid., 33.
6. Ibid., 11.

"Pentecostal experience without a relation with Christ is like a sailboat with neither oars nor rudder—it can only move when there is a wind, though it cannot steer when it is moving. An orthodox Christology without Pentecostal experience is like a barge of coal anchored to shore. It has fuel but no fire, and even if it should burn, it has no engine to turn water into steam and steam into power. And so, not being able to transport people, it takes on more coal."[7] Alan Hirsch insists that "the Christendom mode of engagement . . . was simply not up to the type of missionary challenge presented to us by our surrounding context: a context that required more of a cross-cultural missionary methodology than the 'outreach and in-drag' model we have been using to this point."[8]

The challenge remains in the United States, where in many regions the traditional approach still has some traction because the cultural distance between the church and broader society is still sufficiently close. Through the influence of friends and family members, individuals who have distanced themselves from the church can be attracted back into the local church. They are familiar with religious language, symbols, and rituals, so the church world is not alien to them. However, even in the Deep South and rural America, an increasing percentage of the population is proving resistant, and even cynical, to these invitations.[9] This is especially true of the postboomer generations.

Breakthrough in Syrian Antioch

In Luke's account of the expansion of the church throughout the Eastern Mediterranean, the initiative passes from Jerusalem, Judea, and Samaria to Syrian Antioch, where we witness the breaking of ethnic barriers and the expanding of missionary horizons. "Antioch became the center of his [Paul's] activities, perhaps for most of the twelve to fourteen years that he spent 'in the regions of Syria and Cilicia' (Gal. 1:21; cf. 2:1–14 and Acts 11:25f; 13:1). Antioch, center of political, military, and commercial communication between Rome and the Persian frontier and between Palestine and Asia Minor, was one of the three or four most important cities of the empire and the home of a large and vigorous Jewish community."[10]

7. Ibid., 48–49.
8. Hirsch, *Forgotten Ways*, 34.
9. During a visit to a town in northern Tennessee I asked a representative group of pastors for their best estimate of the percentage of the population in church on an average Sunday. They agreed on a figure of 25 percent.
10. Meeks, *First Urban Christians*, 19.

It is significant that the initiative for the further expansion of the church beyond Israel did not come from the apostles in Jerusalem but rather from unnamed churched members who were scattered initially throughout Judea and Samaria (Acts 8:1). They soon ventured farther, traveling up the coast to Phoenicia, and from there some took a ship to Cyprus, while others headed inland to Antioch of Syria (Acts 11:19). At first they confined their mission to fellow Jews. However, a group went from Cyprus and Cyrene in North Africa and began preaching to Gentiles. David Peterson believes they "were doubtless influenced by the ministry of Stephen and Philip before being thrust from Jerusalem."[11] Like them, these missionaries were probably Hellenistic Jews who were in the same circle of acquaintances as Stephen and Philip.

Groundbreaking Initiatives

These missionaries from Cyprus and Cyrene took their groundbreaking initiatives a step further. God affirmed their bold step, for "the Lord's hand was with them, and a great number of people believed and turned to the Lord" (Acts 11:21 NIV). Their taking the initiative to speak to non-Jews "is the first detailed account of evangelism by ordinary believers."[12] Yet again the leaders of the Jerusalem church are not the ones taking the lead in this significant expansion of mission.

In Luke's account we repeatedly see God taking the initiative, for it is by the prompting of the Holy Spirit that the gospel continues to advance. Part of the explanation of this instant success, F. F. Bruce believes, may be "that some of the Gentiles who believed belonged to the class of God-fearers who already knew something of the Old Testament revelation by attendance at Jewish synagogues; it would be in accordance with the analogy of other places if such people formed the nucleus of the Gentile converts in Antioch."[13]

A number of issues, arising out of this significant missionary breakthrough, are relevant to the church across subsequent centuries, and are even more applicable in our day. The first is that mission initiatives more often ascend from the ground level than descend from church hierarchies. Or, as Paul Pierson, veteran missiologist and former dean of Fuller's School of World Mission, describes it, "Mission arises at the margins rather than at the center." In our own day we are finding that emerging churches, both within traditional denominations and as independent groups, come into

11. Peterson, *Acts of the Apostles*, 351.
12. Ibid.
13. Bruce, *Book of Acts*, 239.

being through the initiatives of groups of Christians who sense God's call first to take the gospel to their own contexts, and then to reach out to more distant places.

A second important factor is that many of the teams that take these initiatives are multicultural and even international in composition. This is especially significant when engaging pluralistic urban contexts. The churches birthed in such situations should reflect the racial composition of their neighborhoods and the people they are seeking to engage.

Response of the Jerusalem Church

When the church in Jerusalem heard the news that non-Jews were responding to the gospel in significant numbers, they sent Barnabas to Antioch to check it out, just as they had sent Peter and John to evaluate Philip's missionary outreach in Samaria. Barnabas was a good choice on this occasion in that he had, as a native of Cyprus, a broader cultural understanding and was a warmhearted encourager. In contrast to monocultural Jerusalem, "Antioch was a cosmopolitan city, where Jew and Gentile, Greek and barbarian rubbed shoulders, where Mediterranean civilization met the Syrian desert; racial and religious differences which loomed large in Judea seemed less important here."[14] "When he [Barnabas] arrived and saw what the grace of God had done, he was glad and encouraged them all to remain true to the Lord with all their hearts. He was a good man, full of the Holy Spirit and faith, and a great number of people were brought to the Lord" (Acts 11:23–24 NIV).

This second wave of conversions is especially significant in that it was the result of the witness of new believers and the evidence of God's grace at work in their lives, despite the fact that they resided in a city with a reputation for lax sexual morals.[15] If a person with a critical or suspicious spirit had been sent, they could have squelched this new movement at the outset.

Barnabas had the good sense to recognize that this movement made demands that required a helper. But, significantly, he does not return to Jerusalem for assistance; rather, he goes to Tarsus, the capital of Cilicia, in search of Paul, whom he felt had the upbringing and gifts needed for this situation. "He [Paul] was a Hebrew yet full of Roman sympathies, intimate with Greek thought, and familiar with the neighbourhood."[16] And his cultural context in Tarsus was not so different from that of Antioch.

---

14. This reputation mainly arose from the cult of Artemis and Apollo located at Daphne, just five miles away. Ibid., 241.

15. Ibid., 238.

16. Rackham, *Acts of the Apostles*, 169.

Instructing New Believers

On their return, Paul and Barnabas stayed for a full year in order to establish a firm foundation of knowledge and application of the gospel. Furthermore, they did not restrict their teaching to an elite group but gathered "large crowds of people" (Acts 11:26 NLT). The whole church was "discipled," and if they were to be involved in the ongoing ministry of the church, they would all need to be included in the teaching.

New churches need to be nurtured and discipled from the outset. Today we struggle with the challenge of trying to turn around consumerist churches consisting of undiscipled church members. The apostles first discipled a group of people until they became a church. We face the opposite problem of turning church members into disciples, which is to put the cart before the horse.

The church in Antioch, although mainly composed of non-Jews, did not represent a splinter group wanting to distance themselves from Jewish believers in Jesus as the Messiah. When some prophets arrived from Jerusalem predicting that a great famine was coming on the entire Roman world—which Luke assures his readers was fulfilled during the reign of the emperor Claudius (AD 41–54)—the believers sent famine relief to their brothers and sisters in Jerusalem.

Everyone contributed as much as they were able. Their gifts were entrusted to Barnabas and Paul to take to Jerusalem, probably in AD 48, a visit that Paul describes in greater detail in Galatians 2:1–10. Peterson underlines the significance of this act of generosity: "The sending of a gift from the mixed Jewish-Gentile church in Antioch to the more established Jewish Christian communities in Judea is an important expression of solidarity across social and cultural boundaries."[17]

Releasing Their Best for Mission

Yet again we see evidence that the continuing mission of the church was initiated, not by humans, but by the Holy Spirit, through a prophetic word (Acts 13:1–4). In the church in Antioch were prophets and teachers open to the leading of the Lord. Among them are named Barnabas; Simeon, who was called Niger, probably due to his being a dark-skinned person from North Africa; Lucius of Cyrene, another North African; and Manaen, a member of the court of Herod the ruler. This leadership team is remarkable for its diversity, with the distinctive cultures of North Africa, Cilicia, and Galilee represented. The Antioch church was prepared to release their two key leaders for the work of mission. "The Spirit's charge . . . is for the leaders of the

17. Peterson, *Acts of the Apostles*, 359.

church to acknowledge by their actions what God has already decided and revealed. . . . The Spirit here speaks for the risen Christ, who first separated Paul to himself for a special work."[18] Although the church in Antioch sent out Barnabas and Saul (Paul), they made no attempt to control their movements; they simply released them, sending them out as free agents.

As Barnabas and Paul were sent out by the whole church, it was to the entire church that they made their enthusiastic report when they returned from southern Galatia about a year later (Acts 14:26–28). However, the rapid growth of churches with Gentile majorities caused consternation among leaders of the Jerusalem church who sensed a change in the balance of power.

Fresh initiatives that have not been authorized by the ecclesiastical hierarchy are sometimes opposed because they have not been officially sanctioned by the councils of the church or by its appropriate mission board. At other times, restrictive demands are placed on the pioneers, or they are simply smothered with kindness. Church authorization often depends on ponderous decision-making boards, so that opportunities are missed, or those with the vision simply get tired of waiting.

The church in Antioch evidently regarded the ongoing mission of the church as deserving of their very best. They were prepared to release Barnabas and Paul, who had been their primary teachers and leaders. Contrast this attitude with that of so many church leaders in traditional settings today who regard the pioneering mission of the church as marginal, as the concern of young enthusiasts or "mission types" (who are often snubbed by the local church). A number of significant church leaders also actively oppose taking initiatives to proclaim the good news to people of other faiths on the grounds that such evangelistic activity represents cultural imperialism. In contrast, among the "young, restless, and Reformed" crowd, the pastor-theologian-church planter is *the* rock star and definitely not marginal.

In responding to the mission challenges confronting Western churches, congregations with their leaders must likewise endeavor to identify individuals who have the vision and are convinced of the call of God to embark upon groundbreaking initiatives. They will need the training and the encouragement of Barnabas types to equip and support them in such a challenging endeavor.

Receptive Populations

Each of the evangelistic initiatives out of Antioch resulted in a surprising receptivity (Acts 11:21, 24). Legalistic religion carries little appeal, in that it is

18. Ibid., 376.

judgmental, inward looking, and culture bound. This is in contrast to churches that proclaim the good news of God's grace made available through Christ, which is a message that brings both reconciliation and transformation.

Paul's strategy was unmistakably urban: "In that respect it stood on the growing edge of the Christian movement, for it was in the cities of the Roman Empire that Christianity, though born in the village culture of Palestine, had its greatest successes until well after the time of Constantine."[19] Within that strategic framework, we see in Paul's initiatives consistency coupled with flexibility and opportunism. In every place, he followed the leading of the Holy Spirit, often in the midst of difficult circumstances. We will now trace his journeys to the cities addressed in his follow-up letters.

Conflict and Confusion in Galatia (Acts 13:13–14:20)

After traveling through the island of Cyprus, Paul, Barnabas, and John Mark arrive at Perga (Acts 13:13), the main port of the province of Galatia, at which point John Mark leaves them to return to Jerusalem for reasons that are not stated but evidently caused a rift between him and Paul. From Perga stretched a main trade route through the Atlas Mountains to Pisidian Antioch. From there Paul journeys along a chain of towns, passing through Iconium, Lystra, and Derbe.

The churches addressed in Paul's letter to the Galatians cannot be identified with absolute certainty. Some scholars regard the intended recipients of the letter as the otherwise unknown churches in northern Galatia—that is, northern Asia Minor—where Luke makes no mention of church-planting activities. This was the view principally held by scholars from the patristic period to the Reformation era. They identify the Galatians with the Celts who settled this northern area in the third century BC, whereas the population in the south was not Galatian by race. But Hansen makes the point that "in Paul's time Galatia was the name for the entire Roman province stretching from Pontus in the north to Pamphylia in the south."[20]

Supporting Networks

That Paul visited Pisidian Antioch on each of his missionary journeys, helping to make it a center of the new faith in Anatolia, shows the importance

19. Meeks, *First Urban Christians*, 8.
20. Hansen, *Galatians*, 17.

of the district of Pisidia in the early spread of Christianity. From there, Paul journeyed to the other three nearby cities straddling the same east-west road. This linking made possible mutual support among the churches birthed as the fruit of Paul's missionary journey.

In all church-planting endeavors, it is important for the pioneers to work as a team, for the mutual encouragement of the team members, and to establish faith communities that can support one another once the apostolic team has left the district. Paul demonstrates his further concern for the Galatian churches by retracing his steps to encourage the believers in each place. He did this despite the opposition he had encountered in each location, thereby forgoing the opportunity of a direct, short journey home through the Cilician Gates to Tarsus and on to Caesarea Philippi.

Audience Awareness

Since Pisidia had a large Jewish population, Paul began his ministry in the city by visiting the synagogue, as was his usual custom (Acts 13:5; 14:1; 17:1, 2, 10, 17; 18:19; 19:8). Giving priority to speaking to his fellow Jews about the Messiah was not just a strategic priority but also a theological imperative. The gospel was "for the Jews first," in that the promise of the coming Messiah had been made to them, and God had for centuries prepared them for his coming.

It is significant that Paul did not take the initiative by requesting to be heard, but rather was invited to speak by the leaders of the synagogue. As a distinguished and learned guest, he was someone who was highly respected, a Pharisee from Jerusalem and a former student of the renowned scholar Gamaliel. Paul's opening words established an immediate rapport with his audience: "Fellow Israelites and you Gentiles who worship God, listen to me" (Acts 13:16 NIV).

Paul was aware that he was addressing two distinct audiences. Alongside the Jews were the Gentiles who were attracted to the Jewish faith and needed to know its ancient historic grounding as recorded in the Hebrew Scriptures. What follows in Acts 13 is the only expanded outline of a sermon by Paul in the synagogue, although, as Peterson notes, "there are later, brief summaries which match this model in certain respects."[21] Paul also makes many of the same points throughout his letters.

Paul begins by reminding his audience that God had chosen the Jews from the time of Abraham, and he continues by tracing the subsequent history of Abraham's descendants from the time Israel became a nation. The apostle

21. Peterson, *Acts of the Apostles*, 384.

then brings the message home to his synagogue audience, exposed each Sabbath to that same central theme: "It is to us that this message of salvation has been sent. . . . Therefore, my friends, I want you to know that through Jesus the forgiveness of sins is proclaimed to you. Through him everyone who believes is set free from every sin, a justification you were not able to obtain under the law of Moses" (Acts 13:26, 38–39 NIV). Paul concludes his sermon by cautioning them not to respond as their ancestors had done by scoffing at the message of the prophets, but to be open to the possibility of God doing a new thing in their day.

Paul's address to a predominantly Jewish congregation in the synagogue is in marked contrast to his outdoor message to the pagan audience in Lystra. This town was something of a cultural backwater, with a native population who spoke the local language, Lycaonian. This created a communication barrier that made it difficult for Paul and Barnabas to understand how the population was responding to the miracle they had just witnessed in the healing of the cripple. They needed to know not only the language but also the background history in order to appreciate the significance of the crowd's excited response. They regarded Paul and Barnabas as gods, identifying Barnabas with the Greek god Zeus, who was the patron saint of Lystra, and Paul with Hermes, since he was the chief speaker (Acts 14:12).

The missionaries were unaware of a widely believed legend, recorded by the poet Ovid, that these two gods had previously visited Lystra but were recognized only by an old couple. The population was determined to make amends on this occasion, with the priests of the temple together with the crowds, preparing bulls for sacrifice and making wreaths of flowers to honor their visitors.

Barnabas and Paul were horrified when they eventually realized that they were being made the objects of worship.

> When the apostles Barnabas and Paul heard of this, they tore their clothes and rushed out into the crowd, shouting: "Friends, why are you doing this? We too are only human, like you. We are bringing you good news, telling you to turn from these worthless things to the living God, who made the heavens and the earth and the sea and everything in them. In the past, he let all the nations go their own way. Yet he has not left himself without testimony: He has shown kindness by giving you rain from heaven and crops in their seasons; he provides you with plenty of food and fills your hearts with joy." (Acts 14:14–17 NIV)

Such was the crowd's fear of their gods that even this exhortation was scarcely sufficient to hold them back. In sharp contrast to his approach when addressing a Jewish audience, Paul does not recite the history of God's providential dealings with the Hebrews on this occasion, which would have excluded his pagan audience. Instead, he proffers a common-grace argument.

To both Jewish and pagan audiences, Paul is bringing "good news." However, as Peterson emphasizes, "The message here is not about God fulfilling his promises to Israel and sending the Messianic Savior, but good news about the possibility of escaping from the futility of idolatry . . . and coming to know the living God."[22] Paul stresses that it is the living God who has created all things and continues to care for all the people of his creation by providing rain to ensure the growth of crops. He contrasts the provision of the one living God with the worthless idols that they attempted to please in order to avoid the idols' displeasure. When Paul says, "In the past, he let all the nations go their own way," he is suggesting not that God is indifferent but that he is patient.[23] "What we have here is not evangelism in the normal New Testament sense of proclaiming Christ and his saving work. However, it is a biblical foundation for evangelism in a culture where foundational presuppositions about God and nature and the meaning of human existence need to be challenged."[24]

Receptor-Oriented Communication

Modern communication theory would label Paul's approach "receptor-oriented," meaning his message is consistently adapted to his audience. With his Jewish audience in Antioch, Paul's approach was to remind them of their history and emphasize how God had both guided and protected them as the Lord worked out saving purpose for the nation. Today, even churchgoing people show little appreciation of their place in God's grand narrative, in which they have become adopted sons and daughters of God, the story of God's dealings with God's ancient people now their story too. So within the church we need the kind of preaching that Paul engaged in with his first-century Jewish audience.

We also need to learn from the approach Paul adopted among his pagan audience in Lystra, which focused on "the living God, who made the heaven and the earth" (Acts 14:15). One wonders to what extent a common-grace argument would resonate with twenty-first-century "pagans." When the history proclaimed by the preacher is not your history, it lacks relevance. We need approaches that immediately address the issues that are dominant within a culture.

22. Ibid., 409.
23. Bruce, *Book of Acts*, 294.
24. Peterson, *Acts of the Apostles*, 411.

Poorly aimed preaching raises several questions: To whom are we preaching? Are we preaching to insiders who need to be reminded of God's purposes fulfilled in history and still to be fulfilled as they face the future? Or do we need to start further back with a concept of God who is creator and sustainer of the universe, who challenges our false gods, and who is the Holy One holding us accountable? We talk more frequently to ourselves, about internal church agendas concerned with survival and relational challenges, than to the world, about issues of broad concern on which the Scriptures offer valuable insights.

Paul and Barnabas's experience in Lystra shows us that we need to know people's language and the worldview and stories that have shaped them (whether factual or mythological) in order to be equipped to anticipate and interpret their reactions.

Divided Response

Some in Paul's audience were intrigued by what they heard, so much so that they invited the visitors to share with them on the following Sabbath. Apparently, some were not prepared to wait that long; many followed Paul and Barnabas to learn more. Paul and Barnabas "talked with them and urged them to continue in the grace of God" (Acts 13:43 NIV). The following Sabbath, a great crowd showed up, consisting mainly of non-Jews from the city, to "hear the word of the Lord" (v. 44).

For the Jews in the audience who had rejected Paul's message, the sight of such an unprecedented response, rather than causing them to rejoice, roused their annoyance and jealousy. The crowd of non-Jews virtually took over the synagogue! If only these Jewish leaders had welcomed those who responded, they would have shared in the fulfillment of Israel's role to be a blessing to the nations, as promised to Abraham, and would have been at the forefront of Israel's responsibility to take the saving message to the Gentiles, as prophesied by Isaiah (see Isa. 12:3–6; 42:6; 45:22–23; 49:6). Instead, they did all in their power to undermine the message brought by Paul and Barnabas, contradicting what the two said and becoming personal in their opposition by "heaping abuse" on them.

The word of God received a ready reception among the Gentiles, presumably through the witness of "the devout converts to Judaism," who could speak from personal experience, as well as from what they had learned at the synagogue and from the teaching of Paul. The impact of the ministry of Paul and Barnabas was such that "the word of the Lord spread through the whole region" (Acts 13:49 NIV). Luke acknowledged that this was the Lord's doing, in that "all who were appointed for eternal life believed" (v. 48 NIV). In every town visited by Paul, the majority of the Jewish leaders were determined to do all in their power to oppose the movement, stirring up persecution by gaining the support of the mob and city officials to expel the evangelists from the region.

Among church leaders of every generation are those who feel threatened when new teachers bring a fresh message and gain a wider hearing. They are more concerned about their own personal following than the response of their people to the word of God. They are alarmed when the response comes primarily from the broader community, among which they have little influence.

If the Lord cannot further the divine mission through the leaders and congregations of existing churches, then God will work around them and despite them. Increasingly, this is happening today when historic denominations lose evangelistic vision and sometimes even question the legitimacy of seeking to win those of other faiths or no faith at all in the unique person and saving mission of Jesus Christ. In the present climate of biblical illiteracy, we see instances of theologically heterodox messages proclaimed by high-profile religious leaders gaining a wide public following.

From the outset we notice a distinctive feature of apostolic ministry that the contemporary church needs to emulate. Namely, it had leaders who were going somewhere and refused to give up no matter how hard the going. It has been said that a church that isn't going anywhere doesn't need a leader; a caretaker will do!

Conversions and Opposition in Philippi (Acts 16:12–40; 20:2; 2 Thessalonians 2:2)

The first evangelistic initiative in Macedonia took place in Philippi in AD 49 or 50. As the Jewish population was too small in that city for them to form a synagogue (which required a minimum of ten males), Paul found their place of prayer located on the bank of the River Gangites (now called Angista). This location provided both a quiet place and running water for Jewish purification rites.

In Luke's account we see how the lives of three very different individuals were affected by the gospel: a wealthy businesswoman (Acts 16:11–15, 40), an exploited slave girl (vv. 16–18), and the local jailer (vv. 23–34). In each case we see Paul simply grasping opportunities as they open up.

Here is a reminder that the mission is Christ's own and that his presence always precedes that of the evangelist, by preparing personal encounters and opening minds and hearts to respond to the gospel. In the case of the three individuals identified by Paul, we are also alerted to the power of the gospel to change lives, with deliverances taking many forms. In the case of the slave girl delivered from the spirit of divination, Luke does not mention whether or not she became a follower of Christ. Deliverance does not, in every instance, lead to salvation.

Hospitality

Lydia represents the first recorded convert in Macedonia and is of special significance for a number of reasons. Lydia is a non-Jew, although a "God-fearer" attracted to the Jewish faith, and one the Lord had prepared. "The Lord opened her heart to listen eagerly to what was said by Paul" (Acts 16:14). Her spiritual search, beginning in Judaism, now found its fulfillment in the good news of Jesus's sacrificial death on the cross and his rising from the grave. The first convert being a woman signifies that the gospel—as well as the Holy Spirit—is no respecter of gender. For, as Paul would later write to the Galatians, "There is no longer Jew or Greek, there is no longer slave or free, there is no longer male and female; for all of you are one in Christ Jesus" (Gal. 3:22).

Lydia was also an influential person, owning a business trading in expensive, highly prized purple cloth imported from her home city of Thyatira (Acts 16:14). Following her baptism, she offered hospitality to Paul and his companions, saying, "If you have judged me to be faithful to the Lord, come and stay at my home" (Acts 16:15). In other words, she refused to take no for an answer.

The city's jailer also offers generous hospitality to Paul and Silas following his conversion, which resulted from the praise-filled witness of these two prisoners and their taking charge of fellow prisoners in the aftermath of the earthquake that destroyed the prison. Knowing full well that his life would be forfeited if any of the prisoners escaped, the jailer draws his sword with the intention of committing suicide. But Paul intervenes to reassure him that they are all still present. The jailer escorts them outside, where he asks Paul and Silas, "Sirs, what must I do to be saved?" (Acts 16:30).

It is difficult to ascertain what he meant by this question. At least in the case of this jailer, personal surrender came before intellectual understanding. We can only assume that the two prisoners' worshipful witness that evening gave him some rudimentary understanding of the good news of Jesus Christ. Paul, at least, is assured that the jailer has sufficient understanding to be baptized along with his household. This incident shows us that overheard praise, especially in the face of privation, suffering, and persecution, is often the most effective witness.

No time is lost in baptizing the jailer and his household. Extraordinary circumstances demand urgent measures. The jailer provides hospitality to

Paul and Silas, binding up their wounds and providing a meal. For their part, they waste no time in sharing the word of the Lord with all of the jailer's household. Their baptism creates an instant house church characterized by joy. This incident illustrates the close relationship between the decisions of individuals and the corporate decision-making process.

Conversions Lead to Opposition

The familiar story of opposition is repeated in relation to the slave girl who was possessed by a demon, whose deliverance threatened her owners' commercial interests. Paul's experience in Philippi, of opportunity accompanied by opposition, is a pattern that repeats itself in many locations. On this occasion the local officials become alarmed when they learn that Paul is a Roman citizen and thereby recognize that they have acted illegally in their treatment of Paul. They order the immediate release of Paul and his companions, which triggers crowd protests fomented by Jewish opponents of the evangelists.

The strategic importance of Philippi is reflected in the fact that Paul visited the city on two further occasions—in AD 56 and 57. Paul's letter to the Philippians dates from around 54–55 and shows the immediate impact of his preaching there.

Surviving and Thriving in Thessalonica (Acts 17:1–9)

To all outward appearances, new churches may appear to be very vulnerable, while in reality many are incredibly resilient. The church in Thessalonica emerged out of just three Sabbaths of Paul's preaching in the local synagogue.[25] In his preaching he had argued that the promised and long-awaited Messiah of the Jewish people had come in the person of Jesus of Nazareth. Paul explained and proved that Jesus fulfilled prophecies recorded in the Hebrew Scriptures that the Messiah must suffer and rise from the dead (Acts 17:3).

Opposition Generated in the Synagogue

The gospel message caused division and dissension among the Jewish audience of Thessalonica as elsewhere. Such a divided response, with some accepting the message while many actively opposed the preaching of the good

---

25. Paul's first letter to them, however, suggests a longer period. Time has to be allowed for Paul and Silas to set up shop as leatherworkers in the city (1 Thess. 1:5; 2:9; 2 Thess. 3:8) and for them to engage in a teaching ministry beyond the synagogue (1 Thess. 4:1–2).

news, is not confined to first-century Jewish audiences. It occurs wherever and whenever Jesus is proclaimed as Savior and Lord. The entire church is called in every age to broadcast that message, and we should not be surprised when alongside enthusiastic responses strong negative reactions are also stirred.

Jesus's own ministry triggered the same divisions as that of Paul. To proclaim the uniqueness of Jesus Christ as the Son of God and Savior of the world especially generates opposition in a world characterized by relativism and pluralism. Such a complex context means that the church must bear its witness without compromise and yet with sensitivity. Love and grace go hand in hand with truth.

Despite the relentless opposition of the majority among his Jewish audience, Paul did not give up hope for his people, as we see from his deeply felt concern expressed in Romans 9–11. Paul's persistence provides a lesson for all who endeavor to share the good news with those to whom they feel especially close.

Opposition was not restricted to intellectual debate but boiled over into rabble-rousing. The Jews who had rejected Paul's message succeeded in staging a riot by stirring up individuals who were at a loose end and who welcomed any diversion. They were informed by the Jews that the new believers were meeting in the home of Jason. Their host was presumably a Hellenized Jew, as his name is a Greek version of the Hebrew name Joshua. Unable to locate Paul and Silas, they dragged Jason before the city officials and shouted their accusations that Paul and Silas were troublemakers disturbing the Pax Romana.

Their further accusation represented a half-truth, which if proven would have placed the new believers in a hazardous position. Jesus was in fact proclaimed as "King of kings and Lord of lords," although the Christians did not represent a revolutionary movement actively working for the overthrow of Roman rule. But the Christian movement was nonetheless revolutionary because it hit hard against the idea that Caesar and the state represented the ultimate authority. The charges brought against the small group of believers meeting in Jason's home caused such alarm among city officials that Jason had to provide a guarantee that there would be no further trouble and that Paul and Silas would immediately leave the city.

The church in every age has had to face misrepresentation and opposition. This is especially the case in our media-dominated age that has the power to popularize caricatures and to generate negative images and stir up opposition. It must be admitted that some of the negative publicity experienced by churches today may well be deserved, and for this we must admit responsibility. However, where misrepresentations arise from ignorance, prejudice, and falsehoods generated by biased opinions or vindictiveness, they need to be challenged with carefully reasoned responses.

For instance, in North American media, evangelical Christians are usually associated with right-wing political agendas and anti-intellectual convictions. Such misrepresentations grossly oversimplify a diverse evangelical community. When anyone asks me, with a clearly hostile tone, whether or not I am an "evangelical Christian," I respond by saying, "Before I can answer your question, I need to know what you mean by *evangelical*."

Fruit That Endures

There was some fruit from Paul's preaching in the synagogue, in that "some of the Jews were persuaded and joined Paul and Silas, as did a number of God-fearing Greeks and quite a few prominent women" (Acts 17:4 NIV). We do not know how much additional time Paul and Silas were able to spend in the city before they were forced to leave. They had a brief time to meet with the believers in Silas's home, time they devoted to further teaching of the gospel and practical issues related to living a life consistent with Jesus's teaching and Paul's admonitions. But as Paul and Silas departed for Berea, Paul was understandably anxious about the well-being of this new faith community. He would have liked to visit them personally, but Satan had placed an obstacle in his way in the form of the bond that Jason had been required to post with the city authorities (1 Thess. 2:17–18). So from Berea he dispatched Timothy to Thessalonica to encourage the believers and bring him a report of how they were faring (1 Thess. 3:1–2, 5). Timothy caught up with Paul in Corinth, from where he wrote his two letters to the church.

It is evident that since the departure of Paul and his companions these new believers had maintained their witness among their pagan Gentile associates, even recruiting new members from among them. Paul heard how the Thessalonian believers had turned from idols to serve the living and true God (1 Thess. 1:9).

Time and again we see that new believers make the most effective witnesses. This is due to two main factors: first, their network of relatives, friends, and associates can see the change that has taken place, and their curiosity is aroused; second, this network represents a "fishing ground" of expanding influence. Now that the core of believers was meeting in a private house independently from the synagogue, the message became more widely accessible. Pagan inquirers felt more comfortable in the home of a friend or neighbor. In our own day we see this networking principle applied in such evangelistic programs as the Alpha Course, Christianity Explored, and Introducing God (Sydney, Australia).

The church in Thessalonica provides a challenge to churches today. Can it be said that the message rings out from our faith communities? The term "rang out" (1 Thess. 1:8 NIV, *execheo*) is a strong one that, as John Stott notes, "occurs nowhere else in the New Testament . . . [and] can mean to sound, ring, peal or boom."[26] It may be used to describe the roar of a waterfall, the blast of a trumpet, or a clap of thunder. It is a sound that cannot be ignored. Such boldness in witness in Luke's theology is evidence of the Holy Spirit's empowering for mission in the world.

Growing Pains in Corinth (Acts 18:1–17)

Cities were as diverse in the first century as they are in the twenty-first century. When Paul travels from Athens to Corinth, he enters a very different urban context. Athens prided itself on its intellectual sophistication, whereas Corinth represented political power in southern Greece. As a port city, Corinth was a commercial center, with a reputation for immorality, prostitution, and drunkenness. Paul arrived there around AD 50 and, because of the strategic importance of the city, stayed for eighteen months.

Paul's strategic thinking challenges the parochialism, congregationalism, and denominationalism that characterize so much of urban mission in the twenty-first century. Churches individually and collectively must develop a vision for the city and work together to make a discernible impact. The "white flight" into suburbia that occurred in the twentieth century weakened the church's presence in the cities, which are the centers of cultural influence, political power, and economic and entrepreneurial resources. Over the last decade, many city centers have become "hip" and predominantly white and affluent, whereas the recent economic downturn has altered the demographics of many suburbs and exurbs. Another significant phenomenon is the growth of diaspora churches that have been established by migrants, predominantly from Africa, in the urban areas.

Only when we step out in mission in obedience to Christ, relying on the empowering and guidance of the Holy Spirit, will we discover that the Lord has prepared the way. God both guides according to divine purposes and provides according to our needs. When Paul arrived in Corinth, he discovered that the Lord had provided companionship, for "there he found a Jew named Aquila, a native of Pontus [in Asia Minor], who had recently come from Italy with his wife Priscilla, because Claudius had ordered all Jews to leave Rome" (Acts 18:2). Luke does not inform us how Paul came to hear of them, but subsequent events reveal it was a divine appointment. Like Paul, they were engaged in the trade of tentmaking or leatherworking. As fellow Jews, they were able to

26. Stott, *1 & 2 Thessalonians*, 36–37.

support Paul in his efforts to persuade Jews and God-fearing Greeks in the synagogues, Sabbath by Sabbath. For Priscilla and Aquila also believed in Jesus as Messiah, presumably having come to faith in Rome.

Facing Monumental Challenges

Paul's example demonstrates that a leader need not be a loner. In fact, Paul felt especially inadequate and vulnerable in Corinth without his traveling companions. It was then that the ascended Lord spoke words of reassurance and comfort to him (Acts 18:9–10).[27] He was relieved when Silas and Timothy joined him from Macedonia. They arrived with additional financial resources from the church in Philippi that enabled Paul to devote himself exclusively to preaching, initially confining himself to the Jews in a concerted endeavor to convince them that Jesus was the Messiah (Acts 18:5). Perhaps Aquila and Priscilla were also able to contribute financially from their business profits.

First-century church planting could not rely on the financial and organizational resources of a denomination; neither can their twenty-first-century counterparts. Church planters today often have to live hand to mouth for their support. They may need to be bivocational, trusting in the Lord to provide for their needs when ministry demands mean they can no longer continue in their regular employment. Similarly, faith and flexibility will be required from those who are preparing for ministry and mission in the church today. Churches and denominations can no longer underwrite the initiatives of church planters. Still less can they guarantee a church placement to those in training, due to shrinking congregations and church closures. But, as in the case of Paul, those embarking on church-pioneering initiatives should not be expected, nor should they endeavor, to operate in isolation.

Paul's experience of persecution in Corinth followed a pattern that was becoming familiar. His preaching in the synagogue eventually aroused opposition expressed in personal terms as the Jews became abusive and insulting in their rejection of his message. Paul made it clear that there was no useful purpose in his continuing his ministry among them: "In protest he shook the dust from his clothes and said to them, 'Your blood be on your own heads! I am innocent. From now on I will go to the Gentiles'" (Acts 18:6). In every situation and in any age, discernment is required to know when further efforts would prove futile. We have to be prepared to move on.

27. Whereas on previous occasions Paul had left cities in the face of opposition, here in Corinth "Paul stayed . . . for a year and a half, teaching them the word of God" (Acts 18:11). His prolonged stay indicates the strategic importance of Corinth for the evangelization of Achaia.

Alternative Venues

On this occasion of synagogue opposition, Paul moved next door to the home of Titius Justus, a non-Jew described as "a worshiper of God." This was a significant step as far as the witness of the new believers was concerned. A much wider circle of non-Jews would have felt more comfortable in Titius Justus's home than in the synagogue. Not surprisingly, Paul's setting up shop next door to the synagogue inflamed the ire of synagogue leaders and many others in their congregation. The opposition of these Jewish leaders was further strengthened when Crispus, the synagogue leader, with his entire household came to believe in the Lord. Now that the church had separated itself from the synagogue, many more Corinthians were ready to respond to Paul's preaching, identifying with both the gospel message and the faith community by being baptized (Acts 18:8).

Key persons giving their allegiance to Christ and opening their homes for family, neighbors, and friends to hear the gospel in familiar surroundings often triggers a significant, wider response to the gospel. As twenty-first-century Western societies become increasingly post-Christian and the church more marginalized, a growing percentage of the church's ministry will need to take place away from the church premises, in the everyday living environment of the general population.

The indifferent response of the governor Gallio to the Jews' complaint about Paul persuading people to worship God contrary to the law indicates Gallio's determination not to become embroiled in religious disputes. That he showed no concern when the crowd turned on Sosthenes, the synagogue leader—either the successor of Crispus or one who ruled alongside him—suggests a tolerance for the anti-Semitism demonstrated by the Corinthian crowd, another reason for the Christian movement to distance itself from Judaism.

Social Mix

In writing to the Corinthians, Paul drew attention to the humble social status of the believers in the city: "Consider your own call, brothers and sisters: not many of you were wise by human standards, not many were powerful, not many were of noble birth. But God chose what is foolish in the world to shame the wise; God chose what is weak in the world to shame the strong; God chose what is low and despised in the world . . . so that no one might boast in the presence of God" (1 Cor. 1:26–29).

Gallio's ruling gave Paul the freedom to evangelize and begin a church in Corinth before he left the city. Over the next five years, Paul corresponded with the Corinthians several times and even visited them personally to sort out some of their problems. Guiding his travel plans was his realization that an open door for the gospel awaited in Ephesus (1 Cor. 16:5–9). Similarly, all our plans need to be made in pencil. The church today is just as much in need of humble planning and strategic thinking, yet at the same time putting all things under the sign "if the Lord wills."

Consolidation and Confrontation in Ephesus (Acts 18:19–21, 24–28; 19)

Paul arrived in Ephesus for a brief visit on his return to Jerusalem in AD 51. While in the city, he took the opportunity to minister briefly in the synagogue, which sparked the interest of some of his listeners (Acts 18:19).

Competent Coworkers

Unable to stay longer, it appears Paul left the care and further instruction of new believers to Priscilla and Aquila (Acts 18:18–21). In so doing, Paul demonstrated his confidence in his coworkers, believing that the couple had already provided ample evidence of knowledge and spiritual maturity in their leadership roles in Corinth. One of the crucial tests in any leader's ministry is the extent of that leader's confidence in those he or she has appointed to serve alongside him or her. Controlling leaders tend to surround themselves with persons of lesser ability, who will not pose a threat to their leadership. Paul worked to empower those around him.

Mentoring Future Leaders

Insecure leaders take every opportunity to criticize the shortcomings of others. Priscilla and Aquila demonstrated a positive attitude by inviting Apollos to their home and "explaining the Way of God to him more accurately" (Acts 18:26–27). Having filled in the gaps in his knowledge, they were not possessive, instead regarding him as someone essential to their ongoing ministry, especially in the absence of Paul. Thus when Apollos shared with the members of the newly formed church his desire to go to Achaia, they were prepared to release him. Those who had recently come from Corinth, such as Priscilla and Aquila, would be aware of the needs there.

The church in Ephesus provided Apollos with a letter of commendation. On arrival, he proved to be of great help to the believers and used his apologetic skills in refuting the Jewish opponents in public debate (Acts 18:28). Not only was he learned, but he was also a gifted orator with an influential ministry, testifying to

Christ as Messiah in the synagogue. He was thus able to continue Paul's ministry. In his letter written later from Ephesus, Paul acknowledges the contribution Apollos has made in Corinth. If Paul himself was responsible for the initial sowing of the seed of the gospel, it was Apollos who watered that seed (1 Cor. 3:5–9; 4:1).

There is an urgent need in our day for persons who are prepared to follow the example of Priscilla and Aquila by investing time in individuals who demonstrate ministry potential, specifically, by teaching them one-on-one. We need to recognize that seminaries are of recent origin. Before their emergence, respected and learned ministers would evaluate and mentor individuals who believed they were called by God into the ordained ministry, assessing not only their academic competence but also their character and the authenticity of their call by God.

Currently, many ministry students arrive at seminaries having little knowledge of the Scriptures. This regrettable state of affairs is the result of the decline of the Sunday School movement and the lack of doctrinally rich expository preaching. Reinstating in local churches the mentoring model exemplified by Aquila and Priscilla would provide better screening of candidates for formal theological training. It would also make available opportunities for many more individuals who are already engaged in local church ministry to receive supervised preparation to better equip them for ministry. Among some conservative evangelical churches and networks, candidates for ordained ministry are directed either to "safe" seminaries that uphold their theological position and ecclesial ethos or to their "in-house" training colleges. This trend may result in fewer conservative evangelicals going to interdenominational schools.

Establishing Strategic Urban Centers

On arriving in Ephesus, Paul encountered a group of about twelve disciples who he sensed were deficient in their understanding and experience. He asked them, "Did you receive the Holy Spirit when you believed?" (Acts 19:1 NIV). Evidently they had not, for they had only been baptized according to the rite of John the Baptizer, signifying their intention to repent of their sins. Apparently they knew nothing of baptism in the name of Jesus. Luke records that immediately upon receiving baptism, and with the laying on of hands by Paul, they received the Holy Spirit and spoke in tongues. This incident has been described as the Gentile Pentecost. We must not overlook its missional significance, as Luke relates baptism in the Holy Spirit to commissioning and empowerment for mission rather than inward transformation.

Recognizing the strategic importance of Ephesus in the Roman province of Asia, Paul returned for a longer visit, remaining in Ephesus for more than two years during which he made it the center for his missionary activities:

debating in the synagogue for three months, preaching the gospel "from house to house" (Acts 20:20), and lecturing in the hall of Tyrannus (19:8–10). Those who had been instructed then fanned out to spread the gospel and establish faith communities throughout Asia Minor (Acts 19:10).

From Ephesus, Paul sent several representatives ahead of him into Macedonia and Greece: Gaius, from Derbe; Aristarchus and Secundus, from Thessalonica; Sopater son of Pyrrhus, from Beroea (Acts 19:29; 20:4); and Timothy, Tychicus, and Trophimus, from Asia. Paul stayed in the province of Asia a little longer, and perhaps it was during this time that many of the other six churches mentioned in the book of Revelation were established: Smyrna, Pergamum, Thyatira, Sardis, Philadelphia, and Laodicea (Rev. 2–3).

During the period covered by the New Testament, Aquila and Priscilla, Timothy, and Luke all spent time in Ephesus. It seems that the apostle John later took over the leadership of the churches in the region, judging from the letters he wrote to the seven churches in Asia Minor while in exile on the isle of Patmos. This was during the reign of the persecuting emperor Domitian (AD 81–96). Emperor worship became a significant challenge to Christians toward the end of the first century. Sadly, the church in Ephesus is mentioned in Revelation as a church that had lost its first love (Rev. 2:1–7), and this despite Paul's two years of teaching among them, followed by the ministry of John. Great teachers do not guarantee faithful disciples.

The church in our day must recognize the strategic importance of the city in carrying out its mission. The city remains the center of political and economic power and the birthplace and disseminator of culture. At the same time, we are reminded by Paul's journeys that gospel ministry should not be confined to the city. Once the church has been firmly established there, it becomes a center for outreach to the surrounding region through evangelism, church planting, and the teaching and encouraging of indigenous leaders.

Commercial Interests Threatened

Superstition was apparently widespread in Ephesus, for, when many there became Christians, they brought their magic books to be publicly burned as a witness to their allegiance to Christ. The impact of the Christian missionaries alarmed those who profited from the worship of Diana as a threat to their trade. Chief among them were the silversmiths, who made models of the idols, which were sold to devotees and pilgrims not as souvenirs but as offerings to the goddess. Under the leadership of Demetrius, a great crowd gathered, shouting defiantly in unison, "Great is Artemis [Diana] of the Ephesians!" for a full two hours (Acts 19:34).

Demetrius's nervousness was justified, as he quickly came to realize that Christianity was different from the other religions that abounded in Ephesus. Pagans had no trouble in adding other gods to their pantheon, but Christians gave their total allegiance to Christ and denounced their former pagan gods. This presented a threat not only to the silversmiths but also to the many associated trades providing both accommodation and eating establishments for visitors.

The town clerk intervened to try to calm the situation by reassuring the crowd that Paul and his associates were "neither temple robbers nor blasphemers of our goddess" (Acts 19:37). If the crowd wanted to take the matter further, they should reassemble as a regular assembly (*ekklesia*). Everything should be done in an orderly manner in order not to attract the attention of the Roman authorities. The town clerk was understandably concerned, given that this was not the first occasion when the worship of Artemis was regarded with some concern in Rome. David Peterson provides the following explanation: "We know of two occasions in the first century AD when the Roman authorities questioned practices connected with the temple of Artemis. Against that background, it is easy to see why the city clerk would not want the cult of Artemis to come again to the notice of the proconsul."[28]

Extension to Colossae

The church in Colossae provides evidence that Paul's interest and influence was not confined to the churches that he had personally founded during his missionary journeys, since it was Epaphras, not Paul, who took the good news to Colossae (Col. 1:7). Although Paul had not personally established the church, he kept in close contact with the believers despite the fact of his imprisonment.[29] In all likelihood, Epaphras was a convert from Paul's ministry in Ephesus. Paul took this opportunity to send greetings from his companions in Ephesus to Aristarchus; Mark, the cousin of Barnabas; Jesus (Justus); Epaphras; Luke; and Demas. He also sent greetings to Nympha and the church in her house, in neighboring Laodicea (Col. 4:10–15).

It is evident from Paul's letter to the Colossians that there was a close relationship between the Colossian church and the believers in Hierapolis and Laodicea: "He [Epaphras] has worked hard for you and for those in Laodicea and in Hierapolis" (Col. 4:13).

---

28. Peterson, *Acts of the Apostles*, 551.
29. As we have noted, New Testament scholars are divided as to whether Paul was nearby in Ephesus when he wrote the letter, in which case it dates from AD 63, or writing from Rome during his later imprisonment.

Shifting Centers of Influence

As we look back over nearly two thousand years of church history, we come to the painful realization that churches that played a significant role in the influence and expansion of Christianity must not assume they will continue in their position of prominence into the future. In reviewing the first-century churches in Turkey and Greece, one finds that many of these churches no longer exist or have lost much of their spiritual vitality and evangelistic fervor. Spiritual renewal and revitalization must be a constant concern. Churches can lose their first love and become complacent.

Also, as we see from the history of mission recorded in Acts, the strategic centers of Christianity do not remain static. The prime movers in mission shifted from Jerusalem to Syrian Antioch to Corinth, and then on to Ephesus, and from there to Rome.[30]

From Slave to Son

Paul's letter to Philemon was also sent at this time (AD 63). It was carried by Tychicus, who was accompanied by Onesimus, the runaway slave. In this letter Paul explains that he is returning his runaway slave now as "a beloved brother" in Christ and one who has been his faithful servant. Philemon, it turns out, was a house-church leader in Colossae (Philem. 1–3) who evidently had become a believer himself while visiting Paul (perhaps at Ephesus). In addition, Paul had also met his wife, Apphia, and their son Archippus, who had become partners in the work of the gospel with Philemon. Paul describes Archippus as "our fellow soldier" (v. 2) and Philemon as "our dear friend and co-worker" (v. 1). The military metaphor applied to Archippus is significant, indicating that ministry entails discipline, hardship, and danger. In order to continue in the Christian life and to exercise their ministry, followers needed God's grace and peace.

Paul's Ministry of Reconciliation in Rome

Like Paul's letter to the Colossians, his letter to the Romans is addressed to a location that he had not personally visited at the time of writing. However, Paul is well informed of the issues confronting the believers in the imperial capital. His letter reveals his concern for the tension that has arisen between Jewish and Gentile believers. This has probably been exacerbated by the fact

---

30. An argument can also be made that Paul envisaged the church in Thessalonica playing a significant role as one of the strategic centers.

that Jewish Christians had been banished from Rome, together with fellow Jews, under the edict of Emperor Claudius. This left the church in the hands of non-Jewish believers. As the Jewish Christians began to drift back into the capital, they most likely sensed that power had shifted during their absence, which caused them to emphasize the significance of their Jewishness. Paul's letter addresses at some length the division that has occurred, not just at a pastoral level, but at the deeper level including underlying theological and cultural issues.

Paul resists any attempt to impose a Jewish cultural interpretation of the gospel that emphasizes the importance of the law in securing Gentile believers in a right relationship with God. The conflict is between legalism and grace. At the outset Paul makes it clear that, as a Jew, his calling from God is to take the gospel to non-Jews (Rom. 1:1–7). The tensions and outright opposition between Jewish and non-Jewish believers that erupted in many locations during Paul's journeys are evident in many of his letters. The conflict between a religion based on legalism and a religion based on grace is one that continues throughout the centuries to the present day.

On a number of occasions, Paul mentions his intention of visiting Rome, and Luke's record of the spread of Christianity culminates with Paul's arrival in Rome. Although Paul is keen to visit Rome, he did not intend to make an extended visit, for reasons he explains near the conclusion of his letter: "I make it my ambition to proclaim the good news, not where Christ has already been named, so that I do not build on someone else's foundation. . . . This is the reason that I have so often been hindered from coming to you" (Rom. 15:20, 22).

Importance of Social Networks

Although Paul has not yet visited Rome, the extensive list of personal greetings in Romans 16:1–16 provides ample evidence of his many prior contacts with Christians there. Furthermore, he is not alone in sending greetings; he also names Timothy, Lucius, Jason, Sosipater, fellow Jews, Tertius (Paul's scribe in writing this letter), Gaius, Erastus, the city treasurer in Ephesus, and Quartus (otherwise unknown) as sending greetings (Rom. 16:21–24). Paul, writing from Ephesus, is surrounded by a company of fellow workers. Their being named here perhaps signifies that they too are known to one or more of the believers listed in his greetings.

Throughout the New Testament, the reader is made aware of the existence and importance of social networks. If such networks were possible in the walking culture of the first century, should we not recognize the need to establish and broaden such networks for the encouragement of believers in the twenty-first century? In our day we have far too many stand-alone churches and Christians, who are left to maintain a lonely witness. Mutual support is vital for the well-being of believers and to maintain the momentum of a movement.

Summary and Application

In this chapter we have covered a great deal of ground, both geographically and incidentally. Amid the many stories relating to individual converts and the diverse contexts in which faith communities were birthed, a number of issues stand out that have relevance to the church today.

One such issue is the priority of going to one's own people first. For Paul, as a Jew, this priority was theological as well as strategic. For the church today, family, friends, and work associates comprise the believers' immediate networks. Among these networks believers will make their most immediate impact and have their authenticity tested.[31] Second, those whose beliefs and values differ from, or whose business interests are threatened by, the gospel will inevitably challenge its message. Third, new churches, made up of first-generation Christians who are recent converts, provide a vibrant witness. Fourth, monochrome WASP (white, Anglo-Saxon, Protestant) churches must not abandon the city but must be prepared to face its challenges and opportunities alongside the black churches and those representing diverse immigrant groups. Fifth, church leaders must have a vision for and understanding of cities, establishing in them strategic centers of training and outreach to surrounding areas.

 *Conclusion:*

Twenty-first-century churches must make
urban mission a priority, recognizing the uniqueness
of each location and context.

---

31. See DeYoung and Gilbert, *What Is the Mission of the Church?*

4

Birthing New Churches

The human birthing process is both routine and complex. The moment of conception soon leads to cell multiplication and diversification as various organs are developed. New parents are filled with wonder at the moment of birth. If this is true of natural birth, it is even more evident when it comes to the birthing of new faith communities. These births are the result of the miracles of reconciliation and regeneration (or new birth), which is an action of new creation through the creative initiative of the Holy Spirit. Humans can aid in the process as spiritual midwives, but it is not in their power to actually bring about the regeneration of an individual or to birth a faith community. Those ministries have to be undertaken in complete reliance on the Holy Spirit.

The timing of the birth of a new faith community is much more unpredictable than biological birth. One of the surprises in the book of Acts is the short period of time it takes for a small group of new believers to form into a fellowship. This was due to a variety of factors. In the first place, Paul was able to draw together a group from local synagogues whose hearts had been prepared by their knowledge of the history of God's people and their hope of the coming Messiah. Second, Paul represented a dynamic new movement rooted in the message and ministry of Jesus, which in turn drew upon the vision of the Hebrew prophets. Third, there was a growing cynicism toward many of the pagan religions promoted by Rome. And fourth, the new movement provided a sense of belonging and significance and opened up leadership opportunities, especially among women and slaves.

In the previous chapter, we identified a number of the factors that contributed to the dynamic growth of the early church; among these were opportunism, flexibility, and resilience. In this chapter, we will explore additional elements that made the early Christian movement so prolific, namely, apostolic pioneering, the house-church structure, and the establishing of hub-centered networks.

Birthing Churches through Groundbreaking Leadership

Churches ministering within the later sociopolitical context of Christendom increasingly became static and bureaucratic institutions. In terms of leadership, either providing trained pastors for existing congregations or leading new congregations based on a preexisting model became the main focus of attention. In earlier centuries these leaders were provided by monasteries or a mentoring process; and within the past two hundred fifty years they were prepared by seminaries, initially associated with the universities. The bias of the latter model was toward academia rather than the challenges presented by the daily demands of ministry and mission. Leadership beyond the local level, whether by bishops, superintendents, or denominational bureaucracies, was geared toward the maintenance of the institutions and have more recently become increasingly preoccupied with survival in the face of continuing membership decline and financial shortfalls.

One serious consequence of such preoccupation with institutional survival has been the neglect of groundbreaking initiatives led by individuals and teams of people who are called by God to spread the good news and bring to birth new faith communities. In New Testament terms, we are referring to *apostolic* and *evangelistic* leadership. The first of these terms is a hard one to nail down, as it is used in a variety of ways in the New Testament and is interpreted in different ways by biblical scholars.[1] The term has also become increasingly controversial, in that some modern Restorationist movements use it to describe an authoritarian form of leadership with little accountability and a heavy emphasis on "signs and wonders" as the authentication of leaders' claims. In this view, the resurgence of such apostolic leadership is one of the signs of the near return of Christ to usher in the parousia.[2]

---

1. Hansen notes: "This title was used in the early church in a broad sense to designate missionary leaders (see Acts 14:14). The title was also used in a narrow sense for those who had been given unique authority from Christ to be his representatives and the founders of the church (see Acts 1:21–26). In Galatians 1 Paul claims the title for himself in the narrow sense. He recognizes that there were those who were apostles before him (Gal. 1:17), but he does not see himself as subordinate to the original apostles" (*Galatians*, 31–32).

2. For a fuller discussion of contemporary apostolicity, see Deiros, "Apostolicity, Contemporary," 60–61, and Gibbs, *ChurchNext*, 75–77.

In general terms, *apostle* is used in two senses in the New Testament. In the Gospels it refers to the primary group of twelve disciples, who were apostles-in-training during Jesus's earthly ministry. But when Paul speaks of apostles, apart from himself, he refers to a broader group outside of the Twelve. He himself is both an apostle on par with the Twelve, although "born out of due time," and an apostle in the broader sense of the groundbreaking church planter who takes on the leadership of the churches that have come into being through his evangelistic ministry. Paul's particular calling from God is to take the gospel to non-Jewish people and extend the mission of the church into new geographical areas, rather than to build on the foundational work of other people.

While Matthew, Mark, and John use the term *apostle* only once, Luke, with his strong mission commitment, uses it thirty-four times (six times in his Gospel and twenty-eight times in Acts). Paul also uses the term with some frequency—twenty-nine times in his letters to the churches and five times in his pastoral letters. The basic meaning of *apostle* is a person sent as an authorized representative or "ambassador" of an established church. For Paul, the term designates one sent, not simply by the church, but in response to the personal calling and commissioning by Christ. In the book of Hebrews, the term is also used in reference to Christ himself (Heb. 3:1). Paul often refers to himself by this term, especially in the introductions to his letters, but he widens it to include a circle of missionaries (1 Cor. 12:28; 15:7; 2 Cor. 11:5) and "messengers of the churches" (2 Cor. 8:23; Phil. 2:25).

Renowned Roman Catholic theologian Hans Küng responded to the fifth anniversary of the opening of the Second Vatican Council by writing *The Church*. In that volume he endeavors to set a new direction for the Roman Catholic Church in response to the theological insights and new attitudes stimulated by that watershed council. In his discussion of the dimensions of the church as one, holy, catholic, and apostolic, is a section examining the nature of apostolicity.[3] Despite the explicit command of Jesus, Küng notes that the Twelve did not become missionary pioneers as we might have expected.

The missionary command of Christ (Mk. 16,15 f.; Mt. 28:18 f.; Lk. 24:47 f.; Acts 1:8) seems to reflect the idea and the traditions that the apostles went out into the world as missionaries. But as we have seen, even Acts relates that the apostles stayed first of all in Jerusalem (Acts 8:1) and only undertook with great reluctance the mission to the Gentiles (cf. Acts 10:1–11 and 18). It is only

3. Küng, *The Church*, 344–59.

said of Peter that he left Jerusalem (12:17). The only missionary journeys we hear about are those of Paul and Barnabas. According to accounts which only come down to us from the third and fourth centuries, the apostles stayed for seven, twelve or fifteen years in Jerusalem to begin with. It is only the legends of a later time which portray the twelve apostles as missionaries and founders of Churches throughout the world.[4]

This brings us to the Pauline use of the term. Of the apostles Paul mentions by name, not one is among the Twelve. Including himself, he identifies as apostles Barnabas (Acts 14:14), Andronicus and Junias (Rom. 16:7), Timothy and Silas (1 Thess. 2:6), and Epaphroditus (Phil. 2:25). Some scholars assume that these persons had, like Paul, received a special revelation of the Lord, but the New Testament nowhere mentions such a revelation. Evidently, these named individuals, in response to the call of the risen Lord, were pioneering evangelists who were both preachers of the gospel and church planters, birthing and then nurturing new faith communities. Arthur Patzia comments: "There is no evidence in the New Testament that Paul personally appointed apostles. Apostles always are by God's appointment; they are one of God's spiritual gifts to the church."[5]

In this chapter, concerned with the birthing of new congregations, our emphasis will be on this second use of the term. John R. W. Stott made a distinction between the unique group of the Twelve, describing them as "apostles of Christ," and the other categories, which represented "the apostles of the church."[6] In order to avoid becoming preoccupied with titles, our emphasis will be on the apostolic *calling* of individuals in the church and of the church as a whole, as emphasized by Küng, rather than on the *office* of the apostle.[7]

It is evident that Paul was an apostle in both senses offered by Stott: an "apostle of Christ" and an "apostle of the church." We will first examine the strategic importance of his calling as a missionary to the non-Jews and his bringing to birth new faith communities in many of the major cities in the Roman provinces of Galatia, Asia, and Macedonia and Achaia (modern Greece). Second, we will examine the significance of his priorities for the local churches that he established. One of the functions of leadership is to embody and propagate the institutional culture of the community.

4. Ibid., 345. Küng admits that these "legends of a later time" are without reliable historical foundations.
5. Patzia, *Emergence of the Church*, 160.
6. Stott, *Message of Ephesians*, 160.
7. Gibbs, *I Believe in Church Growth*, 341. See also Gibbs, *ChurchMorph*, 159–61.

As a contemporary example, Martin Garner, a Church Army officer in the Church of England, is an individual with an apostolic calling in the Pauline sense. This is how he identifies apostles:

- They are made for adventure, for taking risks, hardship, and adversity
- They are made for tackling the impossible
- They have eyes of faith for the mission task in a way that leaders of local churches do not:

    for talking to complete strangers

    starting from scratch with no resources

    tackling fear and prejudice

    communicating the good news to those who seem hardest to reach

    living without financial security[8]

Apostolic Calling

Paul traces his call to his encounter with the risen Lord on the road to Damascus, where he was stopped in his tracks in a most dramatic manner (Acts 9:1–19). Paul's conversion from persecutor of Christians to believer in Christ and his call to proclaim the gospel come at the same time. "For several days he [Paul] was with the disciples in Damascus, and immediately he began to proclaim Jesus in the synagogues, saying, 'He is the Son of God.' . . . Saul [Paul] became increasingly more powerful and confounded the Jews who lived in Damascus by proving that Jesus was the Messiah" (Acts 9:19–20). Luke's retelling of the story on two more occasions, quoting at length from Paul's speech before the Roman and Jewish authorities (22:1–21 and 26:1–29), underlines its importance. Also, Paul himself refers to his experience on several occasions in his letters (1 Cor. 15:8–10; Gal. 1:11–17; Phil. 3:4–11).

Within a short period, the opposition to Paul becomes so strong that he has to escape from Damascus and journey to Jerusalem. There, Barnabas becomes Paul's advocate by attempting to overcome the suspicion of the genuineness of his conversion among the believers, who have known Saul only as their deadly enemy. Barnabas assures them that Paul has seen the Lord on the road to Damascus and has preached boldly in his name in the city. As a result, "Paul stayed with the apostles and went all around Jerusalem with them preaching boldly in the name of the Lord" (Acts 9:28 NLT).

8. Garner, *Call for Apostles Today*, 8.

Calling and commissioning are two sides of the same coin. This was true in a unique sense for Paul, considering his role as a pioneering missionary among the Gentiles, but it also holds true in every case of conversion. Conversion calls all believers to play their part in the ongoing mission of Christ, throughout the world and across the ages.

The church in Syrian Antioch later confirms Paul's calling by commissioning and dispatching him and Barnabas after seeking the Lord's will through prayer and fasting. The selection was made not by a joint decision of the leadership but through the direct guidance of the Holy Spirit (Acts 13:1–3). Furthermore, the revelation did not come from the apostles in Jerusalem but through a prophetic word from Simeon, called "a black man," probably from North Africa, and Lucius from Cyrene, the capital of Libya. In mission, strategic initiatives often come from unexpected places. Paul insists to the Galatians that his commission did not come from the apostles in Jerusalem but came directly from the ascended Lord and God the Father (Gal. 1:1–5). Paul is probably writing to the Galatians from Syrian Antioch, the very church that had sent him out. His claim could therefore be verified.

The Lord's calling of individuals as apostles today entails for many churches both a change of direction and reordering of priorities coupled with a recommitment to our commission to witness to God's gracious initiative in our lives. It emphasizes the need for that transformation that only the presence of God's Holy Spirit can bring about, and a continuing response to play our part in Christ's ongoing mission in the place where he has set us, among the people with whom we come into contact.

Paul had the broadest of callings—to the entire Gentile world. But all believers have a more restricted and specific calling—to reach out to the people within their sphere of influence. For some individuals in the church, the distinct apostolic calling is to venture into new situations in order to engage with people who have had no prior contact with the church or are not attracted by the churches or Christians they have met. These apostles are called and equipped to draw alongside such people to gain their respect and trust. They are able to make the gospel understandable and relevant and to draw together a community of believers who can embark on a lifelong journey of faith.

Fresh Insights into the Gospel Revealed

Within the context of the synagogue, Paul is able to proclaim and explain the gospel in terms that his fellow Jews can readily understand, whether they agree with him or not. But he needs fresh insights in order to understand and clearly explain how Gentiles can be included and inherit the covenant promises given by God to his ancient people. Paul's struggle is both intellectual and emotional. It required a "mystery" to be revealed to him by divine revelation. Perhaps this was made known to him during his time in Arabia, a journey made by Saul during his time in Damascus, which, although not recorded by Luke, is mentioned by Paul in his letter to the Galatians (Gal. 1:18).

In Ephesians 3:1–13 and Colossians 1:24–2:5, Paul reflects on the special responsibility that has been entrusted to him to share the good news with the Gentiles. To him, God's mysterious plan—which goes back to the call of Abraham (Gen. 12:2–3; see also Col. 1:25–27; Rom. 16:25) but which Israel had failed to fulfill—came to fruition in Christ. Both Jews and non-Jews are made one body in Christ. In revealing this mystery, Paul recognizes afresh his own unworthiness and inadequacy for the task when he confesses, "Although I am the very least of all the saints, this grace was given me to bring to the Gentiles the news of the boundless riches of Christ, and to make everyone see what is the plan of the mystery hidden for ages in God who created all things" (Eph. 3:8–9).

Notice that Paul does not stand alone in revealing this mystery. Sandwiched between his conversion and his commissioning by the church in Antioch is the account of Peter's response to God's call to share the message of Christ in the home of the Roman centurion, and Peter's report back to the leaders in Jerusalem (Acts 10; 11:1–18). While Peter had been preaching to that non-Jewish audience, the Holy Spirit had come upon them, accompanied by speaking in tongues, just as it had on the Jewish leaders on the day of Pentecost (Acts 10:44–47; 11:15–17). These Gentile believers were then incorporated into God's people through water baptism and the baptism of the Holy Spirit. Peter's actions created a precedent to authenticate Paul's missionary calling.

Such radical initiatives inevitably stir up conflict, both among the Jews and the non-Jews. Paul interprets this as sharing in the sufferings of Christ, which enables him to rejoice rather than complain, because he is involved in this ministry as a servant (literally, "slave"), which entails his unreserved obedience. Slaves do not negotiate their own conditions of service!

The depth and scope of the mystery now revealed must not be underestimated or restricted. It is nothing less than Christ in us, the hope of glory (Col. 1:27). So, Paul's task is not simply to bring people to the experience of conversion but to continue to admonish them, "teaching everyone in all wisdom, so that we may present everyone mature in Christ. For this I toil and struggle with all the energy that he powerfully inspires within me" (Col. 1:28–29). Paul realizes that the believers in Colossae still have a long way to go. Furthermore, they need to be alert to and guard against those who are proclaiming a false gospel.

Communities of Reconciliation

Paul's understanding of the gospel is not individualized or privatized. Rather, it is a message that brings together people who have previously felt their separation and among whom there were cultural tensions and spiritual barriers. The gospel is a message of reconciliation for an alienated people: alienated from God ever since their expulsion from the garden of Eden, and alienated from one another as a result.

Paul addresses the sad situation of the fragmented church in Corinth, where rival groups had formed, with each proclaiming their particular hero in the faith: Apollos, Paul, or Cephas. Kenneth Bailey identifies the significance of these groups within the context of first-century Corinth: "Paul was a Roman citizen. Apollos was a Greek, and Paul refers to Peter as 'Cephas' using his Jewish name. . . . Their various ethnic loyalties were quite likely causing serious tensions in the church and Paul may well have been referring to those loyalties."[9]

Furthermore, the message cannot be reduced to a formula that fits all. There are central truths that apply whatever the context, but those truths need to be explained in ways that make sense within each context. There is an unsearchable mystery at the heart of the gospel that is revealed only through the Holy Spirit. You cannot simply argue or browbeat people to the point of conversion.

The challenge to communicate the gospel in different cultural settings is no less intense in the twenty-first century than it was in the first century. There is no *single* way but *a variety* of ways to convey the gospel, as is evident from the New Testament itself. The starting point will depend on the receivers' understanding of the nature of God—or of the gods in their pagan pantheon and their relationship to creation. The way in which alienation and sin are addressed will differ depending on whether the culture is guilt- or shame-based. How we approach the gospel and its demands will relate to how people within a given culture come to decisions regarding life's important issues. Where we place the emphasis in our sharing of the gospel also hinges on aspects of personal life journeys, including age, life experiences, and present circumstances.

For instance, a seminary colleague of mine was summoned by an inmate on death row who was troubled about whether God could ever forgive him. My colleague asked the man if he thought either his father or mother could forgive him. The man replied that he believed his mother could forgive him. My colleague responded, "Well, do you believe that Jesus can also forgive you?"

There are many ways to say the gospel, depending on the situation, but of course there are core truths relating to the nature of God the Father, the

9. Bailey, *Paul through Mediterranean Eyes*, 70.

person of Christ, and the universal significance both of his death on the cross for the sins of the world and of his resurrection. Our presentation may not start with the cross, but it always leads there.

Inviting Partnership in the Gospel

Paul rejoices at the commitment of the Christians in Philippi to work alongside him in spreading the gospel, and he thanks them for their generous financial support (Phil. 1:3–5). He describes their involvement in business terms—namely, as a "partnership." They are aware of Paul's practical needs of food and other day-to-day requirements while in prison. Notice that he immediately enlists these new believers as partners in his ministry. The sooner new Christ-followers are involved in some form of ministry, especially in witnessing to the gospel, the more quickly they grow as disciples of Christ.

The involvement of the Philippians is not restricted to a brief burst of enthusiasm but is an ongoing commitment "from the first day until now" (Phil. 1:5). Their partnership is also expressed in lives that demonstrate the transforming power of the gospel. Paul exhorts them, saying, "Conduct yourselves in a manner worthy of the gospel of Christ" (Phil. 1:27 NIV). He later adds, "It is by your holding fast to the word of life that I can boast on the day of Christ that I did not run in vain or labor in vain" (Phil. 2:16). Here we see that Paul is just as concerned for the ongoing commitment of believers as he is with their initial response. The turnaround that takes place at conversion is intended to lead to a lifelong journey in a different direction.

Maintaining Independence

A distinctive feature of Paul's apostolic ministry is the measure of independence that he enjoyed, which stems from his being commissioned directly by the ascended Christ. Paul argues this point at length in his letter to the Galatians. However, this freedom does not signify any lack of accountability to the local church. At the conclusion of each of his missionary journeys, Paul reports back to his sending church in Syrian Antioch and spends a considerable amount of time with them (Acts 13:2–3; 14:26–28).

Paul also emphasizes his independence from the churches he established and served by insisting on maintaining his own support. To the recently established church in Thessalonica, he writes, "Surely you remember, brothers and sisters, our toil and hardship; we worked night and day in order not to be a burden to anyone while we preached the gospel of God to you" (1 Thess. 2:9 NIV). In his second letter, Paul returns to the same theme, only this time exhorting the believers in Thessalonica to follow the self-giving example set by himself and his team: "We were not idle when we were with you, and we did not eat anyone's bread without paying for it; but with toil and labor we worked night and day, so that we might not burden any of you. This was not because we do not have that right, but in order to give you an example to imitate" (2 Thess. 3:7–9). Paul expresses the same commitment to the Christians in Corinth, telling them that "we work hard with our own hands" (1 Cor. 4:12 NIV).

This principle is particularly important in pioneering mission work, especially in a suspicious or hostile climate in which people take every opportunity to accuse the evangelists of being motivated by greed. This was indeed the climate in the ancient world, where many itinerant philosophers and faith healers took advantage of people. Paul was determined that their labors should be above such suspicion.

Later in the same letter, Paul provides another reason why he and his colleagues are prepared to set aside their rights, even though they are apostles of Christ. He does this through a series of rhetorical questions, to which the answer is obviously yes.

> Am I not free? Am I not an apostle? Have I not seen Jesus our Lord? Are you not my work in the Lord? If I am not an apostle to others, at least I am to you; for you are the seal of my apostleship in the Lord. This is my defense to those who would examine me. Do we not have the right to our food and drink? Do we not have the right to be accompanied by a believing wife, as do the other apostles and the brothers of the Lord and Cephas? Or is it only Barnabas and I who have no right to refrain from working for a living? (1 Cor. 9:1–6)

Having made his point, Paul also emphasizes the importance of churches providing financial support for those who minister among them. He cites as examples the soldier, the vinedresser, and the shepherd, all of whom receive appropriate rewards for their labors (1 Cor. 9:7). Paul then appeals to the law of Moses, which commands that oxen treading the grain should not be muzzled. If God is so concerned for the well-being of oxen, is not God even more concerned that the farmers who plow and thresh should share in the harvest (1 Cor. 9:9–10)? Paul is writing to those who are the fruit of his ministry as the one who first brought the gospel to them. He thus reminds them: "If we have sown spiritual seed among you, is it too much if we reap a material harvest from you? If others have this right of support from you, shouldn't we have it all the more? But we did not use this right. On the contrary, we put up with anything rather than hinder the gospel of Christ" (1 Cor. 9:11–12 NIV).

The "others" Paul mentions as receiving support are probably the elders who regularly serve the local congregation, whereas the apostle is called to a wider itinerant ministry.

Paul continues to heavily underline the point by providing a further example of the temple servants. "Don't you know that those who serve in the temple get their food from the temple, and that those who serve at the altar share in what is offered on the altar? In the same way, the Lord has commanded that those who preach the gospel should receive their living from the gospel. But I have not used any of these rights" (1 Cor. 9:13–15 NIV).

Paul's declaration of independence must not be interpreted as an expression of his self-sufficiency. He never assumes the stance of a self-confident expert. He repeatedly asks for the prayers of the churches in his letters. To the Corinthians he confesses his awareness of his poor personal appearance and that his speech lacks erudition and style (2 Cor. 10:10). The low self-image he expresses here may have arisen from the hostility he experienced from the Jews in Thessalonica (Acts 17:5, 13). Or it may have been caused by his feeling the oppression of the moral wickedness and spiritual gloom all around him in the city of Corinth (Acts 18:9–10).

Both principles that Paul argues at length are just as relevant today. Pastors and teachers serving the local church need to be valued and paid at an appropriate level, one that enables them to minister without undue financial hardship and anxiety. They should not be taken advantage of as cheap labor. If churches insist that pastors must learn to rely upon the Lord for their maintenance, then congregation members should be held to the same principle!

The situation is different for those called to the pioneering apostolic ministry of birthing new churches. They have to maintain their freedom to follow the leading of the Holy Spirit, avoiding getting bogged down by the demands of any one congregation insisting on ongoing service because it is providing financial support. In Jewish monetary terms, the *shekel* must not become the shackle!

Whereas for the apostle this financial independence represents freedom, such "freedom," to those looking to the church to provide financial security, represents uncertainty and may even cause resentment arising from the church's failure to provide for their present and future support. In the present climate of shrinking congregations and church closures, pastoral openings will most likely continue to decline, and those in training may well find that they do not have churches waiting to interview them. Rather, they will have to think in terms of pioneering, church-planting ministry. But this requires a strong sense of calling, an appropriate set of gifts, and a particular personality. Seminary training will need to be redirected to this end, with appropriate careful screening of applicants.

Heart of a Pastor

Sometimes the apostle Paul is represented as an unfeeling individual, making unreasonable demands of those who work alongside him. Granted, apostolic types are often difficult to work with, being so highly motivated by a single vision and restless in the pursuit of their next task. But Paul assures the Philippians, "I have you in my heart. . . . God can testify how I long for all of you with the affection of Christ Jesus" (Phil. 1:7–8 NIV). A genuine apostle is at the same time a true pastor. In his letters, Paul frequently expresses his heartfelt concern for the spiritual well-being of the church members. Such concern is evident in both the intercessions and thanksgiving he offers for them, and the rejoicing expressed at the conclusion of his letters. Despite his concern for unresolved issues, the churches remain his pride and joy. Here we see the contrast between the true and the false apostle, with the latter constantly making demands.

Even while in prison in Ephesus (or perhaps Rome), Paul is more concerned with the churches' well-being than with his own circumstances. His chains may limit his movements, but they do not circumscribe his world. His eye and mind are on the churches to which he writes during his imprisonment.

Pastors Michael Frost and Alan Hirsch devote the final three chapters of their 2003 book, *The Shaping of Things to Come: Innovation and Mission for the 21st-Century Church*, to "apostolic leadership."[10] One unfortunate consequence of the absence of apostolic leadership has been the marginalizing of the ministry of the evangelist. The pastor-teacher has become the normative expression of ministry in the local church, resulting in the evangelist working either on the periphery or with an independent evangelistic agency.

One of Hirsch's later volumes, *The Forgotten Ways*, describes what he calls the "apostolic environment": "Apostolic leadership, as in all types of influence, is both identified and measured by the *effect* it has on the social environment in which it operates. And in these terms, it is *always* present in periods of significant missional extension. Such people might not always call themselves 'Apostles,' but the apostolic nature and effect of their ministry and influence are undeniable."[11]

The absence of apostolic leadership initiatives at both denominational and local church levels has serious consequences for churches in post-Christendom

---

10. In making their case that reinstating the role of the apostle is crucial for the ongoing mission of the church, they are careful to distance themselves from those who argue for the return of the apostolic ministry as exercised by the Twelve: "In asserting an apostolic dimension to ministry, in no way do we suggest a reinstitution of the apostolic office of the original apostles" (Frost and Hirsch, *Shaping of Things to Come*, 168).

11. Hirsch, *Forgotten Ways*, 151.

contexts. It results in a preoccupation with domestic issues or in frustration, because persons with the requisite gifts and calling are neither recognized nor supported. As a consequence, most of these apostolic types simply take independent initiatives at the local level or begin independent church-birthing networks. Alan Hirsch underlines this point when he says, "Without apostolic ministry the church either forgets its high calling or fails to implement it successfully. Sadly, in declining denominational systems such people are commonly 'frozen out' or exiled because they disturb the equilibrium of a system in stasis. This 'loss' of the apostolic influencer accounts for one of the major reasons for mainstream denominational decline. If we really want missional church, then we must have a missional leadership system to drive it—it's that simple."[12]

Hirsch goes on to assert the important point that apostolic leadership creates the environment in which other ministries emerge.[13] Indeed, it is crucial that they do so because many apostles are restless by nature, always anticipating the next challenge. Their ministry needs to be within the context of the fivefold ministry outlined in Ephesians 4, which also includes the roles of prophet, evangelist, pastor, and teacher. If these four ministries are absent, new churches collapse when the apostle becomes restless and moves elsewhere. Unfortunately, many new churches have failed because of such abandonment.

To be fair to the present leadership of declining denominations, so much of their attention and energy is directed to devising retrenchment measures to help the institution survive that little attention and resources can be given to turnaround strategies. This is especially the case when such a high percentage of their congregations are understaffed, seeking financial support, and requesting consultations and answers to pressing problems.

In response to these challenges, some denominations are appointing parallel leadership to focus exclusively on "fresh expressions" of church and are looking to alternative training models to generate local leadership trained *in* ministry rather than *for* some future ministry.[14] An increasing number of these new models, some based in seminaries, are integrating academic theology with the practice of ministry, following the example of medical, business, and military training.

12. Ibid., 152.
13. Ibid., 157–59.
14. The fresh expressions initiative began in the Church of England and the Methodist Church of Great Britain but has subsequently been adopted by a number of other denominations in England. It originated from the report *The Mission-Shaped Church*, published in 2004. I have summarized it in *ChurchMorph*, chap. 3. The movement is currently achieving wider attention among both the historic denominations and new church networks in an increasing number of places throughout the Western world.

There is a growing disconnect between the needs of declining denominations, with their shrinking and aging congregations, and the kind of persons in training to lead the churches of today and tomorrow. Those attracted to the pastor-teacher role tend to be "settlers," looking for job security, rather than risk-taking pioneers. As a consequence, their education and credentialing do not necessarily translate into competence to meet the challenges of mission in the twenty-first century. To put it bluntly, they soon discover that they were trained for yesterday and to meet the demands of a congregation that absorbs all their energy. Alternatively, many declining congregations place unrealistic expectations on their new leaders to reach the generations they have lost and to attract more of the surrounding community into their churches.

Fruit of Authentic Apostolic Ministry

When we review the fruit of Paul's missionary journeys in Acts and then read through his letters to the churches, we are made aware of the abundant fruitfulness of his ministry. This is demonstrated in the rapid spread of the gospel, the lives transformed, and the faith communities birthed. In this section we will identify and examine Paul's unflagging concern for the advance of the gospel.

We can easily miss Paul's reference to the rapid spread of the gospel throughout Achaia (southern Greece) in his initial greeting to the church in Corinth (1 Cor. 1:1–3; cf. 2 Cor. 1:1–3). This advance occurred within the space of two years, between the writing of his first and second letters.

Paul's approach to mission demonstrates both opportunism and flexibility. There is also a discernible pattern in his initial approach in any new city. He almost always begins his ministry among the Hellenized Jews in the local synagogue. When he no longer gets a hearing or has aroused hostility, he moves into the wider community. On each occasion he takes the receptive Jews and Gentile "God-fearers" with him. From that point on, he follows the guidance of the Holy Spirit in contacting receptive people. Apostles are always eager to break new ground, constantly looking for newly opened doors.

When we compare the results of church planting in Paul's day with contemporary experience, we need to examine what factors today either stimulate or inhibit the advance of the gospel and the birthing of new faith communities. For instance, a number of surveys among the nonchurchgoing population reveal their antipathy to organized religion, yet many still have a high opinion of Jesus and claim to be "spiritual" without being religious. Yet for many Christians, witness still places the emphasis on coming to church, which raises the question: is that an attractive approach in today's world?

Where are the open doors around us? Are we prepared to take the initiative whenever and wherever they open? Opportunities are missed each day by those who turn away too soon. How many missed opportunities are we now aware of, and what can we learn from our lack of awareness? Many churches today are reluctant to venture into the world to participate in the mission of the risen Christ, for much the same reason as the Jerusalem-based Jewish believers; namely, they are locked into their culture and preoccupied with their history.

Urgency in Sharing the Gospel

When Paul opens his heart to the Christians in Corinth, he reveals the sense of urgency he feels to share the gospel as widely as possible and to do all in his power to remove every obstacle standing in the way.

> For though I am free with respect to all, I have made myself a slave to all, so that I might win more of them. To the Jews I became as a Jew, in order to win Jews. To those under the law I became as one under the law (though I myself am not under the law) so that I might win those under the law. To those outside the law I became as one outside the law (though I am not free from God's law but am under Christ's law) so that I might win those outside the law. To the weak I became weak, so that I might win the weak. I have become all things to all people, that I might by all means save some. I do it all for the sake of the gospel, so that I may share in its blessings. (1 Cor. 9:19–23)

The process of winning people entails both patience and sensitivity. It requires the building of trust by developing a genuine understanding and empathy toward those we are seeking to introduce to Christ. Paul, as a Jew who had been released from the bondage of the law by the grace of forgiveness in Christ, when ministering to his own people was prepared to submit to the customs, ceremonies, and rituals of the law in order not to give offense. He realized that the cultural barriers to his people coming to Christ were as significant as the theological obstacles. But when among non-Jews, Paul set aside those regulations of the Jewish law that would have alienated him from those the Lord had commissioned him to reach with the gospel. Indeed, the law, by cultivating a legalistic and exclusive mind-set in many contemporary Jews, had become more of a barrier than a pathway to faith.

Some have misunderstood Paul's bold statement "I have become all things to all people." As N. T. Wright notes, "This statement has sometimes been understood as though it meant that Paul was a mere pragmatist, a spin-doctor, twisting his message this way and that to suit different audiences.

That's not what he's saying. The message remains constant. It is the messenger who must swallow his pride, who must give up his rights, who must change his freedom into slavery. Woe betide those who trim the message so that they don't have to trim themselves."[15] Kenneth Chafin makes much the same point in his commentary on this passage: "Paul was not a chameleon who took on the moral and spiritual climate of his environment. Rather, he was a people-lover who did not let cultural or religious differences become barriers between him and persons for whom Christ died. Because he was a servant of Christ he was able to identify with and love different kinds of people as his Lord had."[16]

In missiological language, Paul's approach represents contextualization, which requires great discernment, under the guidance of the Holy Spirit and in ongoing conversations with the people concerned. The gospel message is not compromised in order to remove the offense of the unique claims of Christ and the significance of the cross and his resurrection; rather, the message is interpreted in order to relate to the distinctive issues in a particular culture.

Transformed Lives

It was customary in the early church for itinerant preachers to carry letters of recommendation from respected leaders and the churches they represented. Such letters of recommendation were especially important in the early church. "This was the only way fledgling congregations had of knowing whether a new prophet or teacher who appeared on the scene had the right credentials and could be trusted."[17]

To the Corinthians, Paul provides a stronger recommendation than a letter. He presents to them as his authentication the transformed lives resulting from his ministry. "Are we beginning to commend ourselves again? Surely we do not need, as some do, letters of recommendation to you or from you, do we? You yourselves are our letter, written on our hearts, to be known and read by all; and you show that you are a letter of Christ, prepared by us, written not with ink but with the Spirit of the living God, not on tablets of stone but on tablets of human hearts" (2 Cor. 3:1–3).

Many attempts to establish missional churches here in the West have suffered reversals and become deviant because the leaders have had no cross-cultural missionary training. As a consequence, they have allowed the cultural

---

15. Wright, *1 Corinthians*, 117.
16. Chafin, *1, 2 Corinthians*, 115.
17. Ibid., 216.

context to override the unique claims of the gospel. They have ended up uncritically affirming the culture, without questioning its underlying assumptions. Perhaps those best equipped to contextualize the message are those who have come to faith in Christ after being immersed in that culture. They have seen and experienced it from the inside. However, some such converts react so strongly in denouncing their former way of life that they are unable to reestablish contact.

There is an urgent need to establish cross-cultural training for mission in the post-Christendom, pluralistic, and increasingly neo-pagan West. In other words, mission training formerly restricted to those called to serve in other countries now needs to be required of those called to be apostles among unreached people groups and cultural enclaves here in the West.

Open Doors for the Gospel

Not only was Paul constantly on the lookout for newly opened doors, but he asks the Christians in Colossae to pray that God would open new doors. It is a mistake to try to force open closed doors; rather, one has to engage in intercession and patiently await God's timing. In writing to the Colossians, Paul not only encourages them in their prayers but also expresses his dependence on them. By their prayers they share in his ongoing ministry. "Devote yourselves to prayer, keeping alert in it with thanksgiving. At the same time pray for us as well that God will open to us a door for the word, that we may declare the mystery of Christ, for which I am in prison, so that I may reveal it clearly, as I should" (Col. 4:2–4).

Devotion to prayer provides the impetus to remaining spiritually alert. Neglecting prayer results in missed opportunities for effective witness. We no longer recognize the opportunities presented to us, nor do we sense their significance and urgency. Paul also takes the opportunity to encourage the Colossians in their own witness, exhorting them: "Conduct yourselves wisely toward outsiders, making the most of the time. Let your speech always be gracious, seasoned with salt, so that you may know how you ought to answer everyone" (Col. 2:5–6). Effective witness is respectful yet never bland. Salt adds flavor, making food appetizing, and, although an expensive commodity in the first century, was worth the expenditure!

We must not overlook that Paul wrote this letter to the Colossians from prison. In other words, he wrote from behind a closed and locked door. Yet he did not allow the door that he faced every day to determine the extent of his vision. Furthermore, it is a sign of his humility that he asked for prayer support from Christians he had never even visited.

Abundant Sowing for an Abundant Harvest

How is it that the church spread so rapidly throughout the Eastern Mediterranean? In the short space of time between the writing of the two letters to the church at Corinth, the gospel had spread out from Corinth into the other population centers of southern Greece. Paul addresses "the church of God that is in Corinth, including all the saints throughout Achaia" (2 Cor. 1:1). The impact Christians make is attributable to more than verbal witness. Rather, their very presence creates a different climate and an occasion for celebration. Using the imagery of a victorious Roman general leading a victory procession, technically known as a *triumph*, Paul writes, "But thanks be to God, who in Christ always leads us in triumphal procession, and through us spreads in every place the fragrance that comes from knowing him. For we are the aroma of Christ to God among those who are being saved and among those who are perishing; to the one a fragrance from death to death, to the other a fragrance from life to life. Who is sufficient for these things?" (2 Cor. 2:14–16). Chafin explains, "For a general to qualify for a 'triumph' celebration, he had to have been a field commander in a victorious campaign where at least five thousand of the enemy had fallen in battle—it had to be a battle where the conquered country was occupied and stabilized to become part of the vast Roman Empire."[18] Paul is a willing bondslave in the general's triumphant procession, over which hangs a pall of incense, which to the victors represents the sweet smell of victory but to the vanquished signifies their doom and death in the arena.

Abundant sowing does not entail covering the same ground time after time but breaking new ground to win unreached people. As we have seen, the calling of every apostle is to be a groundbreaker, constantly moving forward into fresh territory. Paul's pioneering role was to take the good news to non-Jews. He tells the Colossians, "I became its servant according to God's commission that was given to me for you, to make the word of God fully known" (Col. 1:25). His concern is not restricted to a onetime proclamation of the good news but includes "warning everyone and teaching everyone in all wisdom, so that we might present everyone mature in Christ. For this I toil and struggle with all the energy that he powerfully inspires within me" (Col. 1:28–29). Paul recognizes that they still have a long way to go. And he does not confine his concern to an elite leadership group but addresses the entire church.

Paul's task was to proclaim the whole counsel of God and to challenge the ever-present tendency to market a pared-down and distorted version of

18. Ibid., 212.

the gospel, emphasizing personal benefits rather than the costs involved, thereby masking its all-embracing nature by preoccupation with immediate consequences.

In the first half of this chapter, we have provided a detailed examination of the contribution of apostolic ministry in order to draw attention to the serious consequences when such leadership is conspicuous by its absence. We will now discuss structures conducive to the multiplication of faith communities.

Household Structure of Local Churches

The early churches, in addition to demonstrating the leadership dynamic discussed above, also developed a structure that enabled congregations to multiply and maintain momentum, made possible through their foundations in households. In chapter 2, we established the household as a significant building block of both Roman and Greek society that prevailed until the advent of the industrial age. Before large-scale manufacture was introduced, most business was conducted within the household and networks of home-based industries. Those business enterprises conducted outside of the house were mainly confined to building projects, warehousing, government administration, and farming.

When we read that most early Christian groups met in "private houses," we must not interpret this phrase in the modern sense. They were not private in the sense of being domestic units closed off from the outside world, but private in the sense of property ownership and the business conducted from the premises. Roger Gehring emphasizes this point by drawing attention to the fact that "the Pauline, indeed the entire early Christian movement, was able to organize itself as an independent entity not '*alongside* private Christian households but, rather, exclusively *in* them.' By remaining in their *oikoi*, it became clearer than perhaps anywhere else that the first Christians were 'in the world but not of the world.' This is undoubtedly one of the more important reasons why the house church was of such great significance for early Christian missions."[19]

Where Christians Typically Met in the First Century

It seems clear from Acts and the letters of Paul that the early Christians met mostly in private houses. The household structure of the early church meant

19. Gehring, *House Church and Mission*, 228.

that new faith communities were usually birthed within existing households. The core community was already in place, meeting not weekly but daily, because many members of the household were also employed in the business conducted there. In addition, they welcomed other individuals from their network of personal and business contacts to learn about their newfound faith in Christ and observe it in operation in their social interaction and business practices. Meeks makes this same point. "The *kat' oikon ekklesia* is thus the 'basic cell' of the Christian movement, and its nucleus was often an existing household. . . . However, the *kat' oikon ekklesia* was not simply the household gathered for prayer; it was not coterminous with the household. Other preexisting relations, such as common trades, are also suggested in the sources, and new converts could certainly have been added to existing household communities."[20] Paul specifically mentions two households in his list of contacts in Rome, those of Priscilla and Aquila and of Aristobulus, with clear indications of other family networks (see Rom. 16:11, 14, 15, 23).

Unfortunately, since there is no archaeological evidence from the period, we have scant information as to the locations of the majority of early churches. The first meeting in Philippi was in the home of Lydia, a seller of purple dye who was from the city of Thyatira, which was famous for this export. Her house was commodious enough to accommodate Paul, Silas, and Timothy, but also the "brethren" who had responded to Paul's preaching.

We also know that Priscilla and Aquila not only welcomed Paul as a fellow laborer in their tentmaking business, but also opened their premises for the church to meet. They did this in Corinth and Ephesus and most likely in Rome on their return. We don't know whether their various homes consisted of leased villas or were more modest one-room shops with living accommodation in the rear or located in a mezzanine. Many traveling merchants lived in substantial leather tents year-round. A port city, such as Corinth, would have a large tent-dwelling population located outside city walls. This meant a brisk business and a wide network of social contacts, with opportunities to witness and spread the gospel.

Progress of the Gospel

The household was not a place of refuge from the wider world but an integral part of the economic and social network of urban life. Consequently, it makes a significant contribution to the rapid expansion of the Christian movement in a number of ways. In his foundational text, *Understanding*

---

20. Meeks, *First Urban Christians*, 75–76.

Church Growth, Donald McGavran, the father of the Church Growth movement, identifies four obstacles to growth that the church overcame through its household structure.

1. *The cost of a church building.* Without any cash outlay at all, house churches provided as many places to worship as there were groups of Christians.
2. *The obstacle of the Jewish connection.* House churches pushed the church away from the synagogue into the Gentile population.
3. *The obstacle of introversion.* Each new house church exposed a new section of society—a new set of intimates and relatives—to close contact with ardent Christians.
4. *The obstacle of limited leadership.* Each house church thrust the responsibilities and prestige of leadership on able men [*sic*] of the congregation.[21]

To McGavran's list we add five considerations that reinforce the significance of house churches in birthing new faith communities.

1. *Social solidarity and security.* Roman and Greek city populations represented networks of relationships in which an isolated individual was a vulnerable social anomaly. Belonging to a household brought the benefits of membership in an intimate community: a sense of identity that carried social significance, a support network, and a context in which each person could make a distinctive contribution.
2. *Reproducible structures that facilitated exponential growth.* The story of the rapid growth and geographic spread of the gospel throughout the Mediterranean world during the first three centuries is a remarkable phenomenon. The Christian movement began on the margins of society, both Jewish and Roman. It was regarded with suspicion and disdain. It suffered sporadic persecution. Yet it permeated the entire Roman Empire.

   The story of the expansion of the early church underlines the fact that birthing new churches did not rely on the availability and affordability of real estate. Homes were available without the need to own property. This arrangement allowed for exponential growth and maximum flexibility. If one location did not work out, the church could readily move elsewhere. The church today will have to resort to similar flexibility if it is to give birth to new faith communities of sufficient number and imaginative diversity to reach the vast and expanding majority that is either dechurched or never churched.

21. McGavran, *Understanding Church Growth*, 240.

3. *Impact society*. Churches throughout the Western world face a number of tough challenges as they find themselves marginalized in pluralist and relativist cultures. How can urban churches in our day permeate the social and business structures of our society?

The location of churches in households placed them within the regular and wide-ranging activities of the communities of which they were a part. The faith community could be observed at close quarters, including the difference their faith in Christ made in relationships within the fellowship, their business dealings with believers and nonbelievers, and their sexual standards, work ethic, and so on. Their presence in the community, especially during times of crises (e.g., famine, sickness, fire, or earthquake), resulted in their having a positive, even transformative impact.

The household churches were from the very start churches in the marketplace. They did not exist as a ghetto or operate within the safety of their own ecclesial world. In addition to being *gathered* churches, their members were also *dispersed*, engaging with society not as lone individuals but as reproducible units. Each household church was birthed within its own setting and shaped by its social context. Although they had a common commitment to the good news of the reign of God as proclaimed and demonstrated by Christ, they had to work out its practical implications within their own unique contexts. There was no imposition of a one-size-fits-all model of church.

4. *Contexts for evangelization*. When evangelization is conducted on an individual, one-on-one basis unrelated to any faith community, the new believer is placed in a vulnerable position. If the individual loses contact with the person through whose witness she or he has come to faith, the new believer is likely to fall by the wayside. This is in contrast with witnessing households that provide a readily accessible supportive community in which the new believers' faith can be nurtured. Such households also provide a place with which the new believer can readily identify and experience the benefits of Christian community.

The household concept also serves to underline that evangelization is most effectively conducted by the collective witness of the faith community. New believers find it hard to survive on their own in an unsympathetic or hostile environment. Their new allegiance to Christ needs to be nurtured within the faith community. Consequently, evangelization must result in new faith communities being formed, in order to avoid the situation of so many churches today: having largely undiscipled church members. We will explore this challenge in greater depth in the following chapters.

5. *Challenge consumerist mentality.* As we have seen, the vast majority of Roman homes consisted of small rooms in which no more than twenty-five to thirty-five persons could gather. Christians came to know one another on intimate terms, not only because the groups were small, but because they were in regular contact through working together or living in the immediate neighborhood. They were present not as consumers but as full participants. In the language of the New Testament, they were "members"—that is, limbs and organs of a body. There was no place to hide.

What can we learn from first-century churches about how to birth faith communities that are reproducible, especially where real estate is expensive and zoning regulations restrictive? Could a rediscovery of these factors provide some clues for the revitalization of the church in the West in our day?

Hubs and Networks

A careful reading of Paul's missionary journeys reveals that the apostle was not constantly on the move. Paul spent months and even years establishing certain cities as strategic centers for outreach to the surrounding regions. As we have already noted, first-century faith communities were located in households, which severely limited the number that could be accommodated in most cases to roughly twenty to thirty-five persons. In some of these strategic centers, such house churches may have quickly multiplied within the confines of a densely populated city to which the regional population gravitated. If the house churches located there had the missionary vision to reach out to nearby cities, then they became a hub.

For instance, Paul spent eighteen months in Corinth. Although Paul arrived there in fear and trembling, and the house churches established there manifested some serious problems, it apparently became a strategic center for outreach. In his greetings to the Christians there in his second letter, he includes "all the saints throughout Achaia" (2 Cor. 1:1). Evidently, this church was having an impact throughout the southern region of Greece.

A further example is provided by the two years Paul spent in Ephesus (Acts 19:8–10), where he hired a private room in the "lecture hall of Tyrannus." Arthur Patzia notes, "The Western Greek text (D) expands Luke's statement that Paul 'argued daily [*kath hemeran dialegomenos*]' by adding 'from eleven o'clock in the morning to four in the afternoon,' the normal siesta time in Mediterranean countries. If true, Paul may have practiced his trade as a leatherworker during normal working hours and then lectured in the hall when people were free to come and listen."[22] This important city became a strategic center for outreach to the surrounding Gentile population. Evidently, Paul's teaching ministry was intended not to simply provide theological education but to stimulate mission outreach. According to Pliny the Younger's letter to the emperor Trajan in AD 112, the gospel spread from Ephesus to Miletus, Smyrna, Assos, Troas, Pergamum, Thyatira, Sardis, Philadelphia, Hierapolis, Laodicea, and Colossae.[23]

Throughout the Western world, we are aware of megachuches exerting a widespread influence through their conferences, literature, and, less frequently, their church-planting endeavors. However, in more recent decades we have seen small churches establish networks and become an inspiration to other churches that identify with their values and vision. They often provide an inspiring relationship precisely because they do not depend on leaders with outstanding organization and communication abilities. These small churches are reproducible. They do not seek to control but to provide a forum in which experiences can be exchanged. They are often linked by websites and blogs, with frequent communication taking place among the leaders. As Van Gelder and Zscheile insist, "In many church systems, a new congregation becomes officially 'legitimate' only when it comes to resemble the functional Christendom model of church—a congregation that can support a full-time pastor and a building."[24]

Birthing New Churches Today

In many ways the challenges are even greater today than in Paul's day. Cities are much larger in area, more cosmopolitan, and socially diverse. The geographical neighborhood has collapsed in many places into fragmented and competing special-interest groups, resulting in the undermining of civil society. Many people draw into themselves and create especially vulnerable sectors of society, particularly among the aged, the housebound, and the socially marginalized.

As we noted in the opening chapter, there is an increasing awareness that neither big government nor big business has the resources to adequately address the economic and social challenges that face Western societies. Civil society has to be rebuilt at the local level, with churches playing a key role, alongside other local institutions, in bringing this about. Planning blight spread in the

---

22. Patzia, *Emergence of the Church*, 126.
23. Ibid., 128.
24. Van Gelder and Zscheile, *Missional Church in Perspective*, 162.

inner city from the 1950s until the 1990s, at the same time that suburban development attracted significant segments of the residential population and many businesses to these newer areas. This movement of resources created significant social and economic challenges for the inner city that need to be addressed through programs of urban renewal, in which churches can make their distinctive faith-based contribution.

In recent years an urban-design movement known as "New Urbanism" has grown at the expense of older planning philosophies. New Urbanism calls for communities where many of the amenities essential to daily living are available locally; schools, clinics for primary care, shops, restaurants, recreational and sports facilities, libraries, and fitness and leisure centers are all within walking distance. Such communities also provide a range of housing for everyone from first-time buyers and young families to the elderly.[25]

As large sections of the business world move from the industrial complex to the high-tech and information age, with telecommuting replacing freeway commuting and gridlock, the neighborhood comes alive. Furthermore, we must not overlook the fact that 80 percent of new jobs are created not by big conglomerates but by small businesses employing less than fifty persons. In order to be part of this reimagining of the city, churches must learn to work together rather than against one another. They must see themselves, as did the early church, as part of the everyday life of the community. The greater percentage of its manifold ministries will be taking place in the community and not within the fellowship of the church. These ministries must be recognized and resourced.

Unfortunately, neither Luke's account in Acts nor Paul's letters provide precise information on the roles of individual leaders in the churches birthed during Paul's mission. We do know that elders were ordained in each place, which at least emphasizes a plurality of leadership rather than reliance on one individual to meet all ministry demands. Furthermore, the situation was fluid rather than formalized, though we must remember that relationships and roles were already firmly established within the household prior to the baptism of the members. They knew each other's personalities, gifts, and relational skills. Consequently, leadership emerged according to the demands of each situation. The setting aside and official recognizing of persons to serve as elders depends on their spiritual maturity and Christlike character. "The fact that Paul does not mention installing leaders in the house churches in his undisputed letters

---

25. Genuine community requires intergenerational mixing, not segregated accommodation that isolates seniors and separates young families from the support of their wider family and neighbors.

is significant in our context. Even though he was not indifferent to leadership issues, Paul appears not to have concerned himself with the question of the official installation of leaders. This could be related to the fact that it was not necessary because leadership structures were already built into the ancient *oikos* and hence leaders emerged from below, from the household setting itself."[26] The issue for Paul was his recognition of the leadership already in place. It had to be approved by God in terms of each leader's character and calling, which was then affirmed by Paul and the local congregation.

Summary

This chapter has focused on three crucial factors in the church's ability to respond to the urban challenge by birthing new faith communities. The apostle Paul provides both inspiration and insights, in that he had to address the challenge of establishing a visionary and reproducible model to facilitate the rapid expansion of the Christian movement. I believe that today's church needs to rediscover and adapt these insights in order to rejuvenate existing churches and establish new faith communities in reevangelizing the West.

First, apostolic leadership needs to be reinstated in order to release churches from their survival mentality and restore a mission élan. Second, churches must move on from their consumer mentality and institutional confinement to become a dynamic movement in which every faith community has reproducible potential. The following chapters seek to provide additional insights derived from the apostle Paul that fill out and add essential elements to the picture.

 *Conclusion:*

*Visionary leadership, risk-taking,
and enabling skills are needed to initiate
and sustain an expanding movement.*

26. Gehring, *House Church and Mission*, 227.

5

Caring for New Churches

I remember an evangelist commenting, "I love catching fish, but I cannot stand cleaning them!" Fortunately, the apostle Paul did not share his aversion. As an apostle to the churches he had founded, Paul was concerned with their ongoing survival as a community of God's people growing in faith and expanding their witness. He carried in his heart care for all the churches, for which he prayed constantly, and was aware of the many challenges that the growing network of faith communities was facing—both internal tensions and external threats from the surrounding culture. Paul's goal was not simply to gather followers but to ensure that the new believers embarked on a lifelong journey as followers of Jesus Christ, and that their spiritual pilgrimage should lead to their progressive transformation into Christ's image. In order to achieve this high goal, Paul and his team took a number of practical steps.

In the opening chapter, I stressed the need for authentic community and locally based renewal of the city. The dysfunctional nature of Western societies will not be adequately addressed either by top-down political strategies or by market conditions being imposed, whether through financial institutions or the business community. This is not to imply that government, either national or regional, and financial and business institutions have no significant roles to play. But in order for their contributions to have significant impact, a civil society must be in place, one in which people experience authentic community, find support and encouragement, and are held accountable.

As the church in the West becomes increasingly marginalized and numerically depleted, the urgency to provide support networks both for new churches and for traditional churches seeking renewal increases. In responding to these challenges, the contemporary church has much to learn from the various measures employed within the early Christian movement.

Return Visits

Although Paul traveled extensively, he was no fly-by-night evangelist. Despite the rough treatment Paul and his team experienced in the southern Galatian cities of Pisidian Antioch, Iconium, Lystra, and Derbe, they did not take the short journey home through the Cilician Gate to Syrian Antioch. Instead, they retraced their steps through those same towns where they had been poorly treated. On their return visit to the churches resulting from their pioneering evangelism, "they strengthened the souls of the disciples and encouraged them to continue in the faith, saying, 'It is through many persecutions that we must enter the kingdom of God.' And after they had appointed elders for them in each church, with prayer and fasting they entrusted them to the Lord in whom they had come to believe" (Acts 14:21–23).

Paul's second and third missionary journeys both began as follow-up visits to the churches he had already founded in southern Galatia rather than as attempts to break new ground. Some time after returning from the Jerusalem Council, Paul said to Barnabas, "Come, let us return and visit the believers in every city where we proclaimed the word of the Lord and see how they are doing" (Acts 15:36). As it turned out, their journey was not confined to a follow-up visit to southern Galatia. They continued on through the Roman province of Asia (modern western Turkey) and then Macedonia and Achaia (modern Greece). After returning once more to Syrian Antioch to deliver a report on his activities, Paul "departed and went from place to place through the region of Galatia and Phrygia, strengthening all the disciples" (Acts 18:23). It is significant that on both of these occasions the initial impetus for Paul's journeys was the strengthening of existing disciples in churches that had already been established. It was only after this initial purpose had been fulfilled that Paul and his companions extended their mission into new territory.

In the course of his missionary journeys, Paul succeeded in establishing "small cells of Christians in scattered households in some of the strategically located cities of the northeast Mediterranean basin. Those cells were linked to one another and to Paul and his fellow workers by means of letters and official visits and by frequent contact through traveling Christians, and he had encouraged local persons of promise to establish new groups in nearby towns."[1]

Precisely because Paul was an apostle, his ministry was both extensive and intensive. In other words, he was concerned, not just for the geographical expansion of the Christian movement, but also for the quality of life and spiritual progress of all those who identified with Christ's rapidly expanding communities of adopted sons and daughters in the family of God. They took on a new identity that was intended to increasingly reflect the very person of Christ.

In his letters to the churches, Paul sometimes refers to follow-up visits. He made it clear to the Thessalonians in one of his earliest letters that he had made repeated attempts to pay them a return visit (1 Thess. 2:17–18). His first visit had been all too brief, and he had left in a hurry only to avoid exposing them to further danger on his account. G. K. Beale comments, "This is such an emphatic statement about his concern for them that many have perhaps rightly concluded that Paul is offering an implicit defense against Jewish accusations that he did not care about the readers and would never return."[2]

Bearing in mind that the churches of the New Testament were small, newly formed, and widely scattered, frequent visitors were especially important. They brought encouragement by sharing news, conveyed letters from Paul, and inspired local witness and evangelistic outreach to birth new communities of Christ-followers. These same ministries are even more important in our own day.

Today it is the larger churches that attract most of the renowned visiting preachers and teachers. The churches' primary motivation for inviting these visitors is not so much the relevance of their teaching but their ability to draw crowds. They are often described as "much-sought-after speakers," with their publicity including the countries where they have ministered and the best sellers they have authored. The hope is that they will attract a large congregation, often supplemented by Christians from other churches. This is very different from the normal pattern of visiting in first-century churches. As we have noted, congregations then were small, consisting of less than fifty persons. The churches did not swarm around celebrities. Rather, they gathered for instruction and encouragement, to receive news about other churches, and to hear and discuss a letter from Paul addressed to them personally.

Today's churches need that kind of ministry just as much as first-century churches, especially in light of their shrinking numbers, lack of direction, and

---

1. Meeks, *First Urban Christians*, 9–10.
2. Beale, *1–2 Thessalonians*, 90.

low morale. This is particularly true for isolated rural churches and struggling churches in transitional neighborhoods, which are either closing down
or moving elsewhere at an alarming rate. They need frequent visits by people
with special gifts and insights in teaching Scripture and who can help them
overcome denial and defeatism, gain fresh motivation and vision, and develop
contextually appropriate ministries.

Extended Stays

A superficial reading of Acts might give the false impression that Paul was
constantly on the move. A more careful reading reveals that he remained for
longer periods of time in some strategic locations, in order to consolidate
the work he had begun and build up the local church. This practice began
in Antioch before Paul embarked on his first missionary journey. When
Barnabas checked out the new outreach to non-Jews and saw evidence of
the grace of God at work among these new believers, he "went to Tarsus to
look for Saul, and when he had found him, he brought him to Antioch. So
it was that for an entire year they met with the church and taught a great
many people, and it was in Antioch that the disciples were first called 'Christians'" (Acts 11:25–26).

During Paul's subsequent missionary journeys, he made Corinth and
Ephesus centers of regional outreach, spending eighteen months in Corinth
"teaching the word of God among them" (Acts 18:11). From this location the
gospel spread throughout Achaia. While in Ephesus he "argued daily in the
lecture hall of Tyrannus. This continued for two years, so that all the residents
of Asia, both Jews and Greeks, heard the word of the Lord" (Acts 19:9–10).

By means of these extended visits, the apostle Paul demonstrated both
evangelistic urgency and the need to develop local leaders through his teaching, example, and pastoral care. Leadership entails establishing a corporate
culture, or DNA, ensuring the right priorities and comprehensive nature of
ongoing ministry. In Paul's example, we see the distinction between the ministry of the apostle and that of the evangelist. The latter is usually preoccupied
with bringing to birth new believers, whereas the apostle has a much broader
agenda—namely, the nurturing of new believers and forming or incorporating
them into healthy, vibrant churches.

Interim pastors exercise valuable ministries in guiding hurting and dysfunctional churches through painful transitions. They may provide wise counsel
for churches recovering from a previous pastor who suffered burnout or succumbed to sexual or financial temptations. Or the previous pastor may have

been theologically deviant, leaving the congregation in need of biblical teaching to establish a firm foundation in the Word of God.

Coworkers

Rapidly growing and expanding ministry cannot remain dependent on the initiative of one leader. Eventually, the leader will suffer burnout and the whole movement will lose both momentum and cohesion. Often contemporary apostolic types operate as loners, but this was not the case with the apostle Paul. Whenever possible he was accompanied by a select team of coworkers. Barnabas was Paul's close friend and companion during his first missionary journey. Barnabas had been his most loyal supporter and encourager from his first contact with the church leaders in Jerusalem. Along with them traveled the young John Mark. Then Timothy joined Paul and Silas (also from Jerusalem). Paul took young believers with leadership potential and trained them by the apprenticeship method.

Evidence from Acts and Paul's letters provides abundant indications of much traffic between the churches. After Paul and his team made their hasty exit from Thessalonica, Paul sent back the young Timothy to encourage the new Christians, and to make a report indicating how they were managing to survive under continuing opposition. Timothy rejoined Paul in Corinth, with the encouraging news that the churches were not only holding their own but were spreading their message throughout the provinces of Macedonia and Achaia (1 Thess. 3:2–6).

Sometimes visitors consisted of traveling Christians seeking hospitality. At other times the delegates were sent either by Paul personally or on behalf of churches, to bring instructions, deliver letters from or to Paul from one of the churches, or provide financial support. For instance, we read of Paul sending delegates (Stephanas, Fortunatus, and Achaicus) to Philippi. Epaphroditus was sent to either Ephesus or Rome by the Philippian Christians to take care of Paul's financial needs (Phil. 2:25–30; 4:18). Paul describes him as his "brother and co-worker and fellow soldier" who served at the risk of his life (Phil. 2:25).

Of particular interest is Paul's recommendation of Phoebe, a wealthy benefactor and deacon in Corinth's neighboring port of Cenchrea, who bears on his behalf a letter for the Christians in Rome.[3] Paul commends her warmly, "so that you may welcome her in the Lord as is fitting for the saints, and help her in whatever she may require from you, for she has been a benefactor of many and of myself as well" (Rom. 16:2).

3. See Meeks, *First Urban Christians*, 16–17.

The widespread nature of Paul's ministry, and the fact that he was such a key figure in spearheading the mission to the non-Jewish world, necessitated frequent changes in plans. He has to defend sudden changes in his itinerary on a number of occasions, explaining that his absences were not due to neglect. For instance, Paul responds to criticism by the Corinthians in both his first and his second letters (1 Cor. 4:18–19; 2 Cor. 1:15–17). His absences are due to pastoral emergencies, physical sickness, legal bans, or other means that Satan is using to place obstacles in his way. With so many new churches largely composed of recent converts from the pagan world, problems and challenges abounded. It is not surprising that Paul gives such high priority to identifying and appointing local leadership to handle as much as they are able.

One of the persistent challenges facing all itinerant ministers is remembering those they have left behind. This challenge balloons with every new visit, as the list of places and people lengthens with each passing week. Making follow-up visits becomes increasingly demanding, until leaders find themselves caught in their own web. This inevitably entails church leaders having to make strategic centers their base of operations. As we have noted, Paul followed this course of action in the case of Corinth and Ephesus (2 Cor. 1:16–2:5; 11:23–28).

Organizationally, the success of Paul's urban strategy resulted from his making it a collaborative enterprise. Paul began his ministry as a "fellow worker of Barnabas," and "when Barnabas and Paul split after the confrontation described in Galatians 2:11–14, each took one or more partners. In the New Testament reports, none of the other apostles, such as Peter, Apollos, or Philip, seems to have done that."[4] Some of Paul's leaders were local, as was Epaphras in Colossae (Col. 1:7; 4:12), while others were occasionally itinerant, such as Timothy and Epaphras (Epaphroditus), who were dispatched to Philippi (Phil. 2:25–29; 4:18). It is impossible to keep track of all of Paul's numerous coworkers. Many are simply mentioned in passing. Others step in and out of Luke's narrative or Paul's correspondence. The coworkers identified by name include Apollos, Timothy, Silas (Silvanus), Sosthenes, Barnabas, John Mark, Stephanas, Fortunatus, Achaicus, Epaphroditus, Tychicus, and Onesimus.

One of the simplest and most reliable tests to determine whether persons are leaders is to ask, is anyone following them? If the answer is negative, then those individuals are not leaders, no matter how impressive their credentials or titles. We can appreciate Paul's genius as a leader, in that during a short period he gathered a considerable retinue of persons demonstrating deep commitment and reliability. Even more impressive are the clear indications that these associates were not dependent on Paul. They continued to function and

4. Ibid., 133.

take initiative whether or not Paul was present. Not that this was true in every case, as there is always an element of risk. The young Mark failed to live up to Paul's expectations, so Barnabas took him under his wing as an assistant in his ongoing ministry in Cyprus. Then there is Demas, who abandoned Paul because he loved this present world.

Wise leaders avoid building networks of dependency. If they allow that to happen, eventually the whole structure will collapse, due to the numbers of persons clamoring for the leader's attention, and jealousy arising among them when they perceive, or imagine, a pecking order. As today's church leaders face the challenges presented by the need to birth new faith communities and to decentralize their ministry structure in order to reach an ever-increasing un- churched population, they can gain inspiration from the first-century example of the apostle Paul. Similar leadership strategies can also be observed in operation today in regions of the world where significant church growth is taking place.

Team Leadership

One of the consequences of professionalizing ministry has been the establish- ment of the solo pastor as the norm for local church leadership. Such profes- sionalization also leads local churches to look for leadership from outside the membership of the local congregation. From the outset, the apostle Paul established the pattern of a plurality of leadership drawn from among the church members. As we have seen in the previous section, Paul did not work alone but in company with a team of coworkers. This established a pattern of shared leadership that was not confined to the initial apostolic team, which moved elsewhere once the local church was firmly established. To the new believers in Thessalonica, Paul describes the young Timothy as his coworker in proclaiming the good news and in strengthening and encouraging them (1 Thess. 3:2; see also Phil. 2:19–24).

In his opening salutation to the Colossians, Paul writes, "Paul, an apostle of Christ Jesus by the will of God, and Timothy our brother, To God's holy people in Colossae, the faithful brothers and sisters in Christ: Grace and peace to you from God our Father" (Col. 1:1–2 NIV). Here as elsewhere Paul's letter is not confined to the leadership of the church but is addressed to the core members, described as "holy" and "faithful." Paul is possibly writing from prison in Ephesus, a hundred miles away from Colossae. He is not seeking to make them dependent on him, but rather prays that they will continue to receive what only God can impart: "grace and peace from God our Father" made available to them through Jesus Christ by the Holy Spirit.

In each of the churches, it was Paul's custom to give local "elders" authority to continue to develop the ministry and mission of the local church after his departure. Paul's introduction to the church in Philippi acknowledges a plurality of leadership: "To all God's holy people in Christ Jesus at Philippi, together with the overseers and deacons" (Phil. 1:1 NIV). Yet such acknowledgment does not lead to the marginalizing of the laity such as we see today in many of our church structures and decision-making processes. As Gordon Fee observes, "After being singled out in the address, they are not hereafter mentioned or spoken to."[5] They are simply reckoned as being within the community.

When the leaders are singled out, as here, they are not said to be "over" the church but are addressed along with the rest. Their authority was both administrative and spiritual. Deacons deal with practical matters yet need to be spiritually qualified by being "full of the Holy Spirit." There is no hint of elitism. However, homegrown leadership raises issues of recognition, respect, and submission (1 Thess. 5:12–13; 1 Cor. 16:15–16). Jesus himself encountered this problem in his own hometown (Mark 6:1–6).

Letter Writing

The twenty-one letters preserved in the New Testament represent a highly relational form of communication. New believers gathered in faith communities, and young leaders ministering among them needed guidance to keep them on track and to address issues they were confronting, either among the members or in relation to the wider community. A prompt response was required. Letters are far less formal than general theological statements, pastoral guidelines, or policy statements.

Paul's letters included intercession, teaching, information, and admonishment. During his brief visit to Thessalonica, Paul gave teaching high priority. He was concerned for individuals not just to make an initial decision for Christ as their Savior, but also to embark on a life of discipleship as apprentices of Christ. The word that was taught had to be received (1 Thess. 2:13–14). Paul was concerned about not only his delivery of the message but also their reception of it, wanting them to live in order to please God.

Effective communicators are always sensitive to the needs and attitudes of those they are addressing. They are concerned not just to impart information but to facilitate formation. The received word enables followers of Christ to grow in their relationships with God. Paul describes a fruitful response to the

5. Fee, *Philippians*, 42.

word of God in the following terms: "As you therefore have received Christ Jesus the Lord, continue to live your lives in him, rooted and built up in him and established in the faith, just as you were taught, abounding in thanksgiving" (Col. 2:6–7).

In his letter to the Philippians, Paul recognizes that fruitfulness is the work of God in the life of the believer: "For it is God who is at work in you, enabling you both to will and to work for his good pleasure" (Phil. 2:13). Fruitfulness is the product of a healthy and abiding relationship. As Beale comments, "Christians who grow up in church sometimes have difficulty making the transition from thinking of their faith as a duty demanded by a divine master to a relationship of love encouraged by a divine Father."[6]

In our day we need to give fresh attention to both the Gospels and the letters of the New Testament in order to counteract the widespread biblical illiteracy among churchgoers. At the other extreme, there is also the problem of preachers who deliver Bible teaching that may be theologically orthodox yet unrelated to life. In his letters, Paul responds to actual questions presented by the recipients, which at times causes difficulty in interpreting Paul's statements. Frequently, we have to guess at the issues the recipients have raised and to which he is responding, since we receive only one side of the communication.

One fruitful way of engaging with Paul's correspondence is to imagine that we are the intended recipients and to respond with our own letter headed "Dear Paul." This approach stimulates our imagination and is especially illuminating when used as a group exercise, with each individual making his or her own response and then sharing with the group. Each person's contribution can throw fresh light on the passage, especially in relation to our personal lives and issues within our church.

Frequently Paul mentions colleagues who share the concerns expressed in his letters. His correspondence does not consist of private communications. For instance, he introduces his letter to the Galatians with the statement, paraphrased in the New Living Translation, "All the brothers and sisters here join me in sending this letter to the churches of Galatia" (Gal. 1:2). The Christian fellowship he refers to is probably the church in Syrian Antioch, the base for his missionary journeys and the original sending body.

In order to specify the intended recipients of his first letter to the Thessalonians, Paul signs off, "I solemnly command you by the Lord that this letter be read to all of them [i.e., the brothers and sisters]" (1 Thess. 5:27; see also Col. 4:16). There is no hint of elitism. Despite the fact that they are all fairly new believers, information is not restricted to the privileged few. Everyone is to be

---

6. Beale, *1–2 Thessalonians*, 79.

"in the know." This open communication ensures that everyone is part of the conversation, empowered to share in decision making and take responsibility for responding appropriately to the issues raised. It is significant that, although leaders in the churches may be acknowledged, they are generally not named.

Paul intended his letters to be discussed, considered carefully, and acted upon. In fact, he issues a solemn warning to those who ignore what he has written: "Take note of those who do not obey what we say in this letter; have nothing to do with them, so they may be ashamed. Do not regard them as enemies, but warn them as believers" (2 Thess. 3:14–15). His concern is to shame them, not to drive them away. They are still members of the adopted family of God, so the goal is their forgiveness and restoration to fellowship.

Paul was fully aware of the apostolic authority that lay behind his letters. He was also a practical man who recognized the possibility of forgeries that could do damage. In his second letter to the Thessalonians, he mentions this possibility (2 Thess. 2:2). To provide evidence of their genuineness, in a number of letters he signs off personally (e.g., Gal. 6:11; 2 Thess. 3:17).

Unfortunately, not all of Paul's letters have survived, such as the "unknown letter" referred to in 1 Cor. 5:9, which Paul had written prior to our 1 Corinthians. In addition, there is the "tearful letter" (2 Cor. 2:3–4), which was composed following his painful visit. Paul asks his readers in Colossae to pass on his letter to the Laodiceans and for the Laodiceans likewise to give to the Colossians his letter to them (Col. 4:16). But Paul's letter to the Laodiceans has not survived.

Paul's letters demonstrate that leaders need to be prepared to find themselves under attack and to take appropriate steps to ward off attempts to undermine their authority. N. T. Wright, in his excellent series of daily devotions on Paul's letters to the Corinthians, strikes a helpful balance. "If the community is simply concerned to have a placid life, and tones down the clear and definite notes of gospel belief and behavior for the sake of that, its effectiveness, its witness and its mission to the world, will be greatly reduced. . . . Equally, if a community becomes so keen on discipline and order that it deals harshly with offenders and allows them no chance to repent, to make amends, and to be welcomed back to full members, the satan will be just as pleased."[7]

We now turn to each of Paul's letters written to churches in specific locations to identify the issues that had arisen in each place, and to see how he responds to their questions. In these letters Paul also takes the opportunity to assure them of his continuing prayers, offer words of encouragement, and provide general guidance on a number of theological, ethical, and practical issues, as well as counsel on specific issues.

7. Wright, 2 Corinthians, 21.

Issues in Galatia

I am assuming that Paul wrote his letter to the Galatians soon after his return to Syrian Antioch. This being the case, we can better appreciate the polemical tone of the letter. For, while Paul was with the church in Antioch, people from Jerusalem arrived, teaching believers in this largely Gentile church that, "unless you are circumcised, according to the custom taught by Moses, you cannot be saved" (Acts 15:1 NIV). Their intervention exacerbated problems between the Jewish and non-Jewish members of the churches. Having experienced so much opposition from unbelieving Jews who insisted they observe the Mosaic Law, these Jewish followers of Jesus stirred up antagonistic debate, as is evident in Paul's letter. This opposition party from Jerusalem was clearly influential, as we see from Peter's trepidation and caving in to their pressure (Gal. 2:11–14).

The Judaizers' insistence on circumcision, the observation of special days in the Jewish calendar, and dietary regulations, represented an imposition of cultural observances that, if they remained unchallenged, would have reduced Christianity to a sect within Judaism. On a deeper level, their demands also undermined the gospel of grace. Paul challenges the notion that such requirements represent an enriching addition to the gospel, insisting they would lead to an undermining, and even betrayal, of the gospel. He describes those who include observance of the law as a necessary prerequisite to salvation as reverting to "spiritual infancy" (Gal. 3:23–25; 4:1–2) and as turning from freedom to "slavery" (Gal. 4:3–8).

The Judaizers pride themselves in claiming Abraham as their father. While identifying with this claim as a Jew himself, Paul also points out that Abraham was justified in the sight of God by faith centuries before the giving of the law of Moses. The true children of Abraham are those who, by faith enabled by the Spirit, identify with Christ as their indwelling Lord and Savior (Gal. 3:6–9). It was by this means that the promise given to Abraham—that all peoples on earth would be blessed through him—came to fulfillment (Gen. 12:3). Christian social anthropologist Melba P. Maggay notes, "The idea that one does not have to be culturally a Jew to be part of the chosen people of God was so new that Paul was attacked for making up a gospel that is easier and more palatable to people (Gal. 1:10–11). In reply Paul asserts that his gospel and the authority to preach it were received directly from God and not from any man" (Gal. 1:1, 12, 15–17).[8]

The threat of the cultural captivity of both the gospel and the church is an ever-present challenge. Legalism is a religious tendency that both restrains

---

8. Maggay, "Message of Galatians," 245.

and retards. In every age it works to undermine the mission of the church. If the Judaizers had won the day, then Christianity would have withered under the constraints of legalism and ritualism.

The message of Galatians is as relevant to the twenty-first century as it was to the first century. Maggay emphasizes the significance of Paul's refusal to yield to the Judaizers for mission in our day. "Without this man's tears and persevering struggle, Christianity could have become just another Jewish sect, a minor tribal religion not very different from all the others whose main teachings have to do mostly with what one may and may not do before God."[9]

Paul resisted all attempts to undermine his authority, claiming that his calling came directly from the ascended Christ, as did his understanding of the gospel of the grace of God. Consequently, he refused to compromise, insisting that "a different gospel . . . is no gospel at all" (Gal. 1:6–7 NIV). The temptation to turn away from the gospel of Christ is not confined to the first century. It can happen with surprising speed with any believer in Christ and within any congregation. Like Paul, we must remain forever vigilant against substituting "gospels."

Issues in Philippi

Philippians is one of the four letters written by Paul during his time in prison. There is no consensus among New Testament scholars as to whether he was incarcerated in Rome or in Ephesus. The traditional view is that the location was Rome, but many modern scholars argue for Ephesus, which is the position taken here. Wherever he was held prisoner, this letter is characterized not by self-pity but by the joy and rejoicing (mentioned ten times) that he experiences himself and also encourages among the believers in Philippi.

There are no doctrinal arguments in this letter; rather, Paul strives to encourage the believers. He is grateful to God for them and assures them of his continuing prayers for their spiritual growth. He draws on his own experience of imprisonment to inspire the Philippians in the midst of their difficulties, explaining how his circumstances have not curtailed the advance of the gospel but resulted in the message continuing to be broadcast: "It has become known throughout the whole imperial guard and to everyone else that my imprisonment is for Christ; and most of the brothers and sisters, having been made confident in the Lord by my imprisonment, dare to speak the word with greater boldness and without fear" (Phil. 1:13–14). He prays for courage to

9. Ibid.

face whatever the future may have in store for him, adding, "For to me, living is Christ and dying is gain" (Phil. 1:21). His option is either to continue here on earth in fruitful labor or to enter into his reward in heaven.

A far greater example than Paul's suffering for Christ is the suffering of Christ himself. The believers in Philippi should stand side by side in mutual support, inspired by the example of Christ that Paul puts before them. Prose is inadequate to describe what Christ was prepared to undergo in order to fulfill the mission entrusted to him by his heavenly Father. Many scholars believe that Philippians 2:6–11 is an ancient hymn, either composed by Paul himself or quoted by him. The fact that Christ left the majestic security of heaven to become a slave prepared to suffer the most painful and shameful of deaths—crucifixion—provides the supreme example of self-sacrifice. It also assures suffering Christians that, as in the case of Christ, the Lord will vindicate them. Death is followed by resurrection.

In the face of the Judaizers' demands of adherence to the law (Phil. 3:1–3), Paul exhorts believers to continue to share in Christ's suffering and death and thereby experience the resurrection power of Christ (Phil. 3:10–11). If this was a difficult step for them to take, it had been even more so for Paul. He had set aside his social status and religious achievements, counting them all as garbage "because of the surpassing value of knowing Christ Jesus my Lord" (Phil. 3:8). He was eventually relieved to exchange his own worthless, works-based righteousness for the righteousness obtained on his behalf by Christ on the cross. In conclusion, Paul encourages the believers to fill their lives with rejoicing, prayerful dependence on God, and gratitude for his provision. Paul also takes the opportunity to thank the Philippian church for its generosity in providing for his material needs while he is in prison.

Philippians provides a much-needed reminder that the gospel is not about our material comfort and that ministry is not about boosting our egos, or our standing within the church. Discipleship, and the service to Christ and his church that this entails, is undertaken at great personal cost. Paul's example and his exhortations challenge all ministry that is ego-driven or undertaken for the sake of personal gain.

Issues in Thessalonica

Paul's letter to Thessalonica is written to recent converts banded together in a church that was only months old at the time of writing. It is sent to them as a joint composition, with Paul mentioning Silas and Timothy, companions who had shared in teaching these young believers. This first letter makes clear that while some Jews were converted through Paul's preaching, most of the converts were Roman and Macedonian Gentiles who had abandoned idolatry in order to follow Christ (1 Thess. 1:9–10). From day one they confronted a hostile society, so they urgently needed encouragement and guidance. They had made a good start but needed to continue as they had begun (1 Thess. 4:1–2).

Paul rejoices in the faith, love, and hope of the new believers, which together provide solid evidence of the genuineness of their conversion, demonstrated as much in their common life as in their individual lives. Their work is faith inspired; their backbreaking toil is love inspired; and their endurance is inspired by their sure and certain hope grounded in the Lord Jesus Christ (1 Thess. 1:3).

The Thessalonians are commended for their witness. They shared their good news throughout Macedonia and Achaia within a few weeks of their own conversions. Their message is authenticated by the great joy they demonstrate despite persecution from their fellow citizens. Their exuberance and empowerment are evidences of the Holy Spirit working among them. Paul recalls their response to his witness among them: "For we know, brothers and sisters beloved by God, that he has chosen you, because our message of the gospel came to you not in word only, but also in power and in the Holy Spirit and with full conviction" (1 Thess. 1:4–5).

Issues confronting these first-century believers are highlighted in Paul's two letters. He exhorts them to live in order to please God, which entails avoiding sexual sin. Promiscuity and prostitution were prevalent in the pagan world, not least because they were an integral part of pagan temple culture. A second issue that Paul addresses has to do with church members who have given up their jobs or are refusing to work. They believe that the Lord is returning soon, so why bother? Additionally, perhaps some unscrupulous individuals within households that had become Christian are taking advantage of the situation by living off the resources of other household members. A third issue concerns believers who had died before the Lord's return. Paul exhorts the community not to behave like pagans who have no hope in life beyond the grave (1 Thess. 4:13). On his return, the risen Lord will bring back with him those who have died, to meet those who are alive at his coming. He also urges them not to speculate about the timing of the Lord's return. It will come as a surprise, so we must remain alert and prepared.

In his second letter, written a year or more later, Paul devotes the main section to further teaching on the Lord's second coming. Evidently, there is still confusion and misunderstanding on this issue; some are teaching that the Lord had already come. But the church is not to be alarmed or deceived by such teaching, "for that day will not come unless the rebellion comes first and the lawless one is revealed, the one destined for destruction" (2 Thess. 2:3). They must remain alert and resilient, for no one knows the hour of the Lord's appearing.[10]

In concluding each of his letters to the Thessalonians, Paul touches on a number of issues that are as relevant to twenty-first-century believers as to those in the first century. They deal with the attitude of members toward leaders and with their mutual ministry. The second letter concludes with a warning against idleness (2 Thess. 3:6–15) and other problems Paul had addressed in his first letter (1 Thess. 5:14) that nevertheless clearly persisted.

In these brief letters, we see something of the range of Paul's concerns, as well as evidence that he is well informed. He combines doctrinal and ethical matters, demonstrating that his theology is always related to life. This balance is equally important for teachers in the contemporary church.

Issues in Corinth

Two of Paul's letters to the Corinthians have survived. The first was written sometime in the period AD 53–55, during Paul's third missionary journey, and was sent from Ephesus, where Paul spent two or three years during his third missionary journey. He had written a previous letter to the church (1 Cor. 2:3), and the Corinthians had replied, asking his advice on a number of points (1 Cor. 7:1). He had also received reports and visitors from Corinth (1 Cor. 1:11; 16:15–17). Stephanas, Fortunatus, and Achaicus may have delivered the letter when they returned to Corinth. Some problems remained unresolved, resulting in a later personal visit to Corinth, and also a strongly worded letter, which has not survived, that Paul refers to in 2 Corinthians 2:1–11 and 7:8–10.

In his first letter, Paul addresses a number of issues that have come to his attention, including sexual immorality and the need to discipline those who indulge in sexual sin. Another matter of concern relates to bringing fellow believers into court to face lawsuits. The Corinthians also have questions of their own, relating to marriage, divorce, and whether to remain single; whether they can eat food that has been offered to idols; and the responsible exercise of freedom in view of believers who might be easily offended. Paul then gives instructions regarding appropriate dress and behavior in worship and the exercise of spiritual gifts in a manner that demonstrates love rather than

---

10. Throughout the ages, and to the present day, there has been a succession of individuals predicting the date of the Lord's return. It is significant that it is invariably within their own lifetimes and that the date is imminent. They have all been proved wrong.

self-advertisement. Paul next deals at length with the matter of the resurrection of the dead, a concern that the Corinthians share with the Thessalonians. Last, he gives instructions regarding the collection of money for the relief of impoverished believers in Jerusalem.

Paul left Ephesus after the riot in the city (Acts 19:1–21:1), traveling north to Troas and then on to Macedonia, where he wrote his second letter to the Corinthians. Between writing the two letters, Paul experienced much opposition, including threats to his life. In this letter he opens his heart to the believers, describing not only the physical hardships he has endured but also the false accusations he has faced from fellow believers.

In Paul's second letter, after describing his suffering and making clear its significance in ministering to others in trying circumstances, he goes on to underline the responsibilities and privileges of a leader as a minister of the new covenant, brought into existence by God's initiative in sending his Son, Jesus Christ. With great eloquence, Paul writes: "But thanks be to God, who in Christ always leads us in triumphal procession, and through us spreads in every place the fragrance that comes from knowing him. For we are the aroma of Christ" (2 Cor. 2:14–15). The believers in Corinth provide the evidence of his authenticity as an apostle, while they themselves are simply "clay jars" containing the treasure of the gospel.

Despite opposition, suffering, and hardship, he is determined to continue his ministry of reconciliation: "For the love of Christ urges us on, because we are convinced that one has died for all; therefore all have died. And he died for all, so that those who live might live no longer for themselves, but for him who died and was raised for them" (2 Cor. 5:14–15). Alongside Paul, all believers are to be ambassadors proclaiming the message of reconciliation through Christ. The believers in Corinth are called upon to live holy lives and to be generous to those in need, especially the poor in Jerusalem. The predominantly Gentile Christians in Macedonia had come together in collecting for the Jewish believers in Jerusalem. Paul urges the Corinthians to join them in this practical outpouring of love.

In both letters Paul addresses a wide range of issues, including debilitating and painful divisions in the church. Each group claims one or another of the church leaders as its champion. Paul steadfastly refuses to be drawn into personality conflicts, emphasizing instead that his ministry among them rests on the wisdom of God as demonstrated in the cross. He does not rely on eloquence or impressive personal appearance. He and his fellow missionaries are simply servants among them. There is timeliness in the Corinthian correspondence, in that many of the topics covered continue to surface in the life of the church.

Issues in Asia Minor

The Roman province of Asia Minor (modern western Turkey) became an important region for the spread of Christianity. The churches birthed throughout the region resulted mainly from the evangelistic outreach of the church in Ephesus. The letter addressed to the Ephesians may not be as localized as the heading implies. Due to some of the earliest manuscripts not containing the ascription "to Ephesus," many scholars conclude that it was in fact a circular letter addressed to the churches in Asia Minor. For example, Papyrus 46, which is one of the earliest and most reliable, does not mention the city.

It is evident from Paul's first letter to the Corinthians, written from Ephesus, that he was having a difficult time in that city. He writes: "And why are we putting ourselves in danger every hour? I die every day! That is as certain, brothers and sisters, as my boasting of you—a boast that I make in Christ Jesus our Lord. If with merely human hopes I fought with wild animals at Ephesus, what would I have gained by it?" (1 Cor. 15:30–32). Despite this ferocious opposition, Paul is determined to stay on because of the continuing opportunities for the proclamation of the gospel: "I do not want to see you now just in passing, for I hope to spend some time with you, if the Lord permits. But I will stay in Ephesus until Pentecost, for a wide door for effective work has opened to me, and there are many adversaries" (1 Cor. 16:7–9). In every age, opportunity and opposition typically go together.

In his letters to both the Ephesians and the Colossians, Paul devotes the opening sections to the amazing grace God demonstrates in the gospel. Through the power of that message, sinners, who once were spiritually "dead," are made alive by being united with Christ. Paul's deep desire is that these believers continue to grow in wisdom and knowledge. The mystery revealed in the good news announced by Jesus Christ makes known how Jews and Gentiles are united in him. Consequently, they must lay aside their differences; they are now united in one body, that of Christ himself, and must make every effort to preserve this unity.

To the Ephesians, Paul especially emphasizes the supremacy of Christ as the visible image of God, the one in whom all of creation holds together and finds its meaning. Christ is not only supreme in creation but head of the church. The body metaphor represents both unity and diversity, for each member of the body is given a special gift from God so that they might function together, providing all that is necessary for the body to function.

Some members are pioneering types (apostles); some will be given special wisdom and knowledge regarding God's will for his church (prophets); some will be specially gifted in sharing the good news and in winning people to

Christ (evangelists); some will be caring and discerning shepherds, providing support and guidance to those who are stumbling or wandering from the path (shepherds/pastors); and some will be gifted in proclaiming, explaining, and applying the Word of God as revealed in the Hebrew Scriptures and in Jesus Christ (teachers). Each member must be engaged in one or more of these areas of ministry for the community of Christ-followers to function in a balanced way.

As an apostle, Paul also demonstrates heartfelt pastoral concern for the believers in Colossae and Laodicea, and for the many other believers that he has not met personally. Similarly, all believers exercising ministry in their particular area of calling are not locked into only that sphere, but they will also exercise ministry in other areas from time to time, as situations demand or opportunities present themselves. They must remain concerned for the entire scope of ministry.

Paul is aware that there are ongoing relational problems in the church, especially when the majority have so recently emerged from paganism and continue to be surrounded and tugged by its influence. They are to live in the light and not revert to the works of darkness. This transition is only possible by the Spirit's power. In writing to the Colossians, a church that he had neither founded nor visited, Paul is aware of the presence of false teachers. He warns against the influence of their human philosophies and superstitious ritual observances. Such teaching and practice detract from Christ and lead to spiritual bondage.

In both letters, Paul concludes by giving practical guidance to wives, husbands, parents, children, and slaves regarding their relationships and how these are to be expressed now that they are followers of Christ. The transformation of society is possible only when these primary relationships are brought within the scope of the gospel. The civil unrest, mindless violence, and erosion of values and civility increasingly evident in Western societies bear witness to the social consequences that emerge when these primary relationships collapse.

Issues in Rome

As with Colossae, Paul is here writing to a city that he has not yet had an opportunity to visit. Consequently, his letter is less personal. However, as with his other letters, he begins with a greeting and a note of rejoicing and affirmation, first to the Gentile believers in the imperial capital and then to all the believers there. Paul is especially encouraged that their faith has become a topic of conversation throughout the church.

The extensive exposition of the gospel in the first eight chapters of Romans leads many commentators to treat it as a theological treatise. The danger in this approach is that we might overlook that it is a letter written to a specific group of people with their distinctive situation very much in mind. The main issue in Romans relates to how Jews and non-Jews respond to the good news of Jesus Christ and to the grace that he extends to them.

We do not know precisely when or by whom the church in Rome was founded. We do know that among the pilgrims in Jerusalem for the Feast of Pentecost in AD 32 were visitors from Rome, both Jews and Gentile converts to Judaism (Acts 2:10–11), and that there was a very large Jewish community in Rome at that time. We may therefore assume that the church originally consisted mainly of Jews. However, under the emperor Claudius, Jews were expelled from Rome in AD 49, among whom were Priscilla and Aquila, who were to play an important role in assisting Paul in Corinth and Ephesus.

Claudius's edict expelling Jews changed the composition of the church in Rome, making it predominantly Gentile. When the Jewish believers gradually began to return to the capital when Nero came to power after AD 54, tensions apparently arose between the two communities. Paul's letter is largely concerned with an exposition of the gospel, so that each community would come to a fuller appreciation of how it embraced both Jew and non-Jew.

All are equally accountable before God. Jews therefore must not adopt a superior attitude. They have the advantage of being *custodians* of the law, but the important issue is whether or not they are *upholding* that law. Its purpose was to make a person realize his or her need for forgiveness through atonement. For both Jew and non-Jew it is only through faith and by God's grace that sinful people are brought into a right relationship with God.

Only through union with Christ and by the indwelling presence of the Holy Spirit can sinners know freedom from the bondage of sin and, especially in the case of Jews, from the bondage of the law. The presence of God's Spirit assures us of our adoption as sons and daughters of God and that nothing will be able to separate us from God's love.

Paul then moves on, as a Jew himself, to identify with his own people in the realization that the great majority of Jews have rejected the gospel embodied in Jesus as the Messiah. Given the size of the Jewish community in Rome, there must have been great tension and anguish within that community between those who had believed in Christ and those who had not. Paul speaks of the deep-seated longing in his own heart that his people might be saved. He is aware of the increasing hardness of heart of those who have rejected the message, but he refuses to give up hope for them. If their rejection means that the gospel will be proclaimed to the non-Jewish world, this does not signify

God's rejection of his people. Paul is convinced that their hardness of heart is not permanent, for he sees a future when "all Israel" will respond (Rom. 11:26). He confesses that he does not know how this will come about but is confident, leaving the outcome with God.

As with Paul's other letters, the final chapters of Romans are concerned with Christian living at the personal and community levels. He also deals briefly with the Roman Christians' attitude toward secular rulers, an especially pressing matter for the Christian community living at the center of Caesar's rule. Again, Paul demonstrates his concern that the Christian community display both unity among its members and a spirit of mutual service in which others come first. The letter concludes with Paul's travel plans and his greetings to his many friends in Rome.

Communication: Then and Now

When we compare the present age with that of previous centuries, we are struck by the fact that letter writing has become something of a lost art. Until the rise of the industrial age, the pace of life seems to have been much slower, with fewer diversions and a greater emphasis on maintaining a network of personal and social relationships. These were principally maintained by an ongoing flow of correspondence. The topics encompassed intimate matters, political commentary, gossip, and even philosophical speculation. By contrast, in today's fast-paced world, electronic communication tends to be terse and shallow, precisely because it is so instant. Little time is allowed for deeper reflection.

Correspondence has also become devalued because of the avalanche of anonymous correspondence we receive from advertisers and telemarketers, who routinely strike an attitude of assumed intimacy, addressing by first name recipients they neither know nor care about. Then there are the anonymous, bureaucratic letters from taxation and pension officers, which conveniently omit the name of the sender!

The letters of the New Testament are of a different genre. They do not consist of encyclicals addressed to entire denominations, synods, or dioceses but are addressed to individual or groups of congregations. They do not represent political statements made by the church to society at large but are rather far more specific and even intimate in tone. They deal with specific issues with which churches struggle, providing both pastoral guidance and theological insights. Yet, as the discussion in several chapters of this book illustrates, many of the topics recur in different forms throughout the history of the church until the present day.

Whereas letters took days and weeks to deliver in the ancient world, today we live in an era of instant communication through texting, email, blogs, and social-networking websites. Suddenly everybody wants to be your friend, even people you have never heard of. But so much of that communication consists of trivia and is a colossal waste of time—although perhaps this view reflects my generation's outlook. The internet does, however, allow information to be made instantly available, most of it beyond the control of oppressive governments. We are witnessing significant freedom movements generated from the ground level, most of them led by tech-savvy under 35s.

Although online communication provides instant and worldwide opportunity to disseminate a message, it also has its downsides. Individuals and groups have the freedom to say what they like. They do not have to substantiate their opinions and can spread disinformation. They can even invent their own personae.

Among Christian groups, blogs advocating theological positions and promoting church and mission networks proliferate. Unfortunately, a growing percentage of these represent attacks against groups with which the author is at odds over some theological point. One consequence of the ease of instant communication is the growing tendency to talk *about* one another rather than *to* one another. It is all too easy to write a blog post based on misunderstanding and caricature. We need to take care to review our language and check facts before launching our thoughts into the world. Blogs need to be places for respectful conversation rather than billboards for denunciation.

In this information age, we have access to powerful search engines that provide information, both historical and the latest scholarly research on any topic. Information has become democratized, being no longer restricted to the privileged few. Yet many churches are still hierarchical, with those in power jealously restricting the flow of information as a means of exercising control and exerting power. This practice is out of step with our culture and is resented by many who are part of the younger generation, who emphasize leadership through networking and empowerment. This tension gives rise to a clash of cultures in many churches, especially those led by persons over fifty whose leadership style is based on an older model.

If multiple channels for networking among churches were of strategic importance for the pioneering phase of mission in Paul's day, it is equally so today. Congregations must see beyond their own situations and concerns and must relate to churches facing similar challenges. By means of blogs, websites, emails, personal visits, and workshops, they can gain valuable insights and encouragement from other churches seeking appropriate responses and answers to shared challenges and opportunities. Such networking is evident among newer networks of young people birthing faith communities and in missional initiatives within the historic denominations.

Nurturing Challenges

The task of caring for new Christians presented a formidable challenge for Paul. All of the churches were of recent origin and consisted of believers who were new to the faith. Paul and his associates were constantly on the move, with the exception of their longer stays in Corinth and Ephesus. Ethical challenges and doctrinal confusion abounded, so a variety of strategies were adopted to deal adequately and promptly with various issues as they arose.

Instruction

We have seen abundant evidence of Paul's concern about issues facing new Christians as they endeavored to live out their faith in a pagan society. During his brief time among the new converts in Thessalonica, he instructed them on a range of practical issues, although he does not specify in his first letter to them what these issues were. He encourages and further exhorts them: "As you learned from us how you ought to live and to please God (as, in fact, you are doing), you should do so more and more. For you know what instructions we gave you through the Lord Jesus" (1 Thess. 4:1–2).

Conversion is not just a momentary experience. It represents not only an ultimate destiny but also the beginning of a lifelong journey. The gospel message, as proclaimed by the early church, was as much concerned with life *before* death as life *after* death. By contrast, the gospel preached today is often concerned more with the sinner's eternal security than with his or her life transformation and impact on society.

In his second letter to the Thessalonians, Paul again emphasizes the importance of instruction, especially in regard to the return of Christ (2 Thess. 2:5) and the assurance of ultimate victory to the persecuted church. John Stott, in his commentary, emphasizes that "the safeguard against deception and the remedy against false teaching was to hold on to the original teaching of the apostle."[11] Loyalty to the apostolic teaching, now permanently enshrined in the New Testament, is still the test of truth and the shield against error. Some liberal church leaders, exerting apostolic authority, claim prophetic insight even as they deny the plain teaching of the New Testament.

11. Stott, *1 & 2 Thessalonians*, 158.

Teaching, whether by word of mouth or letter, helps new believers stand against opposition and persecution (1 Thess. 1:4–6; 3:2–4), false teaching (2 Thess. 2:2–3), and temptation (1 Thess. 3:13). Paul therefore exhorts the brothers and sisters in Thessalonica to "stand firm and hold fast to the traditions that you were taught by us, either by word of mouth or by our letter" (2 Thess. 2:15). They must brace themselves, standing firm and closing rank in order to withstand the hurricane wind. The apostolic traditions are the very foundation of Christian faith and life.

The tone of Paul's letters to the churches is like that of a parent addressing teenage children. He knows the situations and many of the individuals involved. Consequently, his writing is full of exhortations, encouragement, and warnings. Like any good teacher, he recognizes the importance of repetition. To the pressured church in Philippi, he writes: "Finally, my brothers and sisters, rejoice in the Lord. To write the same things to you is not troublesome to me, and for you it is a safeguard" (Phil. 3:1). The believers need reminders, especially when facing persistent opposition. On six occasions in this letter they are exhorted to rejoice in the Lord despite every adverse circumstance (4:4; 1:18; 2:17–18, 28; 4:10).

Encouragement

The ministry of encouragement is of vital importance, especially in nurturing new, hard-pressed believers. Paul himself benefited from the encouragement of Barnabas in the early days of his discipleship. To the new believers in Thessalonica, Paul offers encouragement (1 Thess. 2:12), while at the same time constantly prodding and urging the weary, discouraged, and downhearted. Precisely because they are called to live in Christ's kingdom and share in his glory, they are to live in such a manner as will bring Christ pleasure.

Encouragement brings joy among God's people (1 Thess. 5:16–17), a characteristic of people at peace with God and with themselves (Rom. 14:17; 15:13). It wells up from within in spite of—and not on account of—favorable circumstances. When Paul calls upon the believers to "pray continually," he is not encouraging uninterrupted prayer but rather that they never give up praying. He is referring to prayer that is frequent and habitual. It should never become something we resort to only when the going gets tough. The ability to "give thanks in all circumstances" becomes possible as we learn to dwell in the presence of God and recognize that God is Lord over all (Phil. 4:4–7).

Paul's example raises a pointed question for today's church leaders: what is the relationship between pastor and congregation? Is it distant and unconcerned, or does it demonstrate the intense feeling of the apostle? In Paul's case, it is remarkable that such depth of relationship should have been forged after so short a visit.

Admonition

Alongside encouragement goes admonition. Paul, the teacher, is not simply a lecturer; he engages his readers out of concern for their response to his letters. In this he demonstrates the close relationship between teacher and pastor. Paul, well aware of the issues new believers need to address, feels a keen sense of personal responsibility for their progress in the Christian life. He is no indulgent parent idealizing his offspring and blind to their faults. Paul likens his relationship to the Thessalonians and the Corinthians to that of a father, who is responsible for guidance, discipline, and encouragement. He gives warm, fatherly admonition, yet does not hesitate to give stern rebukes to troublemakers (1 Thess. 2:11–12; 1 Cor. 4:14–17, 21). Such admonition must be backed up by personal example for the correction to have integrity. N. T. Wright helps put into context and perspective Paul's appeal for the converts to imitate him.

> One of the things we need constantly to remind ourselves when reading Paul (and when thinking about our own Christian living within a hostile world) is that nobody in Corinth, or any of the other towns outside Palestine, had ever before witnessed somebody living the way Paul lived. Nobody had seen someone giving of himself generously, living a life of self-sacrifice, and refusing to play the power-games and the prestige-games that were the stock-in-trade, not only of the sophistic teachers who came and went (and made a lot of money), but of the local rulers, the magistrates and civic dignitaries, and those who promoted and ran the new imperial cult.[12]

Continuing Intercession

Paul's prayers and intercessions are an integral part of every letter. These prayers reveal Paul's knowledge of and concern for the churches. He tells the Thessalonians that he prays for them earnestly night and day (1 Thess. 1:2–3). He longs to see them, as he did the believers in so many of the churches. His prayers and thanksgivings are intertwined. It is self-evident that prayer was the powerhouse of Paul's ministry, and it is out of ground made fertile by continual prayer that thanksgiving originates.[13]

12. Wright, *1 Corinthians*, 53.
13. Beale, *1–2 Thessalonians*, 107.

Paul's prayers provide a reminder that it is only through God's grace and power that anything of significance relating to the reign of God is achieved. One wonders to what extent intercession is neglected today in favor of organizing and social networking. How much more time do we spend sitting at our computers and texting than on our knees praying? Paul's letters provide us with a constant reminder of the priority of prayer and the way in which it permeated his ministry.

Appointing Local Leaders

A church without duly appointed and acknowledged leadership is in a precarious position. The apostle Paul recognized the importance of ensuring that local leadership was in place before moving on to his next city. After traveling through the cities of Galatia, he and Barnabas appointed elders in each church, and "with prayer and fasting they entrusted them to the Lord in whom they had come to believe" (Acts 14:23). Paul's letter to the church in Philippi is addressed to the saints and to "the bishops [or overseers] and deacons" of the church, indicating a plurality of leadership (Phil. 1:1). They were selected through the guidance of the Holy Spirit. Paul reminds the Ephesian elders in his farewell address that their task is "to shepherd the church of God that he obtained with the blood of his own Son" (Acts 20:28).

In small churches, everyone needs to be involved in some kind of ministry. Leaders arise spontaneously and are soon recognized by the other members of the group. If these individuals are to be formally appointed as presbyters and deacons, they must meet the character criteria that Paul outlines to Timothy (1 Tim. 3:1–13). A further point that needs to be underlined is that these early churches were led by a number of elders and not by one solitary individual. Each of these points is as relevant today in the selection of leaders as it was for the first-generation churches.

Through Love

A deep, robust, and practical love permeates all of Paul's letters. His love for the churches stems from the indwelling Holy Spirit, who has infused Paul with the self-giving, initiative-taking love of Christ. In addition to his love for them, Paul speaks often of the love of God displayed in Christ, which has been poured into their hearts. For instance, in writing to the Philippians, he speaks of their love as "overflowing love" coming from the same divine source as his own (Phil. 1:9). Neither his love for them nor their love for others can be characterized as "smother love," for it is expressed with both understanding and wisdom. In other words, it is discerning in nature. Such love is not blind, but clear-sighted and discerning in response to the complex problems of human relationships.

Confidence in the Lord

The nurturing process is not driven by anxiety. In many places in Paul's letters to the churches he expresses his confidence in the Lord to strengthen and protect new believers (2 Thess. 3:3). At the same time, he assures them of his concern for their continued well-being. This confidence arises out of his conviction that the church is the body of Christ and that Christ will not allow it to fail. The Lord has promised to build the church; the gates of hell will not prevail against it.

Paul assures the church in Philippi that the work God (not he) has started, God will bring to completion (Phil. 1:6). From his own experience, Paul assures them that the Lord is at work in all circumstances to fulfill his purposes. Paul's confidence in God's continuing work is not restricted to the immediate future but extends all the way to "the day of Jesus Christ" (Phil. 1:6).

In the following chapters we will consider in greater detail the major areas of ongoing concern revealed in Paul's letters to the churches in terms of Christian discipleship, core beliefs, and their relationships with one another as local fellowships of Christ-followers.

Summary

In order for a movement to retain momentum and cohesion, each unit must be integrated into a network of many strands. The apostle Paul responded to the challenges in establishing connections between churches throughout the Eastern Mediterranean by using several methods. First, he strengthened his personal connection to each faith community through return visits and by making time for extended stays in strategic centers. Second, he established a pattern of team leadership both by his personal example and in the appointing of leaders in each faith community. Third, he wrote letters to churches in the principal cities, to provide encouragement, clear up misunderstandings, admonish them regarding issues and individuals that compromised the witness of the church, and commend them for the impact of their witness in their local communities and beyond.

Despite the greater ease and speed of communication today, too many congregations live for and by themselves. Shrinking and aging congregations need the stimulus of frequent contact with appropriate leaders who can provide much-needed insights and vision, together with the support of a network of churches facing similar challenges. New churches established by young leaders and consisting largely of first-generation Christians likewise need the support of mature leadership. There are some encouraging signs that such networks are being established as part of the church-planting initiatives of new networks and historic denominations. Today's churches need one another just as much as first-century churches did.

 *Conclusion:*

Multiple communication channels must be developed and employed in order to nurture new Christians and guide new faith communities.

6

Welcoming and
Incorporating New Members
into the Body of Christ

This chapter addresses the pressing issue of discipleship. In other words, how do church attendees and members become authentic followers of Christ within their social and cultural contexts? Dwight J. Zscheile provides a succinct definition of discipleship as "following Christ into participation in God's mission in the world in the power of the Spirit."[1] He points out that discipleship is concerned with more than the individual's personal relationship with Christ; it also involves a corporate dimension relating to every area of life. To be a disciple entails growing in relation to other believers and discovering one's role in both serving the faith community and ministering to the needs of the wider community.

Much of the contemporary literature on discipleship and spirituality has focused on the individual, thereby deemphasizing the communal component. This is surprising when one considers the model of disciple making that is clearly evident in the Gospels. There Jesus forms an inner circle whose members learned, not only from listening to him and through what we today call observer participation, but also in the context of their common life. Side by

---

1. Van Gelder and Zscheile, *Missional Church in Perspective*, 150.

side they confronted, challenged, and supported one another amid the wide range of issues they encountered in their daily walk.

In response to the example of Jesus's life and teaching, we must ask, what are the primary influences shaping the identity of Western Christians? Do the relentless forces permeating the surrounding culture govern our values? Sometimes their impact is unmistakably confrontational, while at other times it is subtle and deceptively subversive. When the influence of the surrounding culture predominates, "this leaves God's agenda—the agenda of the kingdom—languishing. The mission of God gets people's leftovers."[2]

Change of Allegiance

Character is developed through a consistent commitment to Christ as Savior and Lord, resulting from a decisive break with the past, and a wholehearted change of allegiance. By contrast, double-minded persons are unstable in all their ways. The new believers in Thessalonica demonstrated a decisive break with their past life when they "turned to God from idols, to serve a living and true God" (1 Thess. 1:9). Their change of allegiance was so noteworthy that the peoples of the regions visited by Paul in Macedonia drew his attention to the fact.

Modern Western readers need to bear in mind that idolatry permeated the whole of society, including the business world and civic, recreational, and family life. It was interwoven in the fabric of society as a powerful spiritual force that first-century believers encountered at every turn.

Furthermore, paganism was intertwined with idolatry in the Roman world. Sex and religion make for a potent mix. For this reason, the New Testament repeatedly warns against idolatry, insisting that Christians break with their idolatrous past. Idolatry was an ever-present and alluring temptation to the Christians in Corinth, a city renowned for its sexual promiscuity, much of it associated with the temple rituals.

Paul reminds the believers that idolatry brought about the downfall of Israel in Sinai and that "these things happened to them to serve as an example, and they were written down to instruct us, on whom the end of the ages has come" (1 Cor. 10:11). Moreover, the influence of idolatry was not confined to pagan temple worship, but was encountered whenever Christians sat down to a meal with pagans in their homes or at a restaurant (1 Cor. 8). Paul is anxious that those Corinthians who are insisting on their "rights" and "freedom" may slide

2. Hirsch and Ford, *Right Here, Right Now*, 71.

back into paganism and become a stumbling block to those who do not want to expose themselves to further temptations and compromises. Christians must never assume that their baptism has made them immune to temptation. As Kenneth Chafin cautions, "We cannot trust in religious ceremony that does not usher us into a different kind of life."[3]

Both family and civic celebrations invariably involved drinking and sex, and when such behavior is excused on religious grounds, it becomes a powerful temptation, for such celebrations were held in honor of the pagan gods. N. T. Wright draws attention to the close ties between the temple and everyday life: "What people don't realize is that in the ancient world the temples normally *were* the restaurants."[4] Moreover, appearance at such meals was of more than social significance; it also had political implications. "Roman citizens in Corinth had a special right to share in meals connected with imperial festivals. If they didn't go along with it, people would notice and there might be trouble."[5]

For those Christians who succumb to the inevitability of being overwhelmed by such pervasive and powerful influences, Paul reminds them that God is with them to strengthen them. "No testing has overtaken you that is not common to everyone. God is faithful, and he will not let you be tested beyond your strength, but with the testing he will also provide the way out so that you may be able to endure it" (1 Cor. 10:13). Paul also reminds the Colossians to give "joyful thanks to the Father, who has qualified you to share in the inheritance of his holy people in the kingdom of light. For he has rescued us from the dominion of darkness and brought us into the kingdom of the Son he loves, in whom we have redemption, the forgiveness of sins" (Col. 1:12–14 NIV).

Twenty-first-century Christians cannot afford to become complacent concerning the issue of idolatry. We must recognize that idolatry takes many forms but basically is present whenever we allow anything to replace our allegiance to God. It is easier to recognize the presence of idolatry in another culture than in our own. We can make an idol out of anything: work, family, body, house, hobby, or even our religion. Our hedonistic and materialistic culture constantly seeks to entice us from our primary allegiance and to separate us from the grace of God.

Changing allegiance entails renouncing false or unreliable sources of identity and security. For some Christians, ritualism provides their primary identity. Rituals are significant in facilitating corporate responses to spiritual truths. Churches of every tradition have developed their own distinctive rituals.

3. Chafin, *1, 2 Corinthians*, 121.
4. Wright, *1 Corinthians*, 98.
5. Ibid., 99.

Ritual*ism*, however, goes much further, by elevating those rituals to the point that their observance is made essential to authentic faith. The ritual is thereby substituted for the reality. If the ritual is not correctly observed in detail, or led by a duly authorized celebrant, it is deemed invalid. Paul, in his day, had a constant battle with the ritualism of the Judaizers who infiltrated the churches.

Legalism represents a second manifestation of false security. It frequently goes hand in hand with ritualism, representing Christianity as a list of dos and don'ts, with the emphasis very much on the latter. It draws a clear boundary line between those individuals who are included and those who are excluded. To both the Galatians and the Romans, Paul contrasts living under the law with the liberating power of Christ through the gospel and the indwelling of the Holy Spirit. Whereas the law condemns all who fail to fulfill its unachievable demands, the gospel brings both forgiveness and liberating power.

Nevertheless, liberty in Christ does not signify a do-as-you-like lifestyle. Rather, it entails living under the lordship of Christ: "So if you have been raised with Christ, seek the things that are above, where Christ is, seated at the right hand of God. Set your minds on things that are above, not on things that are on earth, for you have died and your life is hidden with Christ in God" (Col. 3:1–3). Such a change of allegiance embraces the whole of life, as Paul makes clear at the conclusion of this passage: "And whatever you do, in word or deed, do everything in the name of the Lord Jesus, giving thanks to God the Father through him" (Col. 3:17).

Jesus, in the course of his earthly ministry, had to deal with both ritualism and legalism. In addition, he had to deal with a third explosive issue: nationalism was also a source of false security for some Jews of his day. By the time of Paul, nationalism was less of an issue, as Jewish messianic expectations had begun to wane. Furthermore, it was much less relevant in the churches addressed in his letters, as these were predominantly Gentile in composition. But in the subsequent history of the church, nationalism has periodically emerged as a significant issue.

In nineteenth-century Britain, under the influence of an expanding colonialism, the gospel was advanced amid imperialist claims. Such claims subsided with the shrinking and rapid decolonization that followed the Second World War. At that time, the United States emerged as the dominant world power. Especially during the Cold War era, the gospel became identified with the culture and the economic ascendancy of the United States. According to the doctrine of "manifest destiny," the United States understood itself to be uniquely blessed by God. Indeed, one front-running presidential candidate has declared the twenty-first century to be "the American Century!" Such a claim, however, must be measured in terms of the economic and political realities of our times. Also, whereas Christian influence is declining in the West because of the rise of secularism and religious pluralism, some regions of the world are witnessing unprecedented church growth and mission outreach, not only to the Majority World (the developing world) but also to the West.

Incorporation through Organic Connectedness

Unfortunately, the term *corporation* is associated almost exclusively with business or political institutions. This has led to an obscuring of its essential organic significance. *Incorporation* means becoming part of a body, not of an organization or institution. We must keep this basic meaning in mind, recognizing that the church of Jesus Christ is most frequently described throughout the New Testament in organic terms.

In the person of Jesus Christ, the Jerusalem temple was radically redefined. It was no longer the physical structure in Jerusalem to which the people of God flocked at times of festival. Jesus himself became the foundation of the "new temple" (John 2:19–21). Paul continues this same line of thinking. For instance, he writes that the temple in Corinth consists of the believers in that city who make up God's temple. This is made possible by the indwelling of the Holy Spirit both individually in every believer and corporately within the fellowship of believers (1 Cor. 3:16–17). This high doctrine of the church places great responsibility on each member, who forms part of that temple. Maintaining strong relationships among members is essential for the structural integrity of the building.

Jealousy, selfishness, arrogance, and divisiveness will weaken and ultimately destroy the temple of believers. Paul is aware of people infiltrating the church in Corinth in order to spread their own erroneous teaching and to draw off a personal following. He describes the teaching of these false apostles as "the wisdom of this world," which is "foolishness" in the eyes of God (1 Cor. 3:19).

In our own day, many individuals with influence in the church—not to mention those who attack from outside—are claiming "We now know better" as their rationale to discount much of what Paul taught, and they are editing the Gospels to convince themselves of what they consider Jesus reliably said according to their own criteria. Paul answers such revisionism by warning that we are not to be enamored of human leaders who claim superior knowledge.

We do well to heed Paul's warning: "Do not deceive yourselves. If you think that you are wise in this age, you should become fools so that you may become wise. For the wisdom of this world is foolishness with God. For it is written, 'He catches the wise in their craftiness,' and again, 'The Lord knows the thoughts of the wise, that they are futile'" (1 Cor. 3:18–20).

In our post-Christendom and increasingly neo-pagan cultural contexts, we need discernment in confronting "the wisdom of the world." Human knowledge has grown exponentially in this scientific age. Unfortunately, wisdom has not kept pace with the knowledge explosion, resulting in the creation of great moral dilemmas as we debate what to do with what we know or, just as frequently, what we decide not to do with what we know. When it comes to the gospel, human wisdom can offer no additions, adaptations, or alternatives to what God has revealed in Jesus Christ.

The Basis of Belonging

Belonging to a church entails much more than belonging to a human association. We do not simply belong to one another by virtue of birth, as in a human family; we belong through the work of Christ and his indwelling Holy Spirit, through *re*generation rather than generation. It is an identification that only God can bring about. Paul emphasizes this point in the opening words of his first letter to the Thessalonians: "To the church of the Thessalonians in God the Father and the Lord Jesus Christ" (1 Thess. 1:1). Here we see that their belonging arises from their embodiment in God the Father and the Lord Jesus Christ through the indwelling Holy Spirit, who has brought about their adoption and regeneration.

Most Western Christians have either a *casual* or *contractual* relationship with the church, which falls far short of the New Testament norm of a *covenantal* relationship. Casual relationships are both peripheral and shallow. Contractual relationships can be broken when the offended party decides to break it off. Covenantal relationships, however, are binding and survive the severe stresses of community life. As the surrounding culture becomes less tolerant toward the church and the teaching of Scripture, loosely connected church members become increasingly vulnerable. Ties to the faith community have to be exceptionally strong to survive in a hostile environment. They are also needed in order to keep on intimate terms with the Lord.

In addition to emphasizing the believers' identity in God, Paul also stresses that discipleship has a specific context. They are not only "in Christ," but they are also in Galatia (Gal. 1:2), in Philippi (Phil. 1:2), in Thessalonica (1 Thess. 1:1; 2 Thess. 1:1), in Corinth, in Ephesus (Eph. 1:1), in Colossae (Col. 1:2), and in Rome. Paul writes to the church in Rome, "To all God's beloved in Rome, who are called to be saints" (Rom. 1:7). In greeting the believers in Corinth, Paul not only addresses them as citizens of Corinth but also links them with the wider Christian community: "To the church of God that is in Corinth, to those who are sanctified in Christ Jesus, called to be saints, together with all those who in every place call on the name of our Lord Jesus Christ, both their Lord and ours" (1 Cor. 1:2). Churches throughout the Western world need to recapture Paul's broad vision of identity and unity. This is especially relevant for evangelicals, who have a long reputation, not only for "tribal" divisions, but also for boundary fights between tribes.

In his second letter to the Corinthian church, Paul narrows the vision somewhat: "To the church of God in Corinth, together with all his holy people throughout Achaia" (2 Cor. 1:1 NIV). But this limitation reminds us that unity in general must translate into unity with the wider district in which the church is located. The believers in each city are also challenged to live as "holy people," seeking to please God and to reflect the character of Jesus Christ in each place. Their identity is based on the call of God leading to a new allegiance. *Sanctified* signifies separation *for* more than separation *from*.

In addressing the qualifications needed in order to belong to the church of Jesus Christ, the apostle Paul raises an issue that is important for him personally, as it is for church members of every age. Writing to the Philippians in response to the challenges of the Judaizers, Paul first reminds them that he has more reason to place confidence in the flesh than his accusers. "If anyone else has reason to be confident in the flesh, I have more: circumcised on the eighth day, a member of the people of Israel, of the tribe of Benjamin, a Hebrew born of Hebrews; as to the law, a Pharisee; as to zeal, a persecutor of the church; as to righteousness under the law, blameless" (Phil. 3:4–6). Then he goes on to make it clear that his acceptance before God depends on neither his cultural heritage nor his prestigious position in Jewish society. Consequently, he now counts all of his credentials, which were so impressive in Jewish eyes, as debit rather than credit. More than that, he says, "I regard them as rubbish, in order that I might gain Christ and be found in him, not having a righteousness of my own that comes from the law, but one that comes through faith in Christ, the righteousness from God based on faith" (Phil. 3:8–9).

Paul is not trashing his heritage. His writings indicate how his Jewish background and education have enriched his understanding of the gospel. He frequently quotes the Jewish Scriptures in order to root the gospel in his tradition and to interpret it to both Jewish and non-Jewish audiences. The issue for Paul, as it is for believers in every age, is how we respond to that religious heritage. On the one hand, it is valuable if it serves to enrich our understanding of the gospel, as we draw from the insights of those who carved out our tradition, be that Martin Luther, John Calvin, Thomas Cranmer, John Wesley, or any other individual our particular tradition reveres.

On the other hand, if we cling to our tradition with a judgmental attitude toward others, or rely upon our heritage to gain prestige and position within our church hierarchy, then we need to learn from Paul's example. Our heritage is no longer our treasure, but has become our burden and our garbage that will impoverish our spiritual lives, making us more of a liability than a resource in furthering the mission of Christ.

Making Spiritual Progress

Spirituality is not a static condition but a condition that is dynamic, vulnerable, and in need of constant nurturing. Spiritual maturity requires continuing progress in the Christian life. It does not signify that we have arrived but entails the constant challenge to live up to what we have already attained. It also does not mean one has all the answers or fully lives up to what one knows. The Christian life is always a walk of faith requiring complete reliance upon God. We must persist in living up to what we have already attained and detect every temptation to backslide. We will encounter many perplexing questions and situations about which we must ask God for guidance. Spiritual progress entails lifelong learning; fresh challenges and new questions regularly offer opportunities for growth. The answers to such challenges may not always reside in the past.

Paul provides examples from his own spiritual pilgrimage and ministry journey, likening his life to running a race, which must be run with determination. When you watch school children on the athletic field, you see some running with great determination and in competition with their classmates, while others are just sauntering along, filling in time until the end of the physical education period. Paul reminds the Corinthian Christians, "Do you not know that in a race the runners all compete, but only one receives the prize? Run in such a way that you may win it. Athletes exercise self-control in all things; they do it to receive a perishable wreath, but we an imperishable one. So I do not run aimlessly" (1 Cor. 9:24–26). Life is a long-distance race; discipline and determination are required in order to complete the course and finish well. The aim is to cross the finish line, neither giving up early nor fading within sight of it. We cannot achieve this level of performance in our own strength; it is possible only through knowing personally Christ's resurrection power and sharing in his suffering (Phil. 3:10).

Paul's words challenge our lackadaisical attitude to spiritual disciplines. Consumer Christianity is basically self-focused, highly selective, and preoccupied with what meets the needs of the individual. It is a pick-and-choose religion, which is a far cry from discipleship as described by the New Testament and demonstrated in the lives of the vast majority of early Christians. In a number of passages, Paul describes the Christian life as being prepared to die with Christ—considering it as a privilege—in order that we might live victoriously in Christ (Rom. 6:4–14; 8:10–11).

Paul exerts every effort to bring new believers to spiritual maturity. To the Colossians, he writes, "It is he whom we proclaim, warning everyone and teaching everyone in all wisdom, so that we may present everyone mature in Christ. For this I toil and struggle with all the energy that he powerfully inspires within me" (Col. 1:28–29). Ministry within the local church must engage every member, providing guidance and instruction. In practical terms, this goal can be achieved only as growing churches multiply leaders who are equipped to model these functions.

We have noted the many words of encouragement that Paul brings to new believers. But he does not hesitate to admonish them for their shortcomings. He expects the Thessalonian Christians to respect their leaders and willingly receive admonishment from them (1 Thess. 5:12–13). He has some harsh words for those who refuse words of correction regarding issues he raises in his second letter (2 Thess. 3:14–15). In both letters Paul rebukes those who are embroiled in sin (1 Thess. 5:14; 2 Thess. 3:15).

In our "anything goes" society, the church ignores at its peril actions and attitudes that challenge and undermine the life of Christian discipleship. The individualism and relativism that characterize our society tend to foster a lack of mutual accountability, and under the pressures of cultural relativism, tolerance, and political correctness the lines between right and wrong become blurred and open to ongoing negotiation.

Evidence of Transformed Living

A number of studies comparing churchgoers with nonchurchgoers have revealed that there is no statistically significant difference between the two in terms of values and lifestyle. Both groups are equally materialistic, live according to the same mores, and have the same divorce rates. It is only when churchgoers are further categorized, separating those who only attend services from those who are also involved in small groups and ministries, that the difference becomes statistically significant.

Within our post-Christendom cultural context the church can no longer assume that society at large will support some of their long-held Christian values, which leaves the church struggling to argue and defend its position.

Darrell Guder draws attention to the changing position of the church in North American society:

> Two things have become quite clear to those who care about the church and its mission. On the one hand, the churches of North America have been dislocated from their prior social role of chaplain to the culture and society and have lost their once privileged position of influence. Religious life in general and the churches in particular have increasingly been relegated to the private spheres of life. Too readily, the churches have accepted this as their proper place. At the same time, the churches have become so accommodated to the American way of life that they are now domesticated, and it is no longer obvious what justifies their existence as particular communities.[6]

In addressing this sad state of affairs, the church could learn much from the experience of the early church. The church at that time recognized the pervasive influence of the pagan society that surrounded it and realized the vital importance of relating the gospel to the whole of life. It also welcomed and supported those entering the church from that toxic environment. Paul's first letter to the church in Corinth provides the most detailed account of the issues believers faced in that notoriously immoral city. That this letter was intended for wider circulation indicates that other churches were themselves struggling with many of these same issues. Two millennia later they have not gone away!

Before dealing with these concerns, Paul characteristically begins with a word of encouragement to the Corinthians, reminding them of what God has already accomplished in their lives. He gives thanks to God "because of the grace of God that has been given you in Christ Jesus, for in every way you have been enriched in him, in speech and knowledge of every kind—just as the testimony of Christ has been strengthened among you—so that you are not lacking in any spiritual gift" (1 Cor. 1:4–7).

They have proved themselves eager to learn and able to articulate the knowledge they have gained. Yet they are still struggling to put into practice what they have learned. They retain their blind spots and blinkered vision and are also willfully disobedient in regard to some important issues. Before launching into criticism, Paul assures them that God loves them despite everything and continues to extend grace to them. They are waiting in eager anticipation of the Lord's return (1 Cor. 1:7), which should provide them with the incentive to ensure they are living here and now in accordance with God's will. That

---

6. Guder, *Missional Church*, 78.

which God has begun in their lives, God intends to bring to completion: "God is faithful; by him you were called into the fellowship of his Son, Jesus Christ our Lord" (v. 9).

The call to the life of holiness is a constant refrain in Paul's letters. To the Ephesians, Paul blesses his God and Father for choosing both himself and his readers "before the foundation of the world to be holy and blameless before him in love" (Eph. 1:4). As God's children, they are to live "according to the good pleasure of his will, to the praise of his glorious grace" (vv. 5–6). Paul is acutely aware of the constant pressure for the church to conform to the world's standards and of the danger of the church's ranks being infiltrated (Eph. 4:17–22). He reminds them, "You were taught to put away your former way of life, your old self, corrupt and deluded by its lusts, and to be renewed in the spirit of your minds, and to clothe yourselves with the new self, created according to the likeness of God in true righteousness and holiness" (Eph. 4:22–24).

Paul follows this exhortation with some specific rules for the new life in Christ. They are to put away falsehood and be open, honest, and genuine in their relationships. Thieves must give up their easy living by renouncing their stealing; they must instead be prepared to roll up their sleeves and do an honest day's work. And the Ephesians must replace their former foul language and destructive talk with conversation that builds one another up in the faith and establishes their new honorable identity in Christ (Eph. 4:17–32).

Paul's challenge and encouragement are as relevant for followers of Christ today as for the original recipients of his letters. He reminds us that we can live in an affluent society, which provides great material benefit, while at the same time allowing it to bankrupt us spiritually. The distinctions between right and wrong are fudged in the interest of expediency and the temptation to compromise. Paul reminds us that we are to live here on earth in anticipation of eternity.

The church in Thessalonica receives Paul's message of encouragement with his insistence that the Holy Spirit will inspire joy in their hearts to enable them to overcome whatever adversity they face (1 Thess. 1:6). Paul is well aware of the shortcomings in the lives of these new believers, yet assures them that far from abandoning them, he longs to visit them again: "For what is our hope or joy or crown of boasting before our Lord Jesus at his coming? Is it not you? Yes, you are our glory and joy!" (1 Thess. 2:19–20). In his second letter, Paul assures the Thessalonians of his prayers that God will make them worthy of his call: "To this end we always pray for you, asking that our God will make you worthy of his call and will fulfill by his power every good resolve and work of faith, so that the name of our Lord Jesus may be glorified in you, and you in him, according to the grace of our God and the Lord Jesus Christ" (2 Thess. 1:11–12).

The church is a community of the Holy Spirit, who provides the resilience, discernment, and hope that allow it to face whatever challenges it encounters along the way. On the evidence of their transformed lives, Paul can say that the Thessalonian believers are his "glory and joy" (1 Thess. 2:20). Herein lies the challenge. Of how many churches could Paul say that today? Do we live in such a way as to bring glory to God, or do we bring dishonor to God's name? As Paul reminds us, we are called to live before a watching world in a manner that is worthy of the gospel of Christ.

Paul urges the Philippians, as he would urge us today, to "live your life in a manner worthy of the gospel of Christ, so that, whether I come and see you or am absent and hear about you, I will know that you are standing firm in one spirit, striving side by side with one mind for the faith of the gospel, and are in no way intimidated by your opponents" (Phil. 1:27–28). Mindful that Satan's strategy is to divide and conquer, the church must ensure that it doesn't break rank.

We have already noted that the tendency to divide into rival groups is one of the disturbing trends in the church today. Such divisiveness is often occasioned by a conservative reaction to liberal movements in the church, especially within the historic denominations. The focus is on boundary fights rather than on seeking our common roots in the gospel and in the urgency of the mission challenges facing the church in the West. Often the consequence of separation is polarization, with those on each side becoming narrower and more strident in their beliefs because they now spend too much of their time talking to themselves and caricaturing the position of the opposing party.

Sexual Mores

It is self-evident that Paul devotes a significant portion of his teaching to sexual matters. He does this not because he has a personal preoccupation with the subject, but because it posed such a constant and serious challenge to Christian communities.

In our own day, with the social acceptability of multiple partners, of sexual relationships outside of marriage, and of regarding marriage as no more than a contract that either partner is free to dissolve at any time, the church finds itself under constant pressure to adapt to accepted norms or to reexamine Scripture and tradition in order to maintain its distinctive witness. However, in opting for the second, it must avoid a judgmental stance, recognizing that an increasing number of people entering the church will already have partners with whom they have a sexual relationship, or that they come with addictive sexual behaviors that have led them into a life of promiscuity. The gospel requires that the church fellowship welcome people as they are, yet without condoning their lifestyles. The church must be both unshockable and unshakable. Paul's letter to the Thessalonians draws a clear line for new believers to walk.

> For this is the will of God, your sanctification: that you abstain from fornication; that each one of you know how to control your own body in holiness and honor, not with lustful passion, like the Gentiles who do not know God; that no one wrong or exploit a brother or sister in this matter, because the Lord is an avenger in all these things, just as we have already told you beforehand and solemnly warned you. For God did not call us to impurity but in holiness. Therefore whoever rejects this rejects not human authority but God, who also gives his Holy Spirit to you. (1 Thess. 4:3–8)

Fornication (*porneia*) refers to any sexual union outside of marriage. Paul addresses the issue head-on in the plainest possible terms, for prostitution was allowed and widespread in the Mediterranean world. At the same time, sexual relations with another man's wife were prohibited. Roman marriage customs barred women but not men from extramarital affairs. By contrast, Jewish and Christian authors alike prohibited sexual involvement outside of marriage.

The majority of new believers from the pagan world had been embroiled in this lifestyle. Now the holy life to which believers are called entails both separation to God and separation from the mores of the contemporary culture. The Holy Spirit who indwells every believer provides both the desire and the power to live by different standards. Paul returns to this topic in writing to the Corinthians and also to the Colossians. To the former he writes:

> The body is meant not for fornication but for the Lord, and the Lord for the body. . . . Do you not know that your bodies are members of Christ? Should I therefore take the members of Christ and make them members of a prostitute? Never! . . . Shun fornication! Every sin that a person commits is outside the body; but the fornicator sins against the body itself. Or do you not know that your body is the temple of the Holy Spirit within you, which you have from God, and that you are not your own? For you were bought with a price; therefore glorify God in your body. (1 Cor. 6:13–20)

And he orders the Colossians, "Put to death, therefore, whatever in you is earthly: fornication, impurity, passion, evil desire, and greed (which is idolatry).

On account of these the wrath of God is coming on those who are disobedient"
(Col. 3:5–6). As we have already noted, pagan worship was closely associated
with sexual promiscuity.

> The numerous words in the Greek language for sexual relations suggest a preoc-
> cupation with this aspect of life. Homosexuality was a common result in Greek
> society, which considered the noblest form of love to be friendship between
> men. Some of the great names in Greek philosophy regarded it as not inferior
> to heterosexual love, but it was practiced primarily among males between their
> early teens and early twenties. All kinds of immoralities were associated with
> the gods. Not only was prostitution a recognized institution, but, through the
> influence of the fertility cults of Asia Minor, Syria, and Phoenicia, it became
> a part of the religious rites of certain temples. Thus, there were one thousand
> "sacred prostitutes" at the temple of Aphrodite at Corinth.[7]

Illicit and deviant sexual behavior that has become not only excusable
but acceptable in our day would have shocked the generations before the
sexual revolution of the 1960s. In movies, novels, and news commentary, sex
outside of marriage is mentioned without adverse comment, implying social
acceptance—the new norm. Indulging sexual appetite without restraint can
lead to an addictive state of mind. Paul is clear that sexual sin includes both
adultery and homosexual practice. N. T. Wright notes the following: "The
terms Paul uses here include two words which have been much debated, but
which, experts have now established, clearly refer to the practice of male
homosexuality. The two terms refer respectively to the passive or submissive
partner and the active or aggressive one, and Paul places both roles in his list
of unacceptable behavior."[8]

In tight-knit, stable communities in which people live from day to day under
the watchful eye of those who know them, it is more difficult to hide a sexually
addictive lifestyle. By contrast, in a port city such as first-century Corinth, in
which anything goes, one's life escapes such close scrutiny, and individuals
can all too easily walk away from the consequences of their casual sexual relationships. In reality, there is no such thing as "casual sex," for "to trivialize
sex is to trivialize our God-given humanness."[9] Just like the Corinthians, we
too live in Western cultures obsessed with sex. Today there are people who
treat sex as an appetite to be satisfied casually, just as the need for food is met
by having a snack. "If it feels good, do it."

7. Ferguson, *Backgrounds of Early Christianity*, 70.
8. Wright, *1 Corinthians*, 69.
9. Ibid.

Marital Relationships

We have noted that the concept of discipleship cannot be restricted to the individual's relationship with the Lord, but it must embrace the believers' wider network of associations. The most challenging of these networks is often the family, as it represents the most intimate group in which the genuineness of a person's faith is most clearly demonstrated. This was especially true in the case of preindustrial societies, given that the household consisted of the extended family and was the location for much of the business and manufacture.

Within the confines of the extended household, relationships between people were closely observed. Paul addresses the issue of sexual intimacy between husband and wife (1 Cor. 7:1–7). On the one hand, he commends the option of celibacy in light of the expectation of the Lord's imminent return, ushering in the end of the age (7:29–31).

Another pressing consideration, which Paul does not mention, was the widespread famine conditions existing at the time of writing. "Paul left Corinth, most likely, in AD 51. Right around that time, and for a few years afterwards—exactly the period between his leaving and his writing this letter—there was a severe shortage of grain, the most basic foodstuff, around the Greek world. . . . The poor in particular—and most of the Christians in Corinth were poor (1:26)—would be feeling the pinch." N. T. Wright believes the grain shortage may have left engaged couples wanting "to think hard about postponing their marriages."[10] On the other hand, Paul encourages couples feeling the strain of unexpressed sexual intimacy to get married. He recognizes that both the single and the married life represent God's gift to the individual. One must not be elevated to a superior position above the other.

Some teachers in Paul's day strongly maintained that celibacy provided the way to new depths of personal holiness and spiritual maturity. In this passage, Paul upholds the traditional teaching concerning marriage as a monogamous relationship; consequently both premarital and extramarital sex violate God's norm, and both husband and wife have to be sensitive to one another's needs. Chafin offers some cautionary words in the interpretation of this passage.

> We need to remember some things that are very elemental in all interpretation of the Scripture passages. First, Paul was not writing a general treatise on marriage. He was answering very specific questions, which had been asked of him. Second, we must understand his answers in terms of some of the very

10. Ibid., 91.

twisted views that some of his readers had about marriage. Third, we have to isolate from the whole situation those aspects which were obviously local and temporary. Fourth, all that he said to them must be interpreted in the light of his feelings that he had about the imminent return of Christ to the earth and the inevitability of persecution in the days ahead.[11]

Paul also deals with the sensitive issue of mixed marriage, in which a person is married to someone who is not a believer (1 Cor. 7:8–16). No doubt this was a fairly common problem when one of the married partners came to faith before the other and perhaps without the agreement of the spouse. This situation, in some instances, can be avoided by ensuring that Christians marry only fellow believers (1 Cor. 7:39; 2 Cor. 6:14). But what about those who are already yoked to an unbeliever? Paul believes that it provides an opportunity for witness in the hope that the unbelieving partner might eventually be brought to faith. But a further question remains: what about the children of such a union? Paul encourages the believing parent that the couple's offspring are covered by God's love, and that they are not disadvantaged in their coming to share the faith of the believing parent.

A further challenge faces Christian couples who rush into marriage and enter into Christian ministry without giving due consideration to the implications of that ministry on their future relationship. "In our own day there are many who have ignored Paul's wise advice and have rushed ahead into marriage and into a new sphere of Christian work or service, assuming that because God has brought them together the complex business of learning to work for the gospel and the complex business of learning to live as a couple will somehow fall into place. This simply cannot be assumed. The sorry story of marriage tensions and breakups among Christian workers in recent times bears witness to the dangers."[12] Work for God must not lead to neglect of one another. It does not honor God if, in our endeavors to win the world, we lose those who are closest to us because we have taken them for granted.

Bearing Fruit

Both Jesus and Paul speak of life transformation in terms of fruitfulness. Fruit provides evidence that a person is abiding in Christ (John 15:5).

11. Chafin, *1, 2 Corinthians*, 87.
12. Wright, *1 Corinthians*, 95–96.

Fruitfulness is the true test of the servant, because it means the reproduction and multiplication of the same kind and quality of life. The fruit a tree bears identifies it unmistakably and provides evidence of its state of health. In another place Jesus said, "By their fruit you will recognize them" (Matt. 7:16 NIV).

Fruit embodies the superabundance of life that the tree cannot contain within itself. It is the tree's give-away life. In the mission of Paul, such abundant fruitfulness is evidenced in the spread of the gospel through the influence of lives turned around and transformed by that message. Writing to the Colossians, Paul assures them, "We have heard of your faith in Christ Jesus and of the love that you have for all the saints, because of the hope laid up for you in heaven. You have heard of this hope before in the word of the truth, the gospel that has come to you. Just as it is bearing fruit and growing in the whole world, so it has been bearing fruit among yourselves from the day you heard it and truly comprehended the grace of God" (Col. 1:4–6). We see here that such fruitfulness was not the exception but was typical of the abundant life arising from the gospel, as God by the Holy Spirit fills them with understanding and with the wisdom to apply what has been revealed to them. Such understanding and wisdom are not the product of human intellect and learning but come about as we learn to listen attentively to God.

Abiding must be distinguished from *hiding*. It does not signify the avoidance of responsibility. It is not an invitation to become cowardly or lazy. It signifies a relationship rather than a refuge, entailing our yielding to Christ's control and drawing our very life and sustenance from him. Such abiding does not consist in a cozy relationship, for it also inevitably entails painful pruning, that is, the stripping away of anything that would hinder the relationship.

We belong to the Christ who was raised from the dead "in order that we may bear fruit for God" (Rom. 7:4). The same challenge faces believers today. Having committed our lives to Christ, we all then need to learn to remain in his presence, drawing strength from him, while resisting the temptation to attempt to go it alone, for that would only result in disaster. Christianity is not a self-help program that we can utilize and then discard at will in our journey toward self-realization. No, the teaching of Christianity emphasizes the need to die to self in order to live the abundant life.

Turning once again to Paul's insights into fruitfulness, we see his emphasis on fruit as evidence of the Holy Spirit's presence. Yet we need to remember that the Spirit to which Paul refers is the Spirit of Christ. Hence, the meaning is the same. Abiding in the Spirit equates to abiding in Christ, and that relationship is evidenced by fruitfulness.

In the first place, fruit consists of character qualities. Paul contrasts the fruit of the Spirit with the works of the flesh, the former consisting of "love, joy, peace, patience, kindness, generosity, faithfulness, gentleness, and self-control" (Gal. 5:22). It is significant that Paul uses the singular "fruit," emphasizing that all need to be present in the life of the believer. They are like the segments of an orange.

Fruit is also evidenced in the works Christians undertake through the inspiration and enabling of the Spirit. The power of the gospel, present in the life of the Thessalonians, generated "work produced by faith, . . . labor prompted by love, and . . . endurance inspired by hope" (1 Thess. 1:3 NIV). The fruit of the Spirit is seen in both action and attitude. Notice that the new believers in Thessalonica are not laboring primarily in interests limited to the church fellowship but are laboring within the surrounding community. In his second letter, Paul is still able to commend them: "Your faith is growing abundantly, and the love of everyone of you for one another is increasing" (2 Thess. 1:3). Paul also looks to the Philippians to produce a harvest of righteousness that comes through Jesus Christ for the glory and praise of God (Phil. 1:11). Fruitfulness inseparably relates quality and quantity. A concern for fruitfulness leads us to ask questions about the kind of influence we are having on those around us, the kind of atmosphere we create when we enter a room, and the kind legacy we are leaving.

Resilience

In reviewing both the Acts chapters that tell the story of the churches founded by Paul and the letters he writes to the various cities, we are made acutely aware of the challenges that those churches faced from day one. They encountered opposition from the surrounding populace, both Jews and pagans, leading to misrepresentation, hostility, and open persecution. Additionally, internal tensions between Jewish believers and pagan converts emerged within the church. Furthermore, many congregations were being disturbed by Jewish Christians insisting on the need for continued observance of the law, not only by Jewish believers but also by non-Jews. All of these tensions threatened to cause confusion and discouragement. The need for resilience among the new believers is therefore strongly emphasized throughout Paul's letters.

In writing to the new believers in Thessalonica, Paul is encouraged by the news brought by Timothy that the church is standing firm and growing in faith and love (1 Thess. 3:6–12). Fully aware that these new believers would be facing hostility, as he himself had in Thessalonica, Paul instructs them in how to live in order to please God. He offers himself as an example to emulate.

What he is urging them to do, they are in fact doing and should "do so more and more" (1 Thess. 4:1). Paul's instructions are rooted in the teaching of Jesus (1 Thess. 4:2), who also cautioned his first disciples that they would encounter much opposition that would be fierce at times.

The challenge to live in order to please God is not an optional extra for Christians; rather, it lies at the very heart of the gospel. Paul goes on to spell out the implications of such a commitment in the following verses (1 Thess. 4:3–8). This is a call that contemporary Western Christians need to heed, for ours is a hedonistic culture in which we are pressured to live for ourselves rather than to please God.

When we live to feed our appetites, we soon discover that those appetites are insatiable. The resilience we need may be less about surviving opposition, ridicule, and persecution and more about resisting the subtle and relentless pressures to succumb to materialism and pleasure seeking. We have to challenge the separation commonly made between conversion and discipleship. If conversion means an about-face, discipleship entails stepping out into "a long obedience in the same direction," to quote the title of a book by Eugene Peterson, which he in turn borrowed from Nietzsche. In other words, you cannot be a church member without becoming a disciple of Christ. Discipleship entails becoming a lifelong learner and apprentice, living within a faith community that provides support and encouragement and requires accountability, and serving the fellowship of believers and the wider community in accordance with one's calling and gifting.

The image of believers shining like stars in a dark world provides a further reminder of the need for resilience (Phil. 2:12–18). They are not like sparklers that shine for a short time only to then sputter and die, but like the prevailing, dependable stars in the sky (Phil. 2:15). In our brightly lit urban world, we are not aware of the night sky. Only in complete darkness, under a clear desert sky, do we become overawed by the spectacular display of the stars of heaven. Paul is concerned that the Philippians continue in his absence to work out their salvation "with fear and trembling," as they consider what it means to live the faith in their daily lives, "for it is God who works in you to will and to act in order to fulfill his good purpose" (Phil. 2:12–13 NIV).

Sanctification signifies the believer being set apart by God and brought into a transformative relationship with Christ through the indwelling Holy Spirit. This is a progressive process, which Paul recognizes in the closing words of his first letter to the Thessalonians: "May the God of peace himself sanctify you entirely; and may your spirit and soul and body be kept sound [or "complete"] and blameless at the coming of the Lord Jesus Christ" (1 Thess. 5:23). *Resilience* is the product of total commitment, in contrast to the instability that is the product of double-mindedness and halfhearted commitment. Paul knows, both from personal experience and from his work among the churches, that only God *can* make it happen, and that God *will* make it happen because God is faithful.

Paul makes the same point to the Corinthians: "God is faithful; by him you were called into the fellowship of his Son, Jesus Christ our Lord" (1 Cor. 1:9). Resilience is the product of the faithfulness of God and not simply human resolve. To prevail we need to be clothed in the whole armor of God, both for our protection in defense and in order to attack the enemy (Eph. 6:10–20). We stand firm not in our own strength but in "the strength of his power" (Eph. 6:10). We need the whole kit, not overlooking the wearing of any piece. If, as Paul assumes, attacks are inevitable, every Christ-follower must make sure to wear this protective clothing and must be skilled in using the weapon that God has supplied; namely, "the sword of the Spirit, which is the word of God" (Eph. 6:17).

Maturity

Closely associated with the need for resilience is *maturity*, which is the fruit of abiding in Christ and resisting the forces that would separate the believer and drag him or her in a different direction. Maturity signifies the process of moving toward consistency and completion. Paul acknowledges to the Philippians his own personal struggle while also encouraging them to follow his example.

> Not that I have already obtained this or have already reached the goal; but I press on to make it my own, because Christ Jesus has made me his own. Beloved, I do not consider that I have made it my own; but this one thing I do: forgetting what lies behind and straining forward to what lies ahead, I press on toward the goal for the prize of the heavenly call of God in Christ Jesus. Let those of us then who are mature be of the same mind; and if you think differently about anything, this too God will reveal to you. Only let us hold fast to what we have attained. (Phil. 3:12–16)

Maturity may be defined as consistently living in the present in the light of the future. It is living as citizens of heaven, on tiptoe, with expectancy as we eagerly await the coming of our Savior, which will bring about the transformation of our bodies.

The Calvinistic emphasis on the perseverance of the saints ("once saved, always saved") enshrines a biblical assurance to the believer under pressure.

But that doctrine should never be used to imply that a believer has arrived spiritually and therefore has no further obligation to make progress in the Christian life. Maturity is the result of a lifetime of applying our faith to the challenges encountered during the course of our spiritual pilgrimage.

Saving faith is challenged, shaped, and strengthened by the situations we encounter. In other words, faith takes on different forms according to the varied experiences of each person; consequently, Paul recognizes that ministry among believers is always mutual. To the believers in Rome he declares, "For I am longing to see you so that I may share with you some spiritual gift to strengthen you—or rather so that we may be mutually encouraged by each other's faith, both yours and mine" (Rom. 1:11–12). An individual's faith is not a carbon copy of the apostle's but is the product of the challenges that person has faced.

Faith sharing plays a significant role in the process of Christian maturity. When believers bear testimony to how the grace of God has sustained them during various trials, whether sickness, bereavement, loss of a job, or unrealized expectations, their witness brings encouragement to those who are facing similar challenges or who are seeking to support individuals who are engulfed by personal tragedy. When silence and denial prevail, or there is an insufficient level of trust to allow for such sharing, then spiritual casualties mount.

Paul demonstrates an ongoing concern for believers to continue to grow in Christ and become more and more like him. The primary marks of maturity are the evidence of increasing faith and love. Paul commends the Thessalonians in his second letter to them in the following terms, "We must always give thanks to God for you, brothers and sisters, as is right, because your faith is growing abundantly, and the love of everyone of you for one another is increasing" (2 Thess. 1:3). Their steadfastness and faith in the face of persecution is assured as long as they remain faithful to God the Father and the Lord Jesus Christ and continue to dwell in their presence.

By way of contrast, personality clashes demonstrate one of the marks of spiritual immaturity. Church members sometimes behave like children rather than adults toward each other. Paul humbles the Corinthians, who pride themselves in their knowledge and wisdom, arguing that if they persist in squabbling like infants, they will have to be treated as such.

And so, brothers and sisters, I could not speak to you as spiritual people, but rather as people of the flesh, as infants in Christ. I fed you with milk, not solid food, for you were not ready for solid food. Even now you are still not ready, for you are still of the flesh. For as long as there is jealousy and quarreling among you, are you not of the flesh, and behaving according to human inclinations?

For when one says, "I belong to Paul," and another, "I belong to Apollos," are
you not merely human? (1 Cor. 3:1–4)

Being a follower of Jesus has a great deal to do with relationships, as is evident
in Jesus's calling and training of the Twelve. Personality clashes among his
followers have to be ironed out.

Intelligence takes many forms. Believers may demonstrate *rational* intelligence, with their sophisticated grasp of theological issues, broad knowledge,
and doctrinal discernment, and yet at the same time evidence poor *relational*
intelligence. They may either avoid contact with people as much as possible
or act in divisive and combative ways in their relationships. If, like the Corinthians, they are jealous of one another and quarrelsome, then they are simply
living like everyone else. They may boast of spiritual giftedness yet still be
controlled by their old natures. As they persist in behaving like infants, they
are in no condition to build up one another in the faith. One cannot be an
authentic Christian without becoming a disciple—that is, an apprentice of
Jesus with a commitment to lifelong learning and following.

The church is not just a human institution, despite being made up of forgiven sinners still undergoing formation. It is the Spirit of Christ that gives
the church its unique identity. Paul repeatedly reminds the churches that it is
the presence of God among them that makes them both an inspiration and
a challenge to society at large. At the same time, the church is shaped by its
context and has been entrusted with a God-given mission. As it undertakes
this mission, it must depend on God's grace and demonstrate God's peace.
Consequently, disciples need a dynamic understanding of both faith and love
as expressed in different contexts in response to particular circumstances.

Discernment

Discernment is not necessarily commensurate with giftedness. Indeed, believers
need spiritual discernment in order to receive the Spirit's gifts and to use them
appropriately. Paul makes these points clear to the Corinthians. "Those who
are unspiritual do not receive the gifts of God's Spirit, for they are foolishness
to them, and they are unable to understand them because they are spiritually
discerned. Those who are spiritual discern all things, and they are themselves
subject to no one else's scrutiny. 'For who has known the mind of the Lord so
as to instruct him?' But we have the mind of Christ" (1 Cor. 2:14–16).

The idea of discernment is closely connected with maturity and wisdom.
It denotes the ability to see beneath the surface and shallow symptoms to

deep-rooted causes. Spiritual discernment represents an added dimension. In relation to the gifts of the Holy Spirit, discernment recognizes whether or not they are authentic and being employed appropriately. Spectacular gifts might be demonstrated by spiritually immature persons or by deceivers. The gifts of the Spirit must never be disassociated from the fruit of the Spirit. Charisma and character are indissolubly linked.

In the fourth chapter of Ephesians, Paul establishes a pattern of fivefold ministry: apostles, prophets, evangelists, pastors, and teachers, all of which are essential for the equipping of the saints for life and ministry. Without their collective contribution, the church will not come to spiritual maturity. It will lack discernment and perspective and, in the absence of purpose and direction, will fragment and succumb to the pressures around it. As with the Corinthians, so with the Ephesians: Paul cautions them against remaining as spiritual infants. "We must no longer be children, tossed to and fro and blown about by every wind of doctrine, by people's trickery, by their craftiness in deceitful scheming. But speaking the truth in love, we must grow up in every way into him who is the head, into Christ, from whom the whole body, joined and knit together by every ligament with which it is equipped, as each part is working properly, promotes the body's growth in building itself up in love" (Eph. 4:14–16).

In this passage, Paul once again stresses the relational dimension of discipleship. By strengthening relationships, the faith community will gain resilience to weather storms and maintain its direction, no matter how dark the night or how mountainous the waves. Notice also how Paul balances holding true to sound doctrine and defending such nonnegotiable foundations in a spirit of love. It is often said that little has been achieved if we have won the argument yet antagonized our opponent by our combative attitude. We are always to speak the truth in love (Eph. 4:15). By so doing, the body of Christ will grow as it identifies with Christ and its members are joined together in strong, mutually supportive relationships. When disagreement divides the body of Christ, each part will be weakened and left to limp along, feeling the absence of the members that it has ostracized. Love is the connecting fiber and superglue that binds together the members.

The prevailing emphasis in local church ministry is usually placed on the teacher, on the assumption that church members simply need to be taught the faith. There is some justification for this emphasis, considering the increasingly biblically illiterate culture in which we live, with so many people having bought into an individualistic, therapeutic, and life-beyond-death version of the gospel. Such misguided teaching has come at the expense of the grand narrative of Scripture. The missional challenge we face today in the West is not only to care for the needs of congregations but also to equip them to take the message of the reign of Christ into the everyday worlds they inhabit.

Alertness and Self-Control

Paul describes believers as "children of light and children of the day" (1 Thess. 5:5), living the kind of personal and corporate life that stands out in contrast to the surrounding night and darkness. In order to maintain their witness as light-bearers, they must keep awake and remain sober (vv. 6–8), always vigilant so as to be aware of their surroundings at all times. Sleep represents moral indifference; drunkenness, a failure to exercise self-discipline and control. When people get drunk, they either become aggressive or lapse into a stupor. Once again, Paul employs the image of spiritual armor to represent the protective covering that believers must wear to ensure their survival and distinctive character (1 Thess. 5:8).

The Philippian Christians adopt a laissez-faire approach, believing they can sit back now that they have been reconciled to God and rescued from sin. Instead, they are to work out their own salvation with fear and trembling. This *out*working is a direct result of the *in*working of God, "enabling you both to will and to work for his good pleasure" (Phil. 2:13). On the one hand, we can be assured of the presence of God in our lives; on the other hand, we must accept responsibility for ourselves and address the particular situations in which God has placed us. We do this in relation to one another in the Christian fellowship and by engaging with the world. The fact that we are to do this "with fear and trembling" (Phil. 2:12) emphasizes the seriousness of the challenge, and the sense of responsibility we should feel. Salvation, although intensely personal, can never be privatized. The deepening relationship with God that we experience must be expressed in our deepened relationships with the persons we relate to daily. We stand in awe in the presence of God, made nervous by the sense of our inadequacy.

At the same time, we recognize that God, who has called us into service, has also equipped us to meet the demands that calling will bring. Within every church "there are varieties of activities, but it is the same God who activates all of them in everyone" (1 Cor. 12:6). Here we see the outworking of our salvation in a manner that preserves unity while promoting diversity.

Paul himself testifies to God's enabling in his life when he says, "But by the grace of God I am what I am. . . . I worked harder than any of them [i.e., his critics and opponents]—though it was not I, but the grace of God that is with me" (1 Cor. 15:10). Again, in his second letter to the Corinthians, he reminds them that "our competence is from God, who made us competent to be ministers of a new covenant, not of letter but of spirit; for the letter kills, but the Spirit gives life" (2 Cor. 3:5–6).

Character Formation

Character is one of the four foundation pillars of leadership, along with competence, charisma, and commitment. Character is developed through consistency and resilience in the face of the barrage of challenges that face leaders in the course of daily life. Character builds trust. Stephen Covey helpfully links together character and competence: "Trust is a function of two things: character and *competence*. Character includes your integrity, your motive, your intent with people. Competence includes your capabilities, your skills, your results, your track record. And both are vital."[13] He goes on to make an important distinction between the two: "While character is constant, competence—at least most competence—is situational. It depends on what the circumstance requires."[14]

Within the faith community, one of the key components of character is the ability to rejoice in the face of difficulties. Our moods need not be determined by circumstances; rather, we have learned to rejoice in the Lord, no matter how adverse our circumstances. Writing from prison, Paul is able to encourage others to rejoice in the Lord: "Rejoice in the Lord always; again I will say, Rejoice" (Phil. 4:4). Paul also provides the antidote to worry: "In everything by prayer and supplication with thanksgiving let your requests be made known to God. And the peace of God, which surpasses all understanding, will guard your hearts and minds in Christ Jesus" (Phil. 4:6–7).

Character is forged in the furnace of adversity. It is hammered out on the anvil of suffering. Throughout Paul's letter to the Philippians, *joy* and *rejoicing* are words that peal forth with bell-like clarity. Like Paul, our rejoicing may not derive from our circumstances, which often give no cause for comfort. Rather, our rejoicing is in the Lord, as we abide in God's presence. It is all the more impressive in that such rejoicing makes us more sensitive to the people around us, by releasing us from self-preoccupation and self-pity. "Let your gentleness be known to everyone," Paul exhorts the Philippians (Phil. 4:5). Prayer that is the outpouring of a joyful heart releases us from being demanding and complaining. When we are abiding in the Lord, we know that our petitions have been heard, and we are prepared to leave the outcome in the hands of God. It is not for us to tell God what to do.

13. Covey, *Speed of Trust*, 30. Italics in the original.
14. Ibid., 107.

Witness

The discipleship initiated by Jesus with the Twelve cannot be restricted to the individual level. It is both essentially corporate and outward looking. Both the Twelve and the Seventy (or Seventy-Two) were sent out on mission in Jesus's name (Luke 9:1–6; 10:1–17). This same mission focus is evident in both Paul's personal example and his encouragement to the new believers, who were trained as partners with him in spreading the message. He commends Philemon in the following terms: "I always thank my God because I hear of your love for all the saints and your faith toward the Lord Jesus. I pray that the sharing of your faith may become effective when you perceive all the good that we may do for Christ" (Philem. 4–6). Here Paul links love within the fellowship with commitment to sharing faith—the first motivating the second.

By sharing the good news our own understanding of the message is enriched. This comes about as we see its impact in the lives of individuals facing all kinds of challenges, and as we respond to the questions they raise. The message is not limited by our own experience of the grace of God (Rom. 1:11, 12). Philemon is himself about to face the challenge of the good news he proclaimed to others in regard to his runaway slave Onesimus. He will be challenged to put into practice his love for all the saints, including the one person who has caused him so much grief.

Summary

The churches established by Paul and his associates welcomed new converts from the pagan and pluralistic environment of the Greco-Roman world. They welcomed these new members as they were, but always with a view to their transformation through the challenge of the good news and the enabling power of the Holy Spirit. Throughout this chapter, we have seen that Paul presents his readers with extensive evidence that discipleship embraces the whole of life—every relationship and every activity. The demands of discipleship must be worked out within the context of close-knit communities in which it is all too easy for one person to ruffle the feathers of another. But these communities are also where the church can credibly demonstrate an alternative personal and communal lifestyle made possible by the unique impact of the gospel and the indwelling Holy Spirit.

In relation to the basic premise of this book, the call to become lifelong apprentices of Jesus represents an urgent priority. The consumerist model of church that is all too prevalent throughout the Western world has resulted in the church making little impact on wider society. Here in the United States, which has the highest rate of church attendance within the orbit of Christendom, social problems and economic imbalance prevail. In order to challenge and begin to reverse this sad state of affairs, local communities need to be inspired by vibrant Christian communities living out the radical message of Jesus and giving birth to new faith communities. Such churches are noted for the welcome they extend, rather than perceived judgmental attitude, and for the transformation brought about through the challenges and rewards of incorporating newcomers as active members within the fellowship. The health of a church is measured not so much by the number of people that attend as by the impact the gospel is making in their daily lives. As one church reminds the congregation each week, "Come as you are, but do not leave as you came!"

Conclusion:

Ensuring effective strategies are in place to move members from passive presence to active engagement within the local congregation.

7

Upholding the
Apostolic Message

Throughout the letters of Paul we find recurring reference to certain key doctrines, some of which are addressed frequently—although often merely in passing—while others receive extended treatment. These same issues are not confined to the early decades of the Christian church but continue to emerge today. The questions may take on new forms in response to challenges raised by modern scholarship or contemporary culture, but the underlying issues remain.

Hans Küng insists that for any church to claim apostolic succession it must "agree with the apostolic witness" and "must follow the apostles in continually recognizing and demonstrating that it has been sent out into the world."[1] Throughout its history, the church has constantly had to face challenges to its core beliefs and resist temptations to abandon or redirect its mission away from the priorities established by Paul.

In his letters to the churches, Paul refers to false apostles who constantly dog his steps and challenge his apostolic credentials. He is at pains to provide criteria by which genuine apostles can be distinguished from those making false claims. If the distinguishing mark of the true apostle is the calling and commissioning of the risen Lord, then an individual's claim to such a revelation needs to be tested. There are three crucial tests: the approval and commissioning of the church; the character of the apostle, which should reflect Christ's

1. Küng, *The Church*, 356–58.

own as marked by the presence of the fruit of the Spirit; and the fruit of the apostle's ministry, measured in transformed lives and new churches birthed. The key belief Paul expounds and defends at length is the doctrine of salvation by grace through faith, which lies at the heart of the gospel and must therefore be explained and defended in every age.

Salvation by Grace through Faith

The foundational message running through the letters concerns the total work of salvation accomplished by God through Jesus Christ. The main theme of Galatians is the victory over sin that Christ accomplished on the cross, with his work vindicated by his heavenly Father through his resurrection from the dead. It was in obedience to the Father's will that the Lord Jesus Christ "gave himself for our sins to set us free from the present evil age, according to the will of our God and Father" (Gal. 1:4). This atoning work of Christ must be seen in cosmic as well as personal terms. As Hansen comments, "The cross of Christ inaugurated God's new created order in human history."[2]

Paul makes clear to the Corinthians that salvation is through the grace of God and is not based on human merit, whether religious, intellectual, or social. Consequently, the message extends to the despised nobodies of this world (1 Cor. 1:21–29). Neither is the gospel the product of human reasoning. "For since, in the wisdom of God, the world did not know God through wisdom, God decided, through the foolishness of our proclamation, to save those who believe. For Jews demand signs and Greeks desire wisdom, but we proclaim Christ crucified, a stumbling block to Jews and foolishness to Gentiles, but to those who are called, both Jews and Greeks, Christ the power of God and the wisdom of God. For God's foolishness is wiser than human wisdom, and God's weakness is stronger than human strength" (vv. 21–25).

To this day, the message of the cross remains a stumbling block, because it challenges human pride, pricks conscience, and fails to make sense to those who see no need for atonement and to whom the very concept is abhorrent. Notice how Paul identifies himself with the foolish of this world in his ministry of gospel proclamation. In so doing, he deliberately contrasts both the style and the content of his presentation with that of the pagan philosophers. He has not altered his basic message; he presents Jesus not as a great ethical teacher, a moral example, or even a great leader, but as the crucified and risen Christ. We will now examine the key elements in Paul's understanding and presentation of the gospel.

2. Hansen, *Galatians*, 34.

Law, Grace, and Righteousness

The extended treatment Paul gives to the relationship between the Jewish law and the good news of being put in right relationship with God through faith in Christ reveals the supreme importance of this issue for him. Galatians and Romans provide the most extensive exposition of his understanding of the work of Christ on the cross. Although the two letters cover much the same ground, the former is more personal and passionate, while the latter is more comprehensive and reasoned. Perhaps the difference in tone reflects that while Paul had faced fierce opposition in Galatia, he had yet to visit Rome when he wrote to the church there. However, there was an urgency in his addressing the issue in Rome, as the edict of the emperor Claudius in AD 49 expelling the Jews from Rome had left the churches there largely in Gentile hands. When the Jewish believers returned to Rome, apparently friction between the two groups began to develop.

In Galatians, Paul fires a barrage of fourteen rhetorical questions in the space of four chapters, questions designed to highlight the inconsistencies in the reasoning of the Judaizers and to expose their hypocrisy. He goes over the same ground from a variety of angles to ensure that his basic message hits home—namely, that we are brought into a right relationship ("righteousness") with God through faith in Christ, not through human endeavor in attempting to comply with the Jewish law.

Paul declares and defends this message in the face of Judaizers, who had arrived in Galatia from Jerusalem, claiming that Paul had set the law aside in order to make his message more acceptable to the non-Jewish believers and in so doing had departed from the message of the apostles in Jerusalem. They claimed that the gospel of Jesus still required non-Jewish believers to be circumcised and to keep the comprehensive list of requirements of the law of Moses.

Their arrival in Antioch drives a wedge between Paul and Peter, who succumbs to the pressure from the emissaries from Jerusalem and begins refraining from table fellowship with non-Jews. Paul challenges Peter head-on before the church: "If you, though a Jew, live like a Gentile and not like a Jew, how can you compel the Gentiles to live like Jews?" (Gal. 2:14). The Judaizers' insistence on observance of the Jewish law had destroyed the unity the believers enjoyed in Christ, by driving a wedge between Jew and Gentile. It had also led into slavery those who had come to experience the freedom of the grace of God, by binding them to a law with which they could not comply at every point. In other words, they had turned from salvation as an undeserved gift of God to striving for righteousness, based on human effort. This was especially serious in Antioch, where the pioneering initiative to take the gospel to non-Jews had been made. For the unity obtained in Antioch to be now undermined by the divisive teaching of the Judaizers would have had devastating consequences for the mission to the Gentiles that had just gotten under way.

The main points that Paul makes in developing his argument in Galatians 3–5 are as follows. They have received the Holy Spirit as the guarantor of their faith, not through obeying the law of Moses, but through believing the message about Jesus Christ (Gal. 3:2). Paul responds in utter disbelief as to why they turned their backs on that message. It is as though they had an evil spell cast upon them (Gal. 3:1). There seems to be no adequate human explanation for their foolishness. Paul is perplexed: Why, after starting their Christian lives in the Spirit, are they now trying to become perfect by their own human effort? (Gal. 3:3). He challenges them: "Did you experience so much for nothing?—if it really was for nothing" (Gal. 3:4).

Paul goes on to insist that his teaching that sinners are made right with God through faith is no novel departure from the message that runs throughout the Jewish Scriptures. It can be traced back before Moses to Abraham, who is the spiritual father of all God's people. "Just as Abraham 'believed God, and it was reckoned to him as righteousness,' so, you see, those who believe are the descendants of Abraham. And the scripture, foreseeing that God would justify the Gentiles by faith, declared the gospel beforehand to Abraham, saying, 'All the Gentiles shall be blessed in you.' For this reason those who believe are blessed with Abraham who believed" (Gal. 3:6–9). That promise, given long ago to Abraham and his descendants, is like a last will and testament that can never be rescinded. It stands forever as an everlasting covenant between God and God's people.

It is all too easy to overlook the strength of the cultural pressures that new non-Jewish believers had to face when they committed their lives to Jesus Christ as their Savior and Lord. They no longer belonged to the pervasive pagan society permeating trade guilds and social life. At the same time, they now found themselves under suspicion from the Jewish believers in Jesus as Messiah. Had the faith community failed to fully embrace them, they would have faced a profound identity crisis. No wonder images of the church as "the bride of Christ," "the body of Christ," and "the family of God" were so significant to them, as was baptism, representing the dying of the old self and living a new life in the risen Christ.

The Jewish believers in Jesus as Messiah faced their own challenges. Paul reassures them that the law of Moses did not replace the promise given to Abraham four hundred thirty years earlier; rather, its purpose was to reveal to people their sins and to leave no doubt as to God's displeasure and their accountability. Their inability to keep the law revealed that they were indeed prisoners to sin. Human effort provided no escape. The law might curb sin, but it could not eradicate it. It simply placed them under "protective custody," or discipline, until the way of faith was revealed (Gal. 3:23 NLT).

Becoming united in Christ through baptism signified death to those old distinctions between Jew and Gentile, as it did to other divisions. "There is no longer Jew or Greek, there is no longer slave or free, there is no longer male and female; for all of you are one in Christ Jesus" (Gal. 3:28). Their new identity superseded all other potentially divisive elements. The gospel does indeed result in new social relationships in Christ. It eradicates all racial, social, and gender superiority and discrimination.

For those who prided themselves in their endeavors to keep the law, Paul's next statement must have come as a great shock and caused considerable offense: "For all who rely on the works of the law are under a curse; for it is written, 'Cursed is everyone who does not observe and obey *all* the things written in the book of the law'" (Gal. 3:10, quoting Deut. 27:26; italics added). Christ's death on the cross delivers us from the curse by providing atonement—that is, taking the curse from our shoulders and placing it on his.

In addressing the conflict between Jew and Gentile, Paul emphasizes the atoning aspect of the cross. David Wenham comments on this Pauline emphasis. "Although it was central, we should not assume from what Paul says in letters like 1 Corinthians or Galatians that the cross was all of Paul's theology. He stressed the cross in Galatians and Romans in the face of a Judaizing theology that did not (in Paul's view) take the cross seriously; he stressed it in 1 Corinthians to counter the Corinthian boasting. But in other letters, discussing different issues (e.g., 1 Thess.), it is less central."[3] In other words, although the doctrine of substitutionary atonement is central to Paul's theology, it does not represent the totality of his teaching on this topic. Yet the doctrine of the atonement occurs too frequently for it to be expunged by those who find the very idea offensive.

For those who have experienced freedom in Christ through the gospel, a return to the law is a retrograde move to the position of children under the discipline of a guardian. They are no longer of an age to receive their spiritual inheritance. They have failed to recognize that the decisive moment in history has arrived, when God sent his Son, who is fully human while being the only one able to fulfill the requirements of the law and by his atoning death buy freedom for sinners (Gal. 4:4–5).

Furthermore, they have received the Holy Spirit of his Son in their hearts, prompting them to call out, "Abba! Father!" (Gal. 4:6). What a transformation

3. Wenham, *Paul*, 138n.

in status—from slaves to children who enjoy the privilege of an intimate relationship with their heavenly Father! Paul makes the same highly significant point in writing to the Romans (Rom. 8:15–17). *Abba* is the very term of intimacy that Jesus used in addressing his Father (Mark 14:36; Matt. 6:9). No wonder Paul is utterly perplexed when he appeals to them. "How can you turn again to the weak and beggarly elemental spirits? How can you want to be enslaved to them again?" (Gal. 4:9). His deeply felt concern alerts us to the pervasive and powerful pull of the pagan lifestyle they have so recently abandoned.

Paul draws this long section to a close with a personal appeal: "Friends, I beg you, become as I am, for I also have become as you are. . . . What has become of the goodwill you felt? For I testify that, had it been possible, you would have torn out your eyes and given them to me. Have I now become your enemy by telling you the truth?" (Gal. 4:12, 15–16). If Paul has to speak harshly to make them realize the seriousness of the spiritual consequences they faced in returning to the law, he ends with a warm pastoral appeal: "My little children, for whom I am again in the pain of childbirth until Christ is formed in you, I wish I were present with you now and could change my tone, for I am perplexed about you" (Gal. 4:19–20).

In this section we have given more space to Paul's interaction with the Galatians than to his long letter to the churches in Rome. This is because the purpose of this study is to examine the issues Paul faced in connection with the churches he had actually founded or with which he had an ongoing connection. However, this is not to underestimate the significance of his interaction with the church in Rome, which was to have great influence in the future course of Christianity. Clearly, he has a significant number of contacts with the believers in the imperial capital. Some he knows personally, through his encounter with them during his travels, while others he knows by reputation.

Paul's insistence on their being brought into a right relationship with God through faith, and not through the law, arises from his own radical reappraisal as a former Pharisee. In confronting the boastful Judaizers in Philippi, he lays out the many reasons he might claim confidence in the flesh: "circumcised on the eighth day, a member of the people of Israel, of the tribe of Benjamin, a Hebrew born of Hebrews; as to the law, a Pharisee; as to zeal, a persecutor of the church; as to righteousness under the law, blameless" (Phil. 3:5–6). All that was previously on the credit side of the balance sheet, he now transfers to the debit side. "Yet whatever gains I had, these I have come to regard as loss because of Christ. More than that, I regard everything as loss because of the surpassing value of knowing Christ Jesus my Lord. For his sake I have suffered the loss of all things, and I regard them as rubbish, in order that I may gain

Christ and be found in him, not having a righteousness of my own that comes from the law, but one that comes from faith in Christ, the righteousness from God based on faith" (Phil. 3:7–9). Time and time again Paul reiterates that salvation cannot be earned but can be received only as a free gift from God (Rom. 1:17; 3:21–26; 4:5–8; Gal. 2:16; Eph. 2:8–9).

Establishing Our New Identity in Christ

When there is a sharp contrast between the values and lifestyles of the surrounding culture and the values and lifestyles that represent the transforming power of the gospel, members of the faith community are faced with hard decisions and need discernment and resolve to establish their new identity in Christ. Under Christendom, it was assumed that society at large should, at least in theory, represent the West's Judeo-Christian heritage. This is no longer the case in the United Kingdom, and the assumption is increasingly questioned and eroded here in the United States.

Conflicting views on this subject are evident in the current culture wars. Shifting cultural attitudes have resulted in many churchgoers living in two largely unrelated worlds. They conform to the mores of a secular and pluralistic society when outside the fellowship of the church but display a different belief system and lifestyle within the Christian community. Many attendees become nervous when the church crosses this divide, because in so doing their inconsistencies are more likely to be exposed.

Unfortunately, in the process of communicating the gospel cross-culturally, messengers additionally are prone to pass along many of their cultural assumptions. Sometimes they do so inadvertently, while at other times it is deliberate, on the assumption that the Christianization of their culture is part of their mission mandate. This was especially the case during the Victorian era of colonial expansion. Donald McGavran, writing *Bridges of God* in the 1950s, saw the dangers inherent in this approach as well as its consequences in stifling the expansion of indigenous churches.

Throughout most of Europe, North America, and Australasia, this challenge comes much nearer to home. These societies have become much more pluralistic as a result of waves of recent immigration from areas of the world that are either predominantly non-Christian or marked by Christian traditions more spiritually vibrant than the jaded forms in the West.

The challenge is even more complex due to communities having become more tribalized. How are new faith communities to be birthed within the hip-hop, clubbing, NASCAR, and wilderness-trekking cultures, to mention just a few? Such groups are unlikely to darken the doorways of any of our traditional churches. As was the case in the first centuries of the church, "Christians need to discern the difference between their identity as God's children and the identity offered by the dominant forces of the surrounding culture."[4]

Key Elements in Atonement

When the very idea of atonement is downplayed or rejected outright, we lose sight of a whole range of key terms that lie at the heart of the gospel, including *grace, adoption, redemption, justification,* and *regeneration.*

The good news, announced and embodied in the ministry of Jesus Christ, is a message of *grace* to undeserving sinners. That grace of God flows from only one place—the cross of Christ, for "the Lord Jesus Christ . . . gave himself for our sins to set us free from the present evil age, according to the will of our God and Father" (Gal. 1:3–4). Grace represents the unbounded generosity of God in offering salvation we could never earn by our own efforts. The gospel represents nothing less than a rescue operation, originating in the loving heart of God the Father, who so loved the world that he gave his only Son. Grace flows from the Father and Son together.

The significance of Paul's brief statement in Galatians 1:4–5 must not be overlooked, because it presents a direct challenge to distortions and reductions of the gospel so prevalent today. It confronts the notion of a therapeutic gospel, in which we are rescued primarily from our dysfunctions. The gospel message cannot be individualized and privatized; our rescue is not just from ourselves but also "from the present evil age" (v. 4). In a number of places, Paul's letters emphasize the good news that Christ has established a new world order. Although profoundly personal, the gospel also has the broadest of social dimensions. Paul is not changing the emphasis of the gospel but logically extending Jesus's inaugural message that the "kingdom [reign] of God is at hand" by translating it into the much broader social context of the Greco-Roman world.

In Paul's understanding, Jesus gave himself as a sin offering, taking upon himself the penalty of our sins and making atonement for them. In our day, the notion of substitutionary atonement has come under increasing attack from a number of quarters. Some have caricatured the doctrine, misrepresenting it in terms of Jesus turning away the wrath of his Father against sinners. However, the suffering of Christ is matched only by the suffering of his Father, who cannot simply ignore the evil heart and ways of the world. Only the sinless Son can pay the sacrificial price through his atoning blood. As John Stott

---

4. Hansen, *Galatians,* 85.

comments, "In the cross the will of the Father and the will of the Son were in perfect harmony."[5]

A further objection arises from the notion of radical inclusion. The argument is that all may come just as they are to an all-loving Father, without the need for either atonement or transformation. We are referring here to the rejection not of a particular theory of atonement but of the need for any kind of atonement. This position represents a radical departure from the gospel as presented in many places in the New Testament. Those who claim apostolic authority for this change of doctrine have aligned themselves with the false apostles Paul denounces so firmly, even to the point of anathematizing them.

But the gospel is more than a judicial pronouncement that the guilty one is declared not guilty by faith in the atoning work of Christ. It is also a message of *deliverance*. We are released from the shackles of sin in order to live a radically different kind of life. We continue to live in the world because we are called to engage the world as representatives of the coming age already inaugurated by Christ. Christ delivers us from bondage to the world, but we are not distanced from it, in keeping with Jesus's prayer for the disciples in the upper room: "Sanctify them in the truth; your word is truth. As you have sent me into the world, so I have sent them into the world" (John 17:17–18).

The message of salvation provides a solid ground for hope based on well-attested historical events. The incarnation, earthly ministry, crucifixion, and resurrection of Christ make Christianity, along with Judaism, the most historically rooted of the world's religions. The resurrection of Christ represents the firstfruits guaranteeing the resurrection of all of his subsequent followers (1 Cor. 15:20). Jesus didn't raise himself from the dead but was raised by God (Rom. 1:4). So the Thessalonian Christians, despite their distress, were emboldened to "wait for his [God's] Son from heaven, whom he raised from the dead—Jesus, who rescues us from the wrath that is coming" (1 Thess. 1:10). They waited, not in debilitating resignation, but with vibrant expectation.

The early church looked back to this one great event that gave them unshakable hope. Furthermore, Jesus's departure from the scene did not signify remoteness. His followers had not been abandoned. In the upper room, Jesus assured his disciples that it was to their advantage that he go away for a while. His departure was followed by his resurrection appearances that gave them reassurance and were also a prelude to the giving of the Holy Spirit.

Jesus, as the Son of God, was completely dependent on the Father throughout his ministry, so his stumbling followers must recognize they are even more dependent on God. The sequence of crucifixion leading to resurrection is equally true

5. Stott, *Galatians*, 18.

for us. Dying and rising lie at the heart of all ministry. Jesus's ongoing ministry of intercession on behalf of his body, the church, and its ongoing mission in the world also establish the priority of prayer for all who minister in his name.

Incarnation

Matthew's Gospel presents the announcement of the Messiah's forthcoming birth to Mary using words borrowed from the prophet Isaiah: "'Look, the virgin shall conceive and bear a son, and they shall name him Emmanuel,' which means, 'God is with us'" (Matt. 1:23). But we might ask the identity of this "they" who shall so name Jesus. The most obvious answer: those who followed him and thereby had the opportunity to hear his teaching, observe his ministry, and know him intimately. The prologue to John's Gospel, which bears the name of one of the inner circle of the Twelve, provides his personal testimony: "And the Word became flesh and lived [literally, "pitched his tent"] among us, and we have seen his glory, the glory as of a father's only son, full of grace and truth" (John 1:14). Those two short words, *grace* and *truth*, contain a wealth of meaning. *Grace* speaks of the undeserved, overwhelming generosity of God made known in Christ, and *truth* signifies the authenticity and genuineness of Christ. He was what he claimed to be.

Jesus's incarnational ministry does more than provide a model that subsequent generations try to imitate. That course of action would be both presumptuous and futile. Craig Van Gelder and Dwight Zscheile remind us that "the church's incarnate ministry is not merely an imitation of what Jesus did; it is a participation in a much larger movement in which God is the primary actor."[6] John provides the clue to faithfulness and effectiveness when he testifies, "From his fullness we have all received, grace upon grace. The law indeed was given through Moses; grace and truth came through Jesus Christ" (John 1:16–17).

In the final chapter of their book *Untamed: Reactivating a Missional Form of Discipleship*, Alan and Debra Hirsch unpack the significance of the incarnation for the contemporary church. They maintain that incarnation demonstrates the following eight practices: presence, proximity, spontaneity, frequency, powerlessness, prevenience, passion, and proclamation.[7] *Presence* signifies a total commitment for the long term. *Proximity* entails a close encounter rather than attempting to minister from a safe distance. *Spontaneity* is necessary in order to respond rapidly and appropriately to situations as and when they

6. Van Gelder and Zscheile, *Missional Church in Perspective*, 114.
7. Hirsch and Hirsch, *Untamed*, chap. 9.

present themselves. *Powerlessness* requires a vulnerable and humble approach. *Prevenience* reminds us that God arrives on the scene before we do! *Passion* sets before us the cross of Christ and his outpouring of forgiving love, signifying much more than emotional intensity. *Proclamation* points to the fact that Jesus was a teacher who broadcast the good news of the inauguration of God's reign on earth.

When the theological term *incarnation* is unpacked in this way, we begin to feel both its powerful impact and its comprehensive nature. The incarnation challenges us to appreciate that God is not simply among us to provide comfort but may all too often be too close for comfort! As the subtitle of Alan and Debra Hirsch's book emphasizes, the church today needs to move beyond a form of discipleship that is tamed by individualism to one that is outwardly focused. In their words, the challenge is in "reactivating a missional form of discipleship." Van Gelder and Zscheile make the same point. "The missional church cannot participate in God's passion for the world without drawing close to its neighbors. This means surrendering a posture of control, distance, and mere benevolence in order to enter closely into relational community. The legacies of Christendom and colonialism, along with modernity's stress on human agency, programs, and activities, have fostered approaches to mission that tend to keep the church apart from and unaffected by those in need."[8]

In writing to the Philippians, Paul makes it clear that the incarnation was no masquerade. "Christ Jesus, . . . though he was in the form of God, did not regard equality with God as something to be exploited, but emptied himself, taking the form of a slave, being born in human likeness. And being found in human form, he humbled himself and became obedient to the point of death—even death on a cross" (Phil. 2:5–8). These words present a powerful challenge to the casual Christianity of so many Western Christians today.

Contextualizing the Kingdom Message of Jesus

The basis of Jesus's message, which he both proclaimed and embodied, is expressed in terms of the kingdom, or reign, of God. "When Jesus announced the arrival of the kingdom of God, he said '*Repent*, for the kingdom of God is at hand.' Notice, he did not say, 'Adjust.' To repent entails a complete turnaround. It means that our entire life is aimed in a new direction, with new goals and pursuits."[9] Both the language and the substance of that kingdom message have to

8. Van Gelder and Zscheile, *Missional Church in Perspective*, 115–16.
9. Hirsch and Ford, *Right Here, Right Now*, 77.

be understood in terms of its Jewish and Palestinian context. A constant theme in the message of the Jewish prophets was the restoration of the kingdom of God to Israel, which had ethical, ritualistic, and nationalistic overtones. That message was especially significant for Israel during its seventy years of Babylonian captivity, in the three hundred fifty years between the two Testaments, and during the Roman occupation of Palestine that provided the cultural context for Jesus's ministry. Consequently, for Jesus to announce that the kingdom was at hand was welcome news throughout the land. The challenge Jesus faced was redefining that kingdom in terms neither nationalistic nor legalistic.

The apostle Paul faced the further daunting challenge of translating and reinterpreting the kingdom message of Jesus so that it made sense in the Greco-Roman world of his day. To the majority of new Gentile believers in the Mediterranean cities, talk of the kingdom of God would make little sense and would raise false expectation on behalf of the Jews. Thus the term *kingdom* is used rarely by Paul, occurring only eleven times throughout his letters, mainly serving to maintain contact with his Jewish readers (Rom. 14:17; 1 Cor. 4:20; 6:9; 15:24, 50; Gal. 5:21; Eph. 5:5; Col. 1:13; 4:11; 1 Thess. 2:12; 2 Thess. 1:5). But Paul reminds the Corinthians, "the kingdom of God depends not on talk but on power" (1 Cor. 4:20). The kingdom is not a point of discussion or dispute but a powerful reality to be demonstrated in action.

The Triune God: Father, Son, and Holy Spirit

The current focus on the ministry of Jesus as the model for ministry today is a welcome corrective to the triumphalism and organizational approach to ministry and mission that has prevailed in so much of Western Protestant Christianity. However, discipleship and mission in the writings of Paul are rooted in a trinitarian understanding of the nature of God. While the term *Trinity* is of later use, the bringing together of Father, Son, and Holy Spirit in terms that indicate their divine nature provides the biblical basis for that later theological development. The placing together of God the Father, God the Son, and God the Holy Spirit is all the more striking in that it is simply assumed and introduced without explanation, as in the greetings, benedictions, and intercessions of Paul.

Greetings and Benedictions

In the opening greeting of nearly every one of the letters attributed to Paul, Jesus Christ is coupled with the Father as the source of grace and peace, blessings that can come only from God (Rom. 1:7; 1 Cor. 1:3; 2 Cor. 1:2; Gal.

1:3; Eph. 1:2; Phil. 1:2; 1 Thess. 1:1; 2 Thess. 1:2; Philem. 1:3). In his letters to individuals, such as Timothy and Titus, Paul uses the same terminology (1 Tim. 1:2; 2 Tim. 1:2; Titus 1:4). These two recurring greetings—"grace" and "peace"—represent familiar Greek and Hebrew salutations, but they are much more than that in Paul's usage, as these terms summarize his understanding of salvation and form the very heart of his message to the Galatians.[10]

God the Father and the Lord Jesus Christ, mentioned in the same breath, are coequals and together the source of grace and peace. Such an association challenges those who would represent Jesus Christ as just one among a number of inspired teachers. Indeed, the church of the Thessalonians is described in terms of its being "in God the Father and the Lord Jesus Christ" (1 Thess. 1:1).

The same emphasis is found in the benedictions, which provide a climax to so many of Paul's letters. He blesses the Ephesians in the following terms: "Peace be to the whole community, and love with faith, from God the Father and the Lord Jesus Christ. Grace be with all who have an undying love for our Lord Jesus Christ" (Eph. 6:23–24). To the Corinthians, Paul signs off with the following trinitarian benediction, subsequently used so often at the conclusion of times of corporate worship: "The grace of the Lord Jesus Christ, the love of God, and the communion of the Holy Spirit be with all of you" (2 Cor. 13:13).

Intercessions and Thanksgivings

Even more significant, Paul's intercessions and thanksgivings emphasize his trinitarian understanding of the Godhead. He addresses his prayer to the Thessalonians as follows: "Now may our God and Father himself and our Lord Jesus direct our way to you" (1 Thess. 3:11). It is significant that while the subject is plural, the verb in Greek is in the singular (*kateuthynai*), placing Jesus at one with the Father.[11] Paul thanks both God the Father and the Lord Jesus Christ for the faith of the Romans (Rom. 1:8). Again, in writing to the Corinthians, Paul gives thanks "to my God always for you because of the grace of God that has been given you in Christ Jesus" and declares his confidence that "God is faithful; by him you were called into the fellowship of his Son, Jesus Christ our Lord" (1 Cor. 1:4, 9).

Both God the Father and God the Son are Paul's source of rejoicing. "Blessed be the God and Father of our Lord Jesus Christ, who has blessed us in Christ with every spiritual blessing in the heavenly places" (Eph. 1:3). The entire

---

10. Stott, *Galatians*, 16.
11. That "both the Father and Jesus are the subject of the singular verb *clear* (or 'make straight') highlights the unity of their position." Beale, *1–2 Thessalonians*, 108. See also Stott, *1 & 2 Thessalonians*, 67.

redemptive work of God is a result of the combined operations of Father, Son, and Holy Spirit.

If the Son of God was so dependent on his Father and the Spirit, then we are even more dependent on all three persons of the Trinity as we continue the Son's ministry in the world. Consequently, we must avoid a distorted presentation of the ministry of Jesus, as though he acted autonomously, and the misconception that we are called to meet his demands by relying only on our own dedication and resources.

Trinitarian Basis of Mission

Contemporary theological reflection on mission expressed within the emerging church movement has focused on the mission of Jesus providing the model for the church today. This is in part a reaction against the Pauline missional model and the propositional theology associated with that emphasis. It reflects a desire to reach beyond a church-planting priority in mission to one that embraces the good news proclaimed by Jesus in inaugurating the reign of God here on earth. The reign, or kingdom, message stresses the authority of the incarnate and ascended Christ over the whole of life, challenging the individualistic, privatized, and reductionist gospel that prevails among many evangelicals.

The ministry of Jesus also stresses that you cannot have a *king*dom message without acknowledging the centrality of King Jesus. This view challenges the secularized version of the *missio Dei* that became increasingly prevalent in the more liberal wing of the church from the 1960s. In other words, you cannot build the kingdom through human resources. It is God's surprising accomplishment, which comes to us as gift.

There has been a growing realization that mission is the activity of all three persons of the Trinity. If we focus exclusively on the mission of Jesus, we tend to have a rear-view orientation with an emphasis on reproducing his ministry. But we soon discover that *we* are not Jesus! The ministry of Jesus cannot be considered without reference to the other two persons of the Trinity. Jesus was sent by the Father into the world and referred all that he did to his heavenly Father. He communed regularly with God. He did not act independently, being reliant on the power of his heavenly Father (John 5:19–20). Jesus's will was completely in tune with that of his Father.

> Christ lies at the heart of the missional church, but Christology cannot be understood apart from Christ's relationship with the Father/Creator or his being anointed, empowered, and led by the Spirit. . . .

. . . Imitation tends to stress what God *has done*. Participation invites us into what God *is doing and will continue to do* as God's promises in Christ are brought to fulfillment.[12]

At both the time of Jesus's conception and the beginning of his public ministry, the Scriptures draw attention to the role of the Holy Spirit. Mary's conception came about by the operation of the Holy Spirit, as announced to her by the angel (Luke 1:35). Luke informs us that, immediately after refusing the temptations in the Judean wilderness, "Jesus, filled with the power of the Holy Spirit, returned to Galilee" (Luke 4:14). In announcing the beginning of his ministry in the synagogue in his hometown of Nazareth, Jesus opened the scroll to a passage in Isaiah and read, "The Spirit of the Lord is upon me, because he has anointed me to bring good news to the poor" (v. 18). Having completed his reading of the passage, he amazed those present with the announcement, "Today this scripture is fulfilled in your hearing" (v. 21 NIV). Jesus's entire ministry was conducted in reliance on his heavenly Father and was empowered by the Spirit. It was through the Holy Spirit that he was raised from the dead (Rom. 1:4). When we examine how Jesus prepared his own disciples for their continuing ministry in his name, we find that he taught them the same dependence on the Father and the Holy Spirit that he exemplified.

Interrelated Roles of All Three Persons of the Trinity

The New Testament strongly emphasizes the involvement of all three persons in the subsequent mission of the church. This has been expressed commonly in a sequential form—namely, in the Father taking the initiative in sending his Son to implement the divine mission, who in turn sends the Holy Spirit to empower the church of Jesus Christ to continue that mission throughout the world until his return. Craig Van Gelder identifies a problem with this representation, in that "this understanding of the Trinity concerns the tendency to view God in modalistic terms. Thus works of the Father, the Son, and the Spirit are subject to being separated and individualized, with God conceived of as one subject who acts in different modes."[13]

The Western formulation of the doctrine of the Trinity was heavily influenced by Greek philosophical categories that emphasized the divine attributes, and in so doing distanced God from engagement in mission. It also gave scant attention to the interaction among the persons of the Trinity. The Eastern

12. Van Gelder and Zscheile, *Missional Church in Perspective*, 111.
13. Ibid., 53.

understanding of the Trinity, however, was highly relational. It emphasized community of being and described the interaction of the three persons as a kind of dance (*perichoresis*). This understanding of God has profound implications not only for the doctrine of the Trinity but also for our understanding of human persons. "We are coming to understand that God's character is defined more by the quality of relational life within the trinitarian community than by certain abstract attributes (such as the classical concepts taken from Greek philosophy of omniscience, omnipotence, immutability, impassibility, etc.). This approach fundamentally changes how we view what it means to be human. Humans are not pale imitations of God's eternal rationality and power but rather find their identity in participating communally in the divine community's life and love as well as in one another's lives."[14]

Understanding of the triune nature of God evolved in the context of mission, rather than as a result of philosophical speculation. Such formulations did not emerge for another two hundred years. It is significant that the resurgence of interest in the Trinity today is within the context of missional engagement. In those segments of the church where mission is deemphasized, modalism continues to prevail.

Attempts have been made to find alternative names for the persons of the Trinity. In place of Father, Son, and Holy Spirit, the descriptive titles Creator, Redeemer, and Sustainer are employed. But such substitutions are not entirely satisfactory, as they reduce the Trinity to a series of job descriptions and create artificial distinctions, in that the work of each person of the Trinity cannot be so neatly compartmentalized. The persons of the Trinity do not act alone.

As we have already noted, when we turn to Paul's letters we do not find a doctrinal exploration of the Trinity. Rather, the persons of the Trinity are introduced in the context of his pastoral ministry among the congregations he is addressing. Readers familiar with the text can all too easily overlook the significance of Paul's trinitarian references, as they appear so frequently in his opening greetings, intercessions, and final greetings and benedictions.

Significance of the Holy Spirit

Those who are serious about discipleship and see its significance for the ongoing mission of the church soon come to appreciate the various ministries of the Holy Spirit within their personal and corporate lives. In the first place, it is the Holy Spirit who imparts understanding and wisdom to grasp the significance of the gospel. As Paul instructs the Corinthians, "No one comprehends

14. Ibid., 108.

what is truly God's except the Spirit of God. . . . Those who are unspiritual do not receive the gifts of God's Spirit, for they are foolishness to them, and they are unable to understand them because they are spiritually discerned" (1 Cor. 2:11, 14). The communication of spiritual truth must be undertaken in complete reliance on the Spirit. It is not accomplished simply by the power of logic or persuasion. The revelations of God are foolish to those without the Spirit; they cannot understand them because the revelations are spiritually discerned. Divine wisdom transcends the limitations of human wisdom.

The revelation brought about by the Holy Spirit not only enlightens the mind but also transforms a person's life: "Now the Lord is the Spirit, and where the Spirit of the Lord is, there is freedom. And all of us, with unveiled faces, seeing the glory of the Lord as though reflected in a mirror, are being transformed into the same image from one degree of glory to another; for this comes from the Lord, the Spirit" (2 Cor. 3:17–18). It is this same Spirit who reproduces in us the very character of Jesus, for "the fruit of the Spirit is love, joy, peace, patience, kindness, generosity, faithfulness, gentleness, and self-control" (Gal. 5:22–23). As David Wenham notes, "For Paul the Spirit is the Spirit of Jesus, whose fruit is, above all, love, and who works in the believer conforming him or her to the image of Christ (Gal. 5:22; 2 Cor. 3:18)."[15] Fruit bearing is an ongoing process that comes about as we learn to live in, and be guided by, the Spirit.

Paul draws a sharp contrast between "natural" and "spiritual" persons. The former live "according to the flesh"—that is, governed by their unregenerate nature—while the latter live under the transforming power and guidance of the Spirit. "Natural" persons, because they have not received the Spirit of God, still have their understanding and their horizons very much limited to this world. They cannot understand spiritual matters unless the Spirit of God helps them. Just as Christ came as the supreme revelation of God's love and found that the minds and hearts of many people were closed to his teaching, so the Spirit must come to open our minds and hearts to the gospel. Such teaching underlines the essential part that the Spirit of God plays, not only in conversion, but also in spiritual development. Every evangelist should therefore realize that he or she cannot engineer a person's conversion using intellectual arguments, promotional campaigns, or emotional appeals. Regeneration is essentially a work of the Holy Spirit; no human being can make it happen. Only the Holy Spirit gives life (2 Cor. 3:6), and it is that same Spirit who makes us competent to minister the heart-changing new covenant to others.

The Holy Spirit is described as a guarantee or down payment of life in the Spirit that will be fully realized at the end of time with the return of Christ

15. Wenham, *Paul*, 231.

(2 Cor. 5:5). David Wenham writes, "The Holy Spirit, the first installment of what is to come, had been given, and so Christians were now longing and groaning for what lay ahead (Rom. 8:23). The resurrection of the dead—very much an end-time event—has begun in Jesus, its firstfruits (1 Cor. 15:20); the gathering in of the Gentiles, which the Old Testament anticipates, is under way, and Paul has a crucial role to play in this."[16] This same point is made in Paul's letter to the Ephesians, where he describes those who believe in Christ as "marked with the seal of the promised Holy Spirit; this is the pledge of our inheritance toward redemption as God's own people, to the praise of his glory" (Eph. 1:13–14). The believers' relationship to the Spirit is a dynamic one, not to be taken for granted. They can both quench (1 Thess. 5:19; "stifle" NLT) and grieve the Spirit (Eph. 4:30).

The church is itself a temple of the Holy Spirit on two levels: the corporate level (1 Cor. 3:16–17) and the individual level (1 Cor. 6:19). At both levels the Spirit's presence is demonstrated by the fruit of the Spirit displayed in Christ-like character and in the gifts of the Spirit that equip the church to engage in the manifold ministries of Christ.

Paul is clear that this many-faceted ministry consists of abilities given by the Holy Spirit (1 Cor. 12:6, 13). It is the Holy Spirit who provides the bonds of unity while facilitating diversity (Eph. 4:4). The one body consists of many *members*—that is, limbs and organs that enable the body to function. Every individual making up the body of local believers is equipped by the Spirit to make a distinctive contribution according to his or her calling and gifting. As we review Paul's teaching on the Holy Spirit in his letters to young churches, we can appreciate the Spirit's crucial role in the illumination and transformation of individuals, and their bonding with other believers in the fellowship of the Holy Spirit, which is indeed the church.

Person and Work of Christ in the Context of Mission

Closely related to our discussion of the missional implications of the doctrine of the Trinity is that of the person of Christ who is the central figure of his message and ministry. This focus is prominent in all four Gospels, with each author identifying Jesus as the long-awaited Messiah of Israel. Later in the Acts account, both Peter and Paul, in their proclamation of the good news, argue from the Jewish Scriptures that Jesus is the long-promised Messiah as they speak to the Jewish authorities in Jerusalem. During Paul's

16. Ibid., 53.

missionary journeys he visits synagogue after synagogue proclaiming the same message.

When Paul enters the Greco-Roman world, he encounters a world of religious pluralism and imperial claims of the Roman emperor. From the time of Augustus, there was an increasing emphasis on his divine status. In confronting the challenge of conflicting allegiances—Christ or Caesar—the early church refused to compromise. It declared defiantly, "Jesus is Lord." In other words, it did not capitulate but insisted that the ascended and enthroned Jesus, the Son of God, was "King of kings and Lord of lords" (1 Tim. 6:15).

We have already noted how the divinity of Christ is assumed in Paul's letters to the Thessalonians (1 Thess. 3:11). Similarly, in his second letter Paul couples the Father and the Son (2 Thess. 3:16). John Stott comments, "It is amazing enough, within twenty years of the resurrection, that Paul should have bracketed Jesus Christ with God; it is yet more amazing that he now brackets God with Jesus Christ. He also goes on, in spite of the plurality of the subject (Father and Son), to use the singular reflexive *who* and the singular verbs *loved* and *gave*."[17]

Paul's prison letters, which are covered in this study, contain the highest Christology. The early church had to be clear about its understanding of the person of Christ as it engaged in mission within a pagan context, in which many gods were acknowledged and placated. Writing to the Colossians, Paul highlights the supremacy of Christ, who is "the image of the invisible God, the firstborn of all creation; for in him all things in heaven and on earth were created . . . all things have been created through him and for him. He himself is before all things, and in him all things hold together" (Col. 1:15–17). This same Jesus is not only the Creator-God but also the Redeemer-God, who is the head of the church and reconciler of sinful humankind (Col. 1:21–22), making peace with those who were former enemies and drawing nearer those who previously were far off.

Ephesus was the center of the Asia Minor region. Located there was the temple dedicated to Diana, whose influence spread around the region, including Colossae. Jesus is no alternative object of devotion but one who challenges Diana's false claims and values. Also, as creator and sustainer of all things, he confronts the claims of the Roman emperor to deity, a challenge that has profound political implications.

Once again we must draw attention to the majestic hymn that Paul references in writing to the Philippians (Phil. 2:5–11). The statements made concerning the identity and mission of Jesus are indeed mind-boggling. The one who was in his very nature God renounced his heaven-given privileges and "emptied

17. Stott, *1 & 2 Thessalonians*, 179.

himself, taking the form of a slave. . . . And being found in human form, he humbled himself and became obedient to the point of death—even death on a cross" (vv. 7–8). Jesus's humiliation leads to his exaltation and his being given a name that is above every name. Before him every knee will bow and every tongue confess that the crucified Savior is indeed Lord, to the glory of God the Father. Such a confession is a direct challenge to Caesar's claim to be lord and also goes far beyond popular adoration, in that it is neither coerced nor a formal display of political correctness. On the contrary, this is an audacious claim on the part of the early church—that the one who in Roman eyes was nothing more than a discarded corpse would become the King of kings ushering in a universal and eternal reign.

Here is a clarion call to the church today to continue to declare Jesus in these same exalted terms. At the same time, this confession poses a challenge to the church—engaging in mission entails dying to self, renouncing power and privilege, and engaging the world as those giving unswerving allegiance to Jesus Christ. In the service of mission, our primary loyalty is to the Lord Jesus Christ, resisting every temptation to submit to the demands of the world we engage.

Backing up his high Christology, Paul emphasizes the central historical events of the gospel, centered in the Messiah, who was crucified, buried, and raised from the dead (1 Cor. 15:1–11). Paul outlines the message that he has "handed on to them" and that he expects them to hand on to others without alteration.

> For I handed on to you as of first importance what I in turn had received: that Christ died for our sins in accordance with the scriptures, and that he was buried, and that he was raised on the third day in accordance with the scriptures, and that he appeared to Cephas, then to the twelve. Then he appeared to more than five hundred brothers and sisters at one time, most of whom are still alive, though some have died. Then he appeared to James, then to all the apostles. Last of all, as to one untimely born, he appeared also to me. (1 Cor. 15:3–8)

Note that Paul says Jesus appeared to the entire band of the apostles. In addition, he made himself known to a much wider group of disciples. The five hundred he mentions were possibly the wider crowd that gathered in Galilee to hear Jesus issue his Great Commission (Matt. 28:16–20). Since most of these were still alive when Paul was writing to the Corinthians between AD 53 and 56, they could verify his story. It also reveals something of the youthfulness of the church, considering the short life expectancy of the times.

The individual identified as James, mentioned by Paul, is almost certainly Jesus's brother, who had become a leader of the church in Jerusalem. Paul is here reminding the Corinthians of facts they already know and is not introducing a new idea. Paul's insistence on the historical basis of the climactic events of the gospel must similarly be guarded and emphasized in the church today, to counter those who would seek to deny its historicity and substitute a spiritualized version, thereby separating the Christ of experience from the Jesus of the Gospels.

Paul's unmistakable insistence on a high Christology must not be overlooked in our day. Unfortunately, many churches in the West have caved in to the relativism of our culture, surrendering this high Christology, making Jesus one religious leader among many. I have heard senior leaders declare that to profess "Jesus is my Lord" is nothing more than the language of personal devotion, thereby denying that those of other religions need to face the claims made by Christ. They speculate that there are alternative and equally valid pathways to salvation. Once the biblical teaching that Christ is the Savior of the world is denied, the task of mission to the world is undermined. Some Western church leaders even apologize to leaders of other religions for attempting to convert them, thus placing Christian minorities in some hostile host cultures in greater jeopardy.

This insistence on continuing the task of mission is not to condone the many cruel and underhand practices that missionaries have employed to make converts during the course of history, for which the church should apologize and repent. There have been conversions brought about under torture, promises of economic advantages, or, most recently, a health-and-wealth enticement to the sick and poor. Such strategies are not confined to Christian missionaries but are employed to advance other religions, especially in impoverished areas of the world or among persecuted minorities. But such horror stories must not be blown out of proportion. The vast majority of Christian mission has been undertaken at great personal sacrifice, resulting in early death through disease and martyrdom for many missionary pioneers. Hospitals, schools, and relief and development projects around the world are the direct result of countless Christians who have obeyed the call of Christ to treat their fellow human beings as persons made in the image of God, and therefore of intrinsic worth. Furthermore, countless numbers of former animists and polytheists rejoice that through the gospel they have been delivered from the fear and power of spirits and demons.

As we reassess our approach to mission in the twenty-first century, we have a lot to learn from the witness of both the early church and Christians in the global South today. In both situations, the churches usually exist at the margins rather than at the centers of power. Their humble and gracious stance challenges our sense of entitlement and arrogance. In examining Acts and the letters of Paul, we find a balance of boldness and grace.

The early church did not operate from a safe distance but was immersed in its culture, with all the vulnerability that such proximity entailed. Contemporary churches that insulate themselves from their cultural context are prone to caricature people of other faiths and to become judgmental. They have to learn to listen respectfully and discerningly. God may already be at work in other persons and communities and may have significant things to say through them that churches urgently need to hear.

Hope and Scope of Salvation

Election

Salvation embraces a cluster of concepts, each one essential to grasping its complexity and comprehensive nature. Paul is clear that it is God who makes the first move in the salvation of humankind. In writing to the Ephesians, Paul employs in his thanksgiving to God a number of key soteriological concepts and terms, beginning with that of *election*: "Blessed be the God and Father of our Lord Jesus Christ, who has blessed us in Christ with every spiritual blessing in the heavenly places, just as he chose us in Christ before the foundation of the world to be holy and blameless before him in love" (Eph. 1:3–4). It is mind-boggling to be informed that God initiated the divine plan even before the foundation of the world.

The evangelist has the privilege and responsibility of making known the saving invitation of God through the preaching of the gospel. "But we must always give thanks to God for you, brothers and sisters beloved by the Lord, because God chose you as the first fruits for salvation through sanctification by the Spirit and through belief in the truth. For this purpose he called you through our proclamation of the good news, so that you may obtain the glory of our Lord Jesus Christ" (2 Thess. 2:13–14). Paul immediately urges the believers to "stand firm and hold fast to the traditions that you were taught by us, either by word of mouth or by our letter" (2 Thess. 2:15).

In our own day, the doctrine of election continues to be challenged and must be defended with the same conviction, for the regeneration of the individual and the birthing of the church is possible only on the basis of the prior call of God. In order for the church to be truly the body of Christ and the fellowship of the Holy Spirit, the effectual call of God is essential.

Adoption

The second key term that occurs in the praise offering that Paul shares with the Ephesians is that of *adoption*: "He destined us for adoption as his children through Jesus Christ, according to the good pleasure of his will" (Eph. 1:5). This term describes the sublime objective of God's call. It is more than a call to draw near and to be associated with God; it is a call to be included in God's family and thereby to have the family likeness bestowed upon us. Such is not our birthright as human beings; it is actualized only through the gospel. It is a *salvation* term and not a *creation* term. Writing to the Galatians, Paul returns to this theme: "But when the fullness of time had come, God sent his Son, born of a woman . . . , so that we might receive adoption as children. And because you are children, God has sent the Spirit of his Son into our hearts, crying, 'Abba! Father!'" (Gal. 4:4–6). And this note sounds yet again in his letter to the Romans: "For you did not receive a spirit of slavery to fall back into fear, but you have received a spirit of adoption. When we cry, 'Abba! Father!' it is that very Spirit bearing witness with our spirit that we are children of God, and if children, then heirs, heirs of God and joint heirs with Christ—if, in fact, we suffer with him so that we may also be glorified with him" (Rom. 8:15–17).

Adoption embraces three foundational ideas. The first of these is *justification*, which refers to sinful humankind being brought into a right relationship with a holy God through reconciliation. Paul continually proclaims and defends justification on the basis of the grace of God made available through faith—both of which are gifts of God. "There is therefore now no condemnation for those who are in Christ Jesus" (Rom. 8:1). Justification is the basis for forgiveness and makes possible reconciliation. Justification by grace—God's unmerited favor—through faith, does not imply that we are then free to do whatever we will. The evidence of grace received is seen in the fruit of the Spirit and a changed life of obedient and humble service. The price that God paid in Christ for our forgiveness is a powerful reminder that forgiveness does not represent God's moral indifference, but rather emphasizes God's abhorrence of evil and the serious nature and consequences of sin.

The second foundational idea embraced by adoption is *reconciliation*. In writing to the Corinthians, Paul links the idea of reconciliation and regeneration ("new creation"). "So if anyone is in Christ, there is a new creation: everything old has passed away; see, everything has become new! All this is from God, who reconciled us to himself through Christ, and has given us the ministry of reconciliation; that is, in Christ God was reconciling the world to himself, not counting their trespasses against them, and entrusting the message of reconciliation to us" (2 Cor. 5:17–19). Notice also the evangelistic implication of becoming reconciled. It is not a privilege that one can keep to oneself. Having received God's peace terms, made known and available through Christ, all must become ambassadors of reconciliation. "So we are ambassadors for Christ, since God is making his appeal through us; we entreat you on behalf of Christ, be reconciled to God. For our sake he made him to be sin who knew no sin, so that in him we might become the righteousness of God" (2 Cor. 5:20–21).

The third term that relates closely to adoption is *regeneration*. The life changes that take place upon submitting one's life to Christ are the result not of moral reformation but of spiritual regeneration. Paul draws a stark contrast between the former life lived by the Ephesians and the new life that they now enjoy in Christ. In terms of their former spiritual state, he describes them as "dead through the trespasses and sins in which you once lived, following the course of this world, following the ruler of the power of the air, the spirit that is now at work among those who are disobedient" (Eph. 2:1–2).

Conformity to the world results in spiritual bondage from which there is no escape apart from the gospel. It is through God's saving intervention that death is replaced by life: "But God, who is rich in mercy, out of the great love with which he loved us even when we were dead through our trespasses, made us alive together with Christ—by grace you have been saved—and raised us up with him and seated us with him in the heavenly places in Christ Jesus" (Eph. 2:4–6).

Widespread apathy regarding the sharing of the gospel with those who are spiritually "dead" is one serious consequence of the contemporary church's lack of appreciation for the depth and scope of the saving work accomplished by the death and life of Christ. There is some substance to the charge that the vast majority of Christians are closet universalists (alongside those who are happy to openly affirm universalism). In one of his book titles, John Stott describes this failure to witness publicly as "our guilty silence."

Nature of the Church

Paul's letters to young churches serve as a reminder that the first churches were birthed and nurtured as a result of mission and in the context of ongoing mission. In his day there was no such thing as "transfer growth," in which one church grows at the expense of others. Consequently, Paul did not have to defend his understanding of the church as "the body of Christ" (1 Cor. 12:12–26) and the "sharing [fellowship] in the Spirit" (Phil. 2:1) against detractors. He simply reminded the believers of the moral and spiritual implications of their identification with Christ through the Holy Spirit, and of their mutual relationships. In the body of Christ, each individual has significance, and none is to be undervalued or despised.

Not only is Christ the head of his body, the church; he is declared to be the head over all things (Eph. 1:22–23). The presence of Christ permeates the whole church yet is not confined to the church. Precisely because Christ is the head of all things, the church must relate its message and its corporate life to Christ's wider concerns. Although Christ owns us, we do not own Christ.

Return of Christ

The early church experienced the freshness and excitement of the "new creation" that the resurrection of Christ had brought into being through the impartation of his Spirit. Believing they were living in the last days, the age when Old Testament prophecies would be fulfilled, they were on tiptoe with expectancy, awaiting the Lord's return to consummate his kingdom here on earth. Such high levels of expectation gave rise to misunderstandings and misrepresentation that Paul has to deal with in his letters.

Certain Hope in a Secured Future

The early Christians cherished a certain hope in a secured future. They looked forward to the day of the Lord with eager anticipation, believing that it would soon take place. The conduct of Christians should be governed by this expectation, for, as Paul asserts, "salvation is nearer to us now than when we became believers; the night is far gone, the day is near" (Rom. 13:11–12). Writing to the Corinthians, Paul advises that they remain single, refraining from marriage, because "the appointed time has grown short" (1 Cor. 7:29).

Because the Lord's coming represents deliverance from suffering, reminding believers in situations of deprivation or persecution of their heavenly citizenship is especially important. While Paul is himself incarcerated, he reassures the Christians in Philippi, "But our citizenship is in heaven, and it is from there that we are expecting a Savior, the Lord Jesus Christ. He will transform the body of our humiliation that it may be conformed to the body of his glory, by the power that also enables him to make all things subject to himself" (Phil. 3:20–21). This message also brings comfort and reassurance to those new believers in the young church in Thessalonica who have lost loved ones (1 Thess. 4:13–5:11).

David Wenham identifies 1 Thessalonians 1:10 as "the classic passage for Paul's expectation of the near end." In this letter, which is one of his earliest, he directly links conversion with anticipation of the Lord's return. "It is notable that in 1:10, when describing the Thessalonians' conversion, he speaks of them as having turned to God 'to wait for his Son from heaven, whom he raised from the dead—Jesus, who rescues us from the wrath to come.' The Thessalonians were waiting eagerly for the Lord's return, so much so, it seems, that they were taken aback when some church members died."[18]

The measure of grief felt and expressed by Christians was in marked contrast to that of pagans. Jesus's triumph over death gives concrete hope of resurrection to all believers. With his triumphant return, "the dead in Christ will rise first. Then we who are alive, who are left, will be caught up in the clouds together with them to meet the Lord in the air; and so we will be with the Lord forever. Therefore encourage one another with these words" (1 Thess. 4:16–18). Unbelievers have no such basis for hope. Paul also provides clear teaching on the resurrection of the body in his two letters to the Corinthians (1 Cor. 15:12–57; 2 Cor. 5:1–10). Clarity on this issue is needed also in these days of much confusing and popular speculation that after death we are translated into angels or stars or are absorbed into Mother Earth.

Addressing Prevailing Confusion

Paul also has to clear up confusion regarding the Lord's coming. Some were spreading the word among the Thessalonians that Christ had already come in an invisible and spiritual manner and that the final resurrection had already occurred (2 Thess. 2:1–2). At a later date Paul instructs Timothy, who succeeded Paul as leader of the churches in Asia Minor, to oppose Hymenaeus and Philetus, "who have swerved from the truth by claiming that the resurrection has already taken place. They are upsetting the faith of some" (2 Tim. 2:18). Such prophecies are not confined to the first century; they are uttered by deceptive speculators today.

In relation to the Lord's return and the endless speculation about its nature and timing, Paul's letters underline three certainties. First, the Lord's return will be unexpected, like a thief in the night (1 Thess. 5:2). But the emphasis is not on *if* but *when*. This latter point is emphasized because it will come suddenly, like labor pains, without warning (1 Thess. 5:3). This means that believers must be on high alert at all times. Second, it will be preceded by the heightened presence of personified evil, described as "the lawless one" (2 Thess. 2:1–12). Third, it will be globally evident and unmistakable—a regal return announced by the trumpet call of the angelic heralds (1 Cor. 15:52). This

18. Wenham, *Paul*, 298.

language is of course figurative, but the significance is self-evident. Christians must therefore remain awake and alert (1 Thess. 5:5–7).

A Day of Disclosure and Accountability

The day of the Lord also signified God's judgment, in the sense of God's testing to reveal the genuineness and true worth of our actions and the purity of our motives. Paul distinguishes his apostolic calling to lay the foundations for the church from that of Apollos, whose God-assigned task was to build on that foundation. Subsequent generations also are called to build carefully on that foundation. "Each builder must choose with care how to build on it. For no one can lay any foundation other than the one that has been laid; that foundation is Jesus Christ. Now if anyone builds on the foundation with gold, silver, precious stones, wood, hay, straw—the work of each builder will become visible, for the Day will disclose it" (1 Cor. 3:10–13). To what extent have we contributed to the building up of the church?

God's Wrath against Unbelief

God's judgment will fall upon all evildoers together with those who have rejected the gospel (1 Cor. 15:25–28; 1 Thess. 5:3; 2 Thess. 1:6, 9). According to Paul's teaching, the Lord's coming will also herald a day of God's wrath and judgment overtaking "at last" those Jews who had violently opposed the spread of the gospel (1 Thess. 2:16). It appears that Paul had subsequent generations in mind and was not confining his statement to his contemporaries. The word translated "at last" in the NRSV (*pantote*) might better be rendered as "always," "throughout time," or, as the NRSV footnote suggests, "completely" or "forever."

Work in Anticipation of the Lord's Coming

Evidently, some new Christians in Thessalonica had decided there was little point in continuing in their daily work, since the Lord was expected to return in the very near future (1 Thess. 5:14; 2 Thess. 3:6–13). "Paul, however, had a strong sense of a mission to be accomplished before the Lord's return. In particular he believed that he had a mission to the Gentile world, and he was motivated by the conviction that 'the fullness of the Gentiles' must come in before the final salvation (of 'all Israel') would happen (Rom. 11:24, 25)."[19]

19. Ibid., 299.

Paul conducts his own pioneering evangelistic and church-birthing ministry in anticipation of the Lord's coming. He is not so preoccupied with the notion of the Lord's return that he neglects his present responsibilities; rather, it gives added urgency and heightened anticipation to his task of proclaiming the gospel. The new believers in Thessalonica represent his preparation for that moment. "For what is our hope or joy or crown of boasting before our Lord Jesus at his coming? Is it not you? Yes, you are our glory and joy!" (1 Thess. 2:19–20). John Stott comments on a similar passage in 2 Thessalonians (1:11–12).

> So how will the coming of the Lord Jesus be glorified in relation to his people? Not "among" them, as if they will be the theatre or stadium in which he appears; nor "by" them, as if they will be spectators, the audience who watch and worship; nor "through" or "by means" of them, as if they will be mirrors which reflect his image and glory; but rather "in" them, as if they will be a filament, which itself glows with light and heat when the electric current passes through it.[20]

Given the prominence of Christ's second coming in the thinking of the early Christians and in the writings of Paul, we might ask, "What significance does it have for the contemporary church?" Nearly two millennia later we might be tempted to abandon that hope, as some believers even in New Testament times had apparently done. On the other hand, we might look at the precarious state of the world—the economic and ecological crises that we face, the natural disasters, and continuing conflicts between nations—and see signs of the near return of Christ.

By embracing the teaching of the New Testament on this topic we will be safeguarded from needless speculation regarding the timing of Christ's return and from self-focused concern about whether we are in danger of "being left behind" when the Lord returns to remove his saints. Rather, we will see Christ's return in cosmic terms, with the Lord bringing into being a new heaven and a new earth—a constant reminder of the universal scope and comprehensive impact of the gospel. It is this vision that must inspire churches to ask, "Where do we go from here?"

"Maranatha!"

The urgent longing for the coming of the Lord is expressed in the appeal rooted in the Eucharist, in which the worshipers cry "Maranatha!" At the

---

20. Stott, 1 & 2 Thessalonians, 149.

conclusion of Paul's first letter to the Corinthians, this expression sounds a note of judgment against those who oppose the Lord: "Let anyone be accursed who has no love for the Lord. Our Lord, come [*Marana tha* or *Maran atha*]!" (1 Cor. 16:22). This Aramaic word can be translated as either "Come, Lord Jesus" or "The Lord Jesus has come!" If the former, it is a petition for the early return of Christ; if the latter, it is either a declaration from an early creed or a celebration of the Lord's presence in the Eucharist, reflecting Jesus's post-resurrection appearances, which transpired often amid a community meal.

These two sentiments, one longing for his appearing and the other celebrating his ongoing presence, are keynotes of Christian worship in every age. Although *Maranatha* occurs only once in Paul's letters, the hope that the term expresses is a theme running throughout his letters, providing strength to Christians in the midst of challenging circumstances.[21]

Summary

In this chapter we have identified the principal doctrines Paul repeatedly returned to during the course of his letters and have related these convictions to the twenty-first-century church. Together they constitute the apostolic tradition, which the church throughout the centuries is called to confess, expound, and defend against all detractors and those who propound deviant teaching. These challengers confront the church today, perhaps more so than in any previous age. They are as much within the church as in the world. The New Testament themes of reconciliation, "new creation," and the Lord's return provide an awe-inspiring agenda for the church as it combats the cynicism, defeatism, and fatalism within which so many are mired today.

 *Conclusion:*

In cultural contexts where basic Christian beliefs and the radical claims of the gospel are constantly being challenged, the church must humbly and boldly stand its ground with conviction, clarity, and credibility.

21. The word *hope* is found in every one of Paul's letters to the churches and occurs a total of twenty-eight times.

8

Relationships within the Church and with the World

Repeated references in Paul's letters to relationships among believers reflect his concern about how these are to be protected and fostered. These relationships were especially important for the first-century church, because the gospel presented a radical challenge to many of the accepted moral standards and religious practices of Greco-Roman society. If the church was to maintain its distinctive lifestyle, then relationship among members had to be strong and provide cohesion on a basis of mutual accountability, encouragement, and shared commitment to mission. Wayne Meeks underscores this point: "One cannot read far in the letters of Paul and his disciples without discovering that it was concern about the internal life of the Christian groups in each city that prompted most of the correspondence. The letters also reveal that those groups enjoyed an unusual degree of intimacy, high levels of interaction among members, and a very strong sense of internal cohesion and of distinction both from outsiders and from 'the world.'"[1]

Paul's emphasis on building and maintaining relationships is equally relevant to the church today. Under Christendom it was assumed that the church acted as the promoter and guardian of Christian values throughout society. But as Western society became more pluralistic and its Judeo-Christian heritage came

1. Meeks, *First Urban Christians*, 74.

under attack or was simply ignored, the church increasingly had to ensure that it remained true to the gospel, rather than succumb to the prevailing views and moral standards. Relationships among Christians are of vital importance in meeting this challenge. Faith communities provide the sense of corporate identity and the support, accountability, and resources needed to sustain a distinctive gospel ethos and mutual ministry and mission in the world.

For Paul, translating the message of Jesus, originally given within a Palestinian Jewish context to the Greco-Roman world, was no easy task. How could Jesus's messianic message of the reign of God, inaugurated during his earthly ministry and to be consummated with his return at the end of time, be presented within Gentile contexts, among people who did not identify with Jewish expectations?

The Reign of God in the Church of Christ

The relationship between the reign of God, proclaimed and inaugurated by Jesus and the subsequent emergence of the church, is a long-debated issue. Indeed, it is one that the apostle Paul must have wrestled with as he birthed faith communities around the Mediterranean world in the course of his mission journeys. Jesus's discourses and parables provide a comprehensive, if at times mysterious, exploration of the kingdom, but the Gospels record him making only three passing references to the church, which isn't much to go on! This disconnect at least meant that Paul could not merely "wind back the clock." He was also working prior to the writing of the Gospels and was therefore heavily reliant on oral sources, which he refers to as the "received tradition" (see 1 Cor. 11:2; 2 Thess. 3:6).

The crucifixion, resurrection, and ascension of Christ inaugurated a new phase or age in God's redemptive plan. Whereas the ministry of Jesus caused Paul to look back for inspiration, the Spirit came to him not out of the past but out of the future. The Spirit of Jesus reinterpreted the message of Jesus for a very different social and political context. Through the mission of the apostles, and especially that of Paul, the church reached beyond the cultural confines of the Judaism of the day. It had to translate the message of the messianic reign of God into the wider Greco-Roman world, which entailed challenging the "Caesar is Lord" authority of Rome with the counterclaim that "Jesus is Lord." How could the reign of the ascended Lord over the whole of life be expressed through these new faith communities seeking to live together in relationship to Christ? What did it mean to be both "in Christ" and "in the world" of their day?

The church must accept that it is made up of forgiven sinners and not perfected saints. It is a pilgrim church witnessing to the coming reign of Christ. Consequently, its witness is partial and compromised from the outset. Thus, it must always point not *to* itself but *beyond* itself. On account of the church's own imperfections, its witness must be humble if it is to be honest. It must also give due recognition to the ascended Lord working in the world apart from his church and, at times, in spite of his church.

The question remains: How can the church discern where and how God is at work in secular history? In order to address this question, the church needs to be listening discerningly to the Holy Spirit. It can explore the complexity of the issues only by actual engagement in the social contexts in which God has placed each faith community. Such participation has two dimensions: "First, it includes an understanding of God as present in the world beyond the church, where God is at work through both the initial life-giving work of the Spirit and the continuing work of the Spirit to bring healing to all creation, with the church participating in that healing. Second, it includes an understanding of God through the Spirit working to bring reconciliation to the world through God's redeemed community."[2] For the church to develop robust and creative relationships, it must address a number of cultural factors that would weaken and undermine that inner strength.

The Challenge to Individualism

In addition to the challenges confronting Paul, the church today has to face an additional complication due to the prevalence of individualism, the emergence of which is described by Rodney Stark. "From its earliest days, Christianity was equally inventive in its conceptions of human nature and in confronting the issues of morality. Chief among these were propositions concerning fundamental human rights such as liberty and freedom. And underlying these ideas was something even more basic: the 'discovery' of individualism—of the self."[3] Stark believes "the Western sense of individualism was largely a Christian creation," explaining, "Jesus taught that each individual must atone for moral lapses precisely because these are wrong *choices*. There could be no more compelling intellectual emphasis on self and individuality than this."[4] But the liberating emphasis on the individual should not be at the expense of affirming the community's essential work of providing identity and resilience.

2. Van Gelder and Zscheile, *Missional Church in Perspective*, 58.
3. Stark, *Victory of Reason*, 23.
4. Ibid., 26.

Within Western societies, the preoccupation with individual well-being leads to self-preoccupation, which impacts society at large and, more than we realize, influences our theological reasoning.

G. Walter Hansen draws attention to the excessive individualism that has resulted from "the Protestant preoccupation with the question 'How can I, a sinner, be right before a just and holy God?'"[5] "In Galatians Paul develops his argument for justification by faith in order to correct a social problem: Gentile believers have been excluded from fellowship with Jewish believers because they did not observe the law. Paul demonstrates that justification by faith means that Gentile believers are included within the people of God; on the basis of this doctrine Gentile believers have the right to eat at the same table with Jewish believers."[6] Western Christians face the challenge of restoring the balance between individual identity and community relationships and participation. As we examined in the opening chapter, the mobility and fragmentation of Western societies have contributed to the erosion of community. Individualism is so prevalent within society that churches struggle to mount an effective challenge.

Extended families and small groups provide contexts in which relationships are established. Small churches located in stable communities face less of a challenge in this regard than do churches located in urban contexts with high mobility and little awareness of or need for local identity and engagement.

One indication of the serious nature of the problem is that churches in these urban locations typically struggle to launch and maintain a small-group network. It is rare for them to be able to convince more than 30 percent of their regular attendees to join a small group. People have so many competing agendas and are involved in such a wide range of activities—often spread over a large geographical area—that their roots within the local community and the church they attend are tenuous at best. They are *involved* everywhere but *belong* nowhere. Consequently those individuals most likely to be committed to a small group are either longtime residents or lonely newcomers to the area and the church.

The Nature of Fellowship (*Koinonia*)

Fellowship (*koinonia*) is an important concept in the New Testament church. The Greek term occurs nineteen times in the New Testament. In secular usage,

5. Hansen, *Galatians*, 24.
6. Ibid., 25.

it can refer to joint participation in a venture and may be applied to a business association. Luke provides an example of this usage in describing the shared fishing enterprise of James, John, and Simon, who are described as *koinonos*, or "partners" (Luke 5:10). But fellowship takes on a much deeper meaning within the context of the church; it addresses a unique relationship stemming from the very nature of God.

In the New Testament, the triunity of God is progressively revealed, signifying separate identity of persons, yet a unity of purpose and actions—a community of being. No one person in the Trinity acts independently of the other two. Within the Eastern tradition, the understanding of the Trinity "is often expressed by the word *perichoresis*, which refers to the mutual indwelling within the threefold nature of the Trinity."[7] Such an understanding of the Trinity also deeply enriches our understanding of the church as essentially a relational community, as Dwight Zscheile explains: "The Orthodox tradition, in particular, has stressed the generative, outward-reaching love (*ekstasis*) and communion (*koinonia*) of the three persons. The Trinity is seen as a community whose orientation is outward, and whose love spills beyond itself. Moreover, the concept of *perichoresis*, or the mutual indwelling/interpenetration of the three persons in a dynamic circulating movement, has offered rich analogies for human interdependence and relational community."[8]

Unfortunately, the word *fellowship* has become trivialized in popular usage. For many church members, it signifies social events providing opportunity for individuals to reconnect. But, as we have seen, it means much more than Christian camaraderie. At a deeper level, fellowship is forged as Christians face challenges they cannot handle by themselves; they are drawn together and bonded when threatened by danger or when undertaking a joint enterprise. These situations cement relationships that endure even when the threat or challenge is over. But this bonding does not get to the heart of fellowship. It signifies more than a "foxhole faith" forged during times of crisis and danger.

Within the context of the church, fellowship stems from the personal and collective experience of the presence of the Holy Spirit. The apostle Paul specifically speaks of "sharing [fellowship] in the Spirit" (Phil. 2:1).[9] It is significant that the first mention of fellowship among the body of believ-

7. Van Gelder and Zscheile, *Missional Church in Perspective*, 54.
8. Ibid., 105.
9. The apostle John also emphasizes the significance of the fellowship that the church enjoys "with the Father and with his Son Jesus Christ" (1 John 1:3). The church issues an open invitation to others to experience this fellowship through believing in the message that it declares. At the same time, John also challenges the faith community to "walk in the light" of the gospel and to reject the darkness of pagan unbelief if they want to continue in fellowship with God (1 John 1:6–7).

ers is found immediately after Pentecost, when the Holy Spirit was poured out on those who had come to Christ as Savior and Lord in repentance and faith. After the baptism of the three thousand new converts, "They devoted themselves to the apostles' teaching and *fellowship*, to the breaking of bread and the prayers" (Acts 2:42; italics added). Van Gelder and Zscheile explain that relational trinitarian theology gives us a vision of God as a dynamic community of mutuality, openness, difference, and love that makes space for others to participate. These qualities define the image of God in which we are created.[10]

From the day of Pentecost forward, fellowship is realized as the followers of Christ devote themselves to the apostles' teaching. Fellowship is here the outcome of *followership*. It is rooted in association with the apostles and commitment to the apostles' message. It is expressed as the followers learn and apply the apostles' message and celebrate the Lord's continuing presence among them in the "breaking of bread" and in their prayers. Their table fellowship represents a shared meal, one in which they eat "their food with glad and generous hearts" (Acts 2:46). Their generosity is expressed in both the pooling of mutual resources so that no one is in need and attracting "the goodwill of all the people" (v. 47).

Fellowship is realized as believers meet around the Lord's Table to remember and celebrate Christ's life-giving love. In the following explanation of the Eucharist, the New Revised Standard Version translates *koinonia* as "sharing": "The cup of blessing that we bless, is it not a sharing in the blood of Christ? The bread that we break, is it not a sharing in the body of Christ? Because there is one bread, we who are many are one body, for we all partake of one bread" (1 Cor. 10:16–17). Here we see that fellowship does not describe a human association; rather, it expresses a supernatural incorporation, which must be expressed in mutual commitment to the ministry of the gospel. Paul thanks God for the Philippians' "sharing [*koinonia*] in the gospel from the first day until now" (Phil. 1:5). It is instructive to recognize that *companionship* literally means those with whom we share bread.

The idea of fellowship, understood in the context of the New Testament, presents a forthright challenge to Western notions of individualism, which are embodied in the architecture and seating arrangements of our churches. Fellowship cannot be actualized as people sit passively in straight rows looking at the back of people's heads! This claim is borne out by research on churchgoers that indicates gospel values are best lived out by those involved beyond the church service. In other words, values have to be explored and established

---

10. Van Gelder and Zscheile, *Missional Church in Perspective*, 110.

by interaction in small groups providing encouragement and opportunities to engage in the ongoing mission of the ascended Lord Jesus. This level of commitment is essential for life transformation to be realized.

Fellowship, the foundation of mutual ministry, is emphasized time and time again throughout the letters of the New Testament. It is not something we receive from a single source as a one-way action, as is evident from the mutual emphasis of the sixteen "one another" passages (Rom. 12:10; 12:16; 1 Pet. 3:8; Rom. 15:7; Gal. 5:13; Eph. 4:32; Col. 3:16; 1 Thess. 5:11; Heb. 3:13; 10:24; 1 Pet. 1:22; 4:9; 1 John 3:11; 3:23; 4:7; 4:11–12). Herein lies a further challenge to the contemporary church: Fellowship is not only something we receive and enjoy but also something in which we participate as we engage in mutual ministry and in the mission of Christ in the world. Jesus told his followers that as they ventured into the world to make disciples they would experience the reality of his assurance, "I am with you always, to the end of the age" (Matt. 28:20).

The Bond of Love

The Greek language has four words translated "love" in English: *agape, eros, philia*, and *storge*.

- *Agape* signifies initiative-taking, unconditional, sacrificial love.
- *Eros* means passionate love, which may or may not have sexual overtones.
- *Philia* designates love between friends, expressed in loyalty and devotion within the family or between friends.
- *Storge* signifies affection or even toleration.

Neither *eros* nor *storge* is used in the New Testament. Christian love (*agape*) is the fruit and evidence of the presence of Christ among his people. Paul writes, "The love of Christ urges us on" (2 Cor. 5:14). The entire redemptive work of Christ among his people arises out of "the great love with which he loved us," bringing resurrection life to the spiritually dead (Eph. 2:4–6).

At the heart of *agape* love is the announcement that "God so loved the world that he gave his only Son" (John 3:16). For Paul, "God demonstrates his own love for us in this: While we were still sinners, Christ died for us" (Rom. 5:8 NIV). These two verses highlight two aspects of *agape* love: it is self-giving, without limits; and it is an expression of the grace of God to the undeserving. God's love and the love displayed by those who love God can be known only in the actions that it prompts.

In the letters Paul addressed to the churches, the noun *agape* occurs forty-four times, and the verb *agapao* is found twenty-four times. They occur in reference to both God's love for us—demonstrated in Jesus Christ—and our love for God, which is God's love shed abroad in our hearts that we return to God. This same love we demonstrate in our love for one another and to the world that Christ came to save.

Paul notes that the source of *agape* love is the Lord (1 Thess. 3:12), who provides the supreme example of how Christians should love one another. Paul's teaching is further reinforced by the example of his love for the Thessalonians. The presence of love within the fellowship is a fruit of the Holy Spirit (Gal. 5:22). It is love that is in no way limited or restricted. It cannot be contained or confined within the fellowship but rather must flow out into the world, even in the face of persecution.

Love provides the fertile soil in which faith is rooted and can grow; as such it is both self-evident and anticipatory. The church fellowship is meant to be a school of love, where it grows and is refined and made robust in order to be released in the world. Consequently, Christians individually and the church collectively must ask, "Do we contribute to love or generate suspicion, prejudice, and judgmentalism?"

The empowering love of Christ is a constant theme throughout the New Testament, especially in the letters of Paul. To the Ephesians he writes, "I pray that you may have the power to comprehend, with all the saints, what is the breadth and length and height and depth, and to know the love of Christ that surpasses knowledge, so that you may be filled with all the fullness of God" (Eph. 3:18–19). The love of God infused in our hearts is quite literally unfathomable—you cannot touch bottom or penetrate its depth. Our understanding of the expansive dimensions of God's love only grows as we are rooted in it. We see in this passage that "the love of Christ is 'broad' enough to encompass all mankind . . . , 'long' enough to last for eternity, 'deep' enough to reach the most degraded sinner, and 'high' enough to exalt him to heaven."[11]

This is a startling insight—namely, that true knowledge is predicated on love. The knowledge to which Paul refers is the knowledge that comes from insight, reinforced by experience. It has to be grasped and held onto whether one is on the exhilarating mountaintop or in the darkest valley.

Within the body of Christ, we find great diversity among the members and in the gifts they have been given to participate in Christ's ongoing mission. But diversity must not result in divisiveness, as it did in Corinth. Sandwiched

---

11. Stott, *Ephesians*, 137.

between the two chapters dealing with spiritual gifts (1 Cor. 12 and 14) is the majestic chapter on love. Unfortunately, this passage, sometimes referred to as a "hymn of love," is often divorced from its context. It does not stand alone but as part of Paul's larger vision that every Spirit-inspired manifestation of ministry be motivated by a love that binds the whole together. For example, the gift of tongues or of prophecy—or even martyrdom—contributes nothing if love is absent. Love is the essential element in all relationships. "Love is patient; love is kind; love is not envious or boastful or arrogant or rude. It does not insist on its own way; it is not irritable or resentful; it does not rejoice in wrongdoing, but rejoices in the truth. It bears all things, believes all things, hopes all things, endures all things" (1 Cor. 13:4–7). Love is the overriding quality that abides and, from the perspective of eternity, is greater than faith and hope, for both faith and hope will no longer be necessary when all things are eventually fulfilled (1 Cor. 13:13).

Love is concerned with the welfare of all and not just for a restricted group within the fellowship (Rom. 15:2). It seeks to do good to all, especially those of the family of faith (Gal. 6:10). Love must endure for the long haul, weathering all circumstances. Paul reminds the Colossians, "Bear with one another and, if anyone has a complaint against another, forgive each other; just as the Lord has forgiven you, so you also must forgive. Above all, clothe yourselves with love, which binds everything together in perfect harmony" (Col. 3:13–14).

Genuine love demonstrates a person's willingness to give up his or her own desires and to show concern for the good of others (Rom. 5:6–8; 15:3; 2 Cor. 8:9; Phil. 2:4–8). It overcomes class, gender, and racial divisions. Such was the significance of the "holy kiss" with which all the brothers and sisters were to be greeted (1 Thess. 5:26). Such an intimate expression of affection and filial relationship signified the bridging of social divisions and reconciliation between former antagonists.

As Paul makes clear, the centrality of love must be maintained at all times and in all circumstances, for the very reason that God is love. The church needs this reminder in these days of severely eroded civility and courtesy. Social groups are preoccupied with their rights and entitlements, sometimes without regard to the corresponding rights and entitlements of those with opposing concerns. Relationships have become self-serving and manipulative. As one African Christian says of his experience of relationships among Christians in the West, "I find people are friendly, but do not make very good friends." Friendships endure as long as they are of mutual advantage, but in a time of need individuals can soon find themselves ignored and abandoned. Love is the basis of all true community. In other words, true community entails a common unity produced by the bond of love.

The Extended Family

In chapters 2 and 3, we considered the significance of the household in Paul's day. The early churches were household churches consisting of the extended family, which included slaves, freedmen, and their regular clientele. In Colossians Paul draws attention to the extended family when he addresses wives, husbands, children, slaves, and masters (Eph. 5:21–6:9; Col. 3:18–4:1). The Western norm of the nuclear family can lead to fragmentation and exclusion, an "us four and no more" mentality. Wayne Meeks comments on the notably different social reality of early churches: "To be 'baptized into Christ Jesus' . . . signaled for Pauline converts an extraordinarily thoroughgoing resocialization, in which the sect was intended to become virtually the primary group for its members, supplanting all other loyalties. The only convincing parallel in antiquity was conversion to Judaism, although adherence to the sects of the Pythagoreans or the Epicureans may in some cases have come close."[12] Paul applies the gospel to every area of life and does not shrink from addressing the complex relationships among those individuals who made up the household. In both the nuclear and extended family, relationships are extremely important. It is no easy task to hold together a community of people that spans the generations and reflects the cultural diversity of its social context.

A Christian fellowship, whose very life demonstrates the impact of the gospel, will display both reconciliation and mutual understanding. As these qualities become self-evident they will be an impressive sign of the reign of God. One large church in Southern California has begun "six-pack" men's groups. Each six-pack consists of one representative from each of six age groups: twenties, thirties, forties, fifties, sixties, and seventies. The groups have no set agenda but share their insights and experiences intergenerationally, as they study the Scriptures alongside life issues and things like music and film.

Onesimus and Philemon

Paul's letter to Philemon provides a further example of Paul's concern for the restoring of relationships. Philemon was a leader in the church in Colossae, and Onesimus was his former slave who had run away and found his way to Paul. At the time, he was not a believer and was apparently taking advantage of his master's conversion to Christ by failing to fulfill his obligations and by

---

12. Meeks, *First Urban Christians*, 78.

stealing from his master. Eventually the enormity of his actions apparently dawned on him, which could have resulted in his execution for desertion.

Knowing that his master, Philemon, held Paul in such high regard, Onesimus apparently sought out Paul in his prison and pleaded with him to intervene. On finding Paul, Onesimus yielded his life to Christ in repentance and faith, and for a time he served the apostle. Paul, convinced of the genuineness of his conversion, recognized the time had arrived for Onesimus to return to his master and face the consequences of his actions. He provided a letter for Onesimus to take to Philemon. That a letter on such a personal matter has been included in the New Testament is in itself a strong indication of its significance as a model of restored relationships.

The Philemon letter also displays Paul's sensitivity and tact in dealing with this delicate matter. In his prayers and thanksgiving for Onesimus, he begins with this commendation, which is significant considering the occasion that has prompted the letter: "I always thank my God because I hear of your love [agape] for all the saints and your faith toward the Lord Jesus" (Philem. 4–5). His love is motivated by faith, which cannot exclude slaves! It is on the basis of this agape love that Paul makes his appeal (Philem. 9–10). Paul informs Philemon that he has become Onesimus's "father" by virtue of leading him to Christ and nurturing his faith. The one who had become "useless" by his rebellious spirit has now become "useful," living up to his name (Onesimus means "useful").

Paul makes it abundantly clear that he is not returning Onesimus in order to be rid of him. Far from it. "I am sending him, that is, my own heart, back to you. I wanted to keep him with me, so that he might be of service to me in your place during my imprisonment for the gospel; but I preferred to do nothing without your consent" (Philem. 12–14).

Paul sees a greater purpose behind the rebellion of Onesimus, suggesting, "Perhaps this is the reason he was separated from you for a while, so that you might have him back forever, no longer as a slave but more than a slave, a beloved brother" (Philem. 15–16). This is striking language describing a significant change of status. At the same time, Paul is very practical in that he offers to repay Philemon for all that Onesimus had stolen. The inclusion of this personal letter within the New Testament illustrates how the gospel was establishing a new pattern of relationships and redefining traditional authority structures. This new pattern and its redefinition of authority was an important factor in the rapid expansion of Christianity from household to household.

In this significant incident, we see the restorative power of the gospel in both repairing broken relationships and setting them on a new plane. Such restorative power is just as significant in our day. A divided church loses its credibility in proclaiming a message of reconciliation. Paul's exhortation to the various members of the extended family should not be divorced from the life of the church. This is all too easy to do when our idea of church is little more than a weekly or occasional gathering in which relationships are shallow and peripheral. The contemporary church has to reinstate the concept of extended family. We do not *go* to church; we *are* the church.

As we established in the opening chapter, our hyperindividualistic Western culture has seriously eroded any sense of community and has undermined relationships. This atomizing of society has undermined long-term relationships built upon mutual accountability, with disastrous consequences for both the individual and the social context. The erosion of the latter has undermined our sense of identity and self-worth. Robert A. Fryling highlights the need to belong when he observes, "We have a need to belong because belonging is really 'a longing to be.' It is a longing to be who we are created to be. It is a longing to be with those who know us and love us, and ultimately it is a longing to be with our heavenly Father."[13]

Dealing with Divisions

In order to preserve and strengthen relationships, disagreements and divisions must be recognized and dealt with promptly rather than ignored. In the face of persecution, Christians are to stand side by side, without breaking rank. The greater the outside pressure, the more church members need to ensure harmony, for the enemy's tactic typically is to divide and conquer. Unity must be preserved both among members and between members and their leaders. The Thessalonian Christians are to both respect and esteem the leaders that have been appointed from among their ranks (1 Thess. 5:13). Divisions are especially prone to occur as the church finds itself under increasing pressure.

The early church was not immune to such tensions. Early in his letter to the believers in Philippi, Paul calls upon them to live in harmony (Phil. 2:2). He later urges them to "stand firm" and to stand together (Phil. 4:1–3). Paul mentions by name two women, Euodia and Syntyche, who are at loggerheads. (One wonders how they would have felt if they had known their disagreement would be recorded in Scripture and thus become so public!) Paul refuses to take sides, instead addressing another coworker—most likely one of his itinerant coworkers on the scene in Philippi—and asking him to intervene.[14]

13. Fryling, *Leadership Ellipse*, 123.
14. See Fee, *Philippians*, 168.

Paul strikes the same note in writing to the fractious fellowship in Corinth. "Now I appeal to you, brothers and sisters, by the name of our Lord Jesus Christ, that all of you be in agreement and that there be no divisions among you, but that you be united in the same mind and the same purpose" (1 Cor. 1:10). He is urging them to settle their differences, for the Lord's people are to live together in harmony.

Churches in our own day, just as in the time of Paul, must strive to live in conformity with the gospel, with their members demonstrating "humility and gentleness, with patience, bearing with one another in love, making every effort to maintain the unity of the Spirit in the bond of peace" (Eph. 4:2–3; cf. Col. 3:12–15). Like any institution, the church must brace itself to resist power struggles and make every effort to resolve personality clashes. Corporate accountability needs to be addressed in order to balance any undue emphasis on individual rights that has a tendency to occur within our individualistic Western cultures.

The overarching theme of the salvation message from Genesis to Revelation is the story of humankind's rebellion and alienation. Yet God does not abandon us. The good news consists of reconciliation offered by a holy God to sinful humankind on the basis of Christ's sacrifice on the cross and his triumphant resurrection. Reconciliation deals with more than separation; it includes transforming outright hostility into love for God. Paul's own journey from being a persecuting Jew to becoming a proclaimer of the gospel provides clear evidence of the reconciling power of his personal experience and the message he subsequently proclaimed. He can therefore convincingly remind the Gentiles, "In Christ Jesus you who once were far off have been brought near by the blood of Christ" (Eph. 2:13). We see here that reconciliation is not through denial or compromise but through the cross of Christ. Those who are reconciled enjoy a new status as adopted sons and daughters of the family of God.

Paul's first letter to the Corinthians gives warning of the damage caused by divisions in the church (1 Cor. 1:10–16). Groups are prone to become ingrown and to establish and guard their own boundaries. By identifying with an acknowledged leader in the church, they enhance their own prestige and reinforce their self-identity.

Apollos was a knowledgeable and eloquent teacher. Coming from Alexandria, he had the benefit of learning from the esteemed Jewish philosopher Philo. When he arrived at Ephesus, he was taught by Aquila and Priscilla, house-church leaders in the city (Acts 18:24–28). From there he had gone to Corinth, with the commendation of the believers in Ephesus, in order to teach the "Way of God," which Aquila and Priscilla had explained to him more accurately (Acts 18:26). His eloquence especially impressed one group, who claimed him as their own.

Others named Paul as their inspiration, while a different party identified with Cephas, and yet another group claimed to belong to Christ, perhaps out of a sense of spiritual superiority. The result of their rallying around a name was that they began to argue with one another in an attempt to establish their superior standing.

Such misplaced loyalty is not confined to the first-century church. Some church leaders seek to attract a following by denouncing others. In contrast, other church leaders do all in their power to discourage such emulation, insisting on making Christ preeminent, just as John the Baptizer did with his disciples. So that none could claim a special advantage, Paul refrained from baptizing. He was determined to do all in his power to avoid attracting a personal following (1 Cor. 1:14–17). His focus remained on the cross of Christ, where true spiritual power was to be found.

The fact that Paul devotes four chapters to the issue of divisions in the Corinthian church demonstrates just how serious he considered the problem. Notice that Paul does not single out any one group but rebukes them all, including the one group that claims him as their celebrity. Strife and jealousy are evidence of carnality, driven by the inclinations of the unredeemed self (1 Cor. 3:3–4). Paul is more concerned about their character and therefore is not blinded by the many gifts displayed by the believers in Corinth. True spirituality is displayed in fruitfulness rather than in giftedness (Gal. 5:22–23). It is the fruit of the Spirit that binds together diverse people into a unity of love and purpose.

Churches ministering within highly mobile urban society, with congregations made up of people representing diverse cultures, have to work hard to establish mutual understanding and empathy. The good news of Jesus Christ is a message of reconciliation. Consequently, churches representing reconciled and reconciling communities must seek to demonstrate before the watching world a unity that endures through tensions and disagreements. We cannot resort to demonizing the opposition but rather must work for mutual understanding and reconciliation.

There must always be room for differences of opinion. We must agree to differ, without losing respect for one another or denying that more knowledge and greater insight might show our position to be wrong. Paul is realistic enough to know that this will require great effort on the part of everyone. Just as in a marriage the partners have to learn to work through their disagreements and personality clashes, so it is in the extended family of the church.

Flashpoints arise between younger and older members of the church, between newcomers and longtime members, and between traditionalists and those who engage contemporary popular culture. These divisions can quickly turn into battlegrounds. In order to avoid this development, leaders need to stand in the gap as agents of reconciliation, interpreting one group to the other.

The focus of every member's attention must be on Christ alone, thereby avoiding the temptation to play one leader off against another. Paul concludes with this admonition: "So let no one boast about human leaders. For all things are yours, whether Paul or Apollos or Cephas or the world or life or death or the present or the future—all belong to you, and you belong to Christ, and Christ belongs to God" (1 Cor. 3:21–23).

The topic of love-forged unity is pertinent to our own day, in which there is an increasing tendency for Christians to go to secular courts to settle their grievances. Here in the United States we have become increasingly litigious: individual confronts individual and denominations take issue with particular churches, resorting to the courts at great financial cost, which only prompts public scorn. Again, this is not a new problem but one that Paul addressed in writing to the Corinthians. He admonishes the church to settle their own differences by internal arbitration rather than by appeals to unbelievers to judge between them (1 Cor. 6:1–11).

Engaging the World

The task of engaging the world in response to God's call to mission is a challenge that faces every follower of Christ and every faith community. The risen Christ has commissioned the whole church to take the whole gospel into the whole world. It is a task in which every member without exception is to be engaged. If we are called to identify with the death and resurrection of Christ in our baptism, we are at the same time called to participate in his mission. Australian missiologists Hirsch and Ford emphasize this principle. "Everyone in this movement, and not just the so-called religious professionals, must be activated and thus play a vital role in extending the mission of Jesus' church. The people involved in this dimension of people movements are those committed to full-time ministry *outside* of the church community . . . but it is still full-time ministry. In fact, this false distinction in what constitutes ministry is one of the major hurdles we have to overcome if we are going to activate as Jesus' people."[15]

Our understanding of mission must not be narrowed in order to pioneer evangelism, as important as that is. Nor must mission be considered an activity of the church in distant locations. The mission of the ascended Lord is

15. Hirsch and Ford, *Right Here, Right Now*, 32.

many sided, engaging every sphere of life, and applies as much to the here and now as to distant locations: "A missional movement must apply the gospel to all spheres of life (business, family, art, education, science, politics, etc.)—it cannot be limited simply to 'coming to church' or participating in building-based programs."[16]

Searching the letters of Paul, we find few exhortations for Christians to engage with the world. The most obvious explanation is that such exhortations were unnecessary precisely because the faith communities were already immersed in the world, and seeking to engage it with the message of the gospel. Such engagement consisted not only of verbal proclamation but also in their living the "abundant life" in all their relationships, brought about by the impact of the gospel on their lives. In theological terms, their witness was incarnational. Hirsch and Ford identify the three core practices of incarnational engagement as "proximity, frequency, and spontaneity."[17] In other words, the faith communities were readily accessible because they functioned in the marketplace and wherever people interacted. These faith communities did not engage in "raiding parties" into mission situations; they were not here today and gone tomorrow. In contrast, they belonged to those communities and engaged every day with the people around them. In addition, their strategy did not depend on artificially conceived programs but arose spontaneously in response to actual needs, some of which came suddenly and unexpectedly. As Hirsch and Ford point out,

> Rodney Stark . . . maintains that the greatest factor in the growth of early Christianity was the example of ordinary Christians living out their faith in their communities. In fact, he documents the fact that Christianity grew substantially at the time of the terrible plagues that swept the Roman Empire in the first few centuries; there were massive spikes in the growth of the church around these times. The reason for these growth spurts, he suggests, was because while all the pagans abandoned their sick and ran to the hills, the Christians stayed behind to care for the sick and many of them died in this sacrificial service. But many of the sick survived to tell the tale, and tell it they did. The sheer mercy and goodness of the ordinary, marginalized Christians stunned the pagan peoples of that time because such Christ-like compassion and service was unknown to them.[18]

The church today has at its disposal undreamt of resources compared to those available to the early church. Such resources are both a blessing and a

16. Ibid., 34.
17. Ibid., 50.
18. Ibid., 243.

drawback. Churches that are numerically strong have a plethora of programs largely for the benefit of existing church members, and those that enjoy a privileged and prestigious position in society can all too easily provide for themselves. These churches live an insular existence, characterized by their own language and preoccupations, with the result that they become increasingly irrelevant in relation to the trends and challenges of wider society. Worse than that, they may even buy into the values of their social context and become subverted by them.

Christians gain respect in the world through their hard work and integrity in their business dealings. Within the church itself, members must work with their own hands and not become dependent on others (1 Thess. 4:11–12). Paul set an example of hard work by supporting his ministry through his leatherworking trade (2 Thess. 3:7–10). Believers were not to make themselves a burden to others.

Offering hospitality to fellow Christians was important among the early churches, because inns were notorious for immoral activities. In order to meet the needs of missionaries and messengers of the church and other Christians who happened to be traveling, churches provided an extended family, giving lodging and assistance for the journey.[19] But traveling Christians were not to trade upon or abuse the hospitality offered. The first generation of Christians had to safeguard their reputations to ensure the credibility of their witness. They were not to become troublemakers among their neighbors, but were to be industrious, making a positive contribution to society.

Paul is so concerned that idleness will bring discredit on the church that he gives a solemn warning in his second letter to the Thessalonians. Apparently, idleness had become ingrained in those whom Paul had addressed in his first letter, and they had failed to respond to his admonition (2 Thess. 3:6–13). G. K. Beale suggests that the warning is issued not so much against the idle as to the disorderly. These busybodies were not productive; they were interferers hindering the spread of the gospel.[20]

Facing Opposition and Persecution

Early churches were birthed in situations of suspicion and hostility. Paul, who before his conversion was a persecutor of Christians, had experienced both sides of the dividing line. The church in Judea eventually heard of Paul's conversion,

19. See Ferguson, *Backgrounds of Early Christianity*, 89.
20. Beale, *1–2 Thessalonians*, 257.

that "the one who formerly was persecuting us is now proclaiming the faith he once tried to destroy" (Gal. 1:23). Now as an apostle, Paul was constantly on the receiving end of accusations and violence, beginning in Jerusalem (Acts 9:28–30) and continuing during his first missionary journey in southern Galatia (Acts 13:50; 14:2–5, 18). During his second and third missionary journeys, he continued to encounter opposition: in Philippi (Acts 16:19; Phil. 3:2–4), in Corinth (Acts 18:12), in Ephesus (Acts 20:19), and in Colossae (Col. 2:1–14).

Paul faced numerous charges from his opponents, including charges of heresy, creating civil disturbances, and treason (Acts 9:28–34; 17:5–9). In case we might think that Paul, because of his personality, brought this upon himself, we need to remember that such opposition predated Paul. Stephen was stoned to death (Acts 6:8–7:60); Peter was imprisoned for his witness to Christ as Messiah (Acts 12:6); and James the brother of John was run through with a sword (Acts 12:2).

The opposition encountered by Paul spilled over to the faith communities that he established. For instance, from the time of its birth, the church in Thessalonica underwent severe suffering. Yet despite this adversity, it demonstrated joy inspired by the Holy Spirit (1 Thess. 1:6–7).

Churches seeking to bear witness to the gospel in the pluralistic West are likely to meet with increasing suspicion, misrepresentation, and hostility. There are already isolated examples of legal action against Christian activities both in the United Kingdom and in the United States. Discriminatory legislation is being drawn up and enacted regarding conditions of adoption, the public reading or display of Scripture passages, and those refusing to affirm homosexual activity and same-sex unions. There are also widespread initiatives to rewrite school curricula in order to mainstream gay and lesbian relationships and to redefine marriage.

If and when hostility increases, Christians must ensure that they bear witness with boldness and grace, remembering Jesus's exhortation to love our enemies. The churches in the West can learn much from examples of Christians who suffer for their faith today in parts of the world where they are a marginalized minority. Just as the early church did, Christians today can experience the joy of the Holy Spirit, which is not dependent on favorable circumstances. When individuals or churches experience opposition or persecution, they need to step back and see it in the broader context of history and of Christians and churches around the world.

In response to a climate that is less tolerant of Christian values and the witness of the church, we Western Christians need to rediscover a theology of suffering, and we need to do so without developing a persecution complex. Sometimes the suspicion and opposition Christians experience is deserved on account of our insensitive attitudes and counterproductive approaches—for instance, when we resort to confrontation instead of engaging in respectful dialogue in taking a stand on those issues that we consider to be nonnegotiable.

Fortunately, the New Testament in general, and the apostle Paul in particular, has a lot to teach with respect to persecution and suffering. In writing to the Thessalonians, Paul offers strong words against both the church's Jewish opponents and its pagan critics. The Thessalonian church's experience of persecution from such critics was not exceptional but was widely shared among the churches recently established by Paul. "For you, brothers and sisters, became imitators of the churches of God in Christ Jesus that are in Judea, for you suffered the same things from your own compatriots as they did from the Jews" (1 Thess. 2:14). He communicates the same message to the Philippians, to whom he is writing while in jail. "For he has graciously granted you the privilege not only of believing in Christ, but of suffering for him as well—since you are having the same struggle that you saw I had and now hear I still have" (Phil. 1:29–30). In the face of Jewish opposition, Paul was determined to continue in his Christ-appointed mission (Acts 11:18; 13:46–49; 28:28; Rom. 1:16).

Suffering, rather than promoting a victim or martyr mentality, is a gift from God for which we should give thanks (Phil. 1:29). Beale issues this solemn warning from Scripture to those who attack the gospel and its faithful adherents: "Never-ending hostility to God and his goal of redemption will warrant never-ending punishment."[21]

In presenting the gospel, we must not hide the costs involved in responding. Following Christ entails taking up our cross daily. Identifying with the crucified Lord means becoming a target of ridicule, mockery, and destructive forces. If we simply emphasize the benefits, then people will feel conned or feel that God has unfairly singled them out.

In contrast to the teaching of the prosperity gospel, Paul's message, not only to the Thessalonians but to many of the churches, clearly conveys that suffering is an unavoidable part of the Christian life (Phil. 1:29; 1 Thess. 3:3, 4; see also 1 Pet. 1:6; 2:21; 3:17; 4:19). In confronting mounting opposition, Christians must ensure that they stand together, maintaining their orderly ranks (Eph. 6:13; 1 Thess. 3:8). Paul encourages the Philippian Christians to rise above present circumstances as citizens of heaven, so that he may know they are "standing firm in one spirit, striving side by side with one mind for the faith of the gospel" (Phil. 1:27; see also 3:20).

Engaging in spiritual warfare must never lead to seeking revenge or retribution; these must be left in God's hands. In the face of persecution, Christians are sustained by Christ's triumph on the cross over evil. Indeed, Christians

---

21. Ibid., 83.

can boast in what Christ has achieved. John Stott strikes the balance in this regard. "When talking to God, we *thank* him for his grace; when talking to human beings, we *boast* of his grace. . . . If we follow his example, we will avoid both congratulation (which corrupts) and silence (which discourages)."[22]

After centuries of cultural affirmation and toleration, the church in the West might be tempted to seek acceptance through compromise or silence. Ultimately, Christians will have to make up their minds about where their true loyalty lies. You cannot both run with the hare and hunt with the hounds for very long. The early church had to decide whether its allegiance was to the Roman emperor or to Jesus.

Building and Protecting Relationships

Establishing one's identity is not simply a matter of independent self-definition. Identity is related to belonging. In order to sustain their distinctive identity, the Corinthians needed to be reminded that they belonged to God. As God's adopted children, they continually call upon God. Paul opens his first Corinthian letter by addressing the church in the following terms: "To the church of God that is in Corinth, to those who are sanctified [set apart] in Christ Jesus, called to be saints, together with all those who in every place call on the name of our Lord Jesus Christ, both their Lord and ours" (1 Cor. 1:2). In this opening greeting, identity is both local and geographically extensive, reaching beyond the congregation and even the city to "every place."

The unique character of the relationships among members of the faith community arises from their being collectively called and set apart by God to develop a transforming relationship, with the potential to significantly impact the world as well. Their calling is not something they have earned but stems from the unmerited generosity of God. In biblical terminology, it is theirs through God's *grace*, which establishes a new relationship that brings *peace*, here signifying wholeness and unity.

Today we need the reminder that whatever Christian fellowship we belong to, we are part of the same church that is Christ's body here on earth. We must never lose sight of this essential global identity, especially when disagreements threaten to cause divisions. What unites us is greater than anything that could divide us.

Because opponents in all locations were trying to drive a wedge between Paul and the faith communities birthed through his ministry, building and

22. Stott, *1 & 2 Thessalonians*, 144–45.

protecting relationships was for him an intensely personal matter. For instance, in his second letter to the Corinthians, Paul paves the way for his third visit to the church by reminding them of his parental relationship with them (2 Cor. 12:14; see also 1 Cor. 4:14; 1 Thess. 2:11). He challenges the claims of "super-apostles" vying for their allegiance by highlighting the signs of an authentic apostle. "The signs of a true apostle were performed among you with utmost patience, signs and wonders and mighty works" (2 Cor. 12:12). These signs and wonders were not to enhance Paul's prestige; rather, they accompanied his ministry as the Holy Spirit brought new life through the gospel among those he had been commissioned to evangelize. Paul makes it clear that the power he demonstrated was not his own but God's power working through him (2 Cor. 13:3–4).

Consideration for others within the fellowship must be the primary concern of every believer, as Paul reminds the Philippians: "If then there is any encouragement in Christ, any consolation from love, any sharing in the Spirit, any compassion and sympathy, make my joy complete: be of the same mind, having the same love, being in full accord and of one mind. Do nothing from selfish ambition or conceit, but in humility regard others as better than yourselves" (Phil. 2:1–3). His use of the word *if* is not to indicate uncertainty but to signify "if as is certainly the case." It is their failure to live out the kind of fellowship the Holy Spirit makes possible that casts the shadow of doubt. Unity is not achieved by simply papering over the cracks. Nor is it achieved by being highly selective in the issues we choose to highlight, in order to exclude those individuals or groups who pose a threat or do not measure up to our expectations.

Relationship building requires the renunciation of any selfish ambition. Even those who proclaim Christ may do so from a variety of motives. Paul is aware of those who proclaim the gospel out of selfish ambition, seeking to enhance their own standing now that Paul is in prison (Phil. 1:17). Although their activities increase his suffering, he puts aside personal considerations. "What does it matter? Just this, that Christ is proclaimed in every way, whether out of false motives or true; and in that I rejoice" (Phil. 1:18).

Those who operated out of questionable motives were taking advantage of Paul's incarceration to promote their own ministry. Perhaps their agenda, as distinct from that of Paul, was to restore the balance by favoring the Jews over the Gentiles. There are people who use the church in order to pursue their own agendas in enhancing their political power, social standing, spiritual status, economic advantage, and so forth.

Whenever there is a leadership vacuum or the church undergoes a time of leadership transition, power struggles are likely. Party interests then take precedence over the wider issue of identifying those most qualified to continue advancing the gospel and the health of the church. Infighting results in more energy being exerted on domestic matters than in carrying out the mission of the church. As Jesus reminded his followers, "If a house is divided against itself, that house will not be able to stand" (Mark 3:25). Aware of this fact, Paul is determined that in the proclamation of the gospel all sections of the church should present a common front.

Building healthy relationships enhances the witness of the church, such that they "shine like stars in the sky" (Phil. 2:15 NIV). When viewing the night sky, the darker the surroundings, the brighter the stars shine, as anyone who has gazed into cloudless heavens on a moonless night from a deserted place, mountaintop, or ship's deck can testify. When Christians grumble, complain, and fight with one another, they no longer shine before the world. Their light is immediately dimmed and eventually extinguished. They do not have the liberty of narrowing the agenda of accountability before God. Rather, they are to "do all things without murmuring or arguing" (Phil. 2:14).

Respecting Diversity among Members

Churches do not have the liberty of screening members to ensure that the new people they receive are socially acceptable. Unity in the church is not achieved through uniformity or even compatibility. To the contrary, the churches of the New Testament were characterized by social and economic diversity. Paul reminds the strife-torn churches of Galatia, "There is no longer Jew or Greek, there is no longer slave or free, there is no longer male and female; for all of you are one in Christ Jesus" (Gal. 3:28).

The founding members of the church in Philippi included a businesswoman from Thyatira and a Roman centurion jailer. The church in Corinth had a former member of the synagogue, a city treasurer, and no doubt other successful businesspeople. But the majority of the members were without formal education, social standing, or cultural sophistication. Yet they were all drawn together by a common calling as sinners who had responded by faith to the good news made known to them by the grace of God (1 Cor. 1:26–31).

By operating from the bottom of society up through the social strata, rather than from the top down, God shows that the advance of the gospel and the evidence of its transformative power are achieved by God's grace and power alone. By this priority God shames the wise and the strong, and reduces "to nothing things that are, so that no one might boast in the presence of God" (1 Cor. 1:29). Evangeline Booth, speaking out of the early experience of the

Salvation Army, reminded the church at large that "Christianity is a going down not a going up kind of religion."[23] The journey to the cross is a painful descent, yet, paradoxically, it is also the pathway to resurrection power.

The diversity of the church's membership also provides evidence that unity is not achieved through uniformity; rather, unity is demonstrated in an amazing diversity essential for the functioning of the body. The human body consists of a skeletal structure, organs, muscles, and so forth, all of which work in harmony in a healthy body. As Paul expresses it, the body does not consist of one member but of many (1 Cor. 12:14). Consequently, diversity among the members must be respected and celebrated by all.

Paul goes on to develop the metaphor with a touch of humor. The foot, for its part, must not think that because it is not a hand it does not belong to the body. A foot is not a clumsy hand. It is designed and placed in the body to perform functions that the hand would be unable to undertake for any length of time. A handstand can be maintained for only a brief period! Similarly, ears and eyes have very different functions, both of which are essential for the body. So neither feet nor ears should make inappropriate comparisons. It is God who arranges the members in the body as God chooses.

If the foot and ear are prone to demonstrate an inferiority complex, the hand and eye may become guilty of a superior attitude. The hand must not look down (literally!) at the foot, saying, "I have no need of you," thus making the foot feel that it has no place in the body. Neither should the head address the feet with the same dismissive attitude (see 1 Cor. 12:14–21). But Paul goes even further, stating that those functions of the body that we consider less honorable or that we take for granted are just as vital for the functioning of the body. Consider, for example, the hidden but vital functions of the kidneys, liver, and thyroid.

The 1 Corinthians 12 passage prompts us to consider which ministries in the church are given the most recognition. It is all too easy to focus attention on those individuals who have a high public profile due to the particular functions they perform: preaching and teaching, performing in the musical program, or running a program. But we can readily overlook, or take for granted, the many individuals who perform humble and thankless tasks, including keeping the restrooms clean and tidy, changing diapers in the nursery, and unstacking and stacking chairs and tables. Furthermore, the church must ask itself whether it recognizes sufficiently those whose ministry takes place outside of the institutional church: public school teachers, law enforcement officers, firefighters, and medical personnel, among others.

23. I was unable to trace the source of this well-known quote.

Maintaining unity also entails showing respect to those whose viewpoints and tastes differ from our own. Such consideration is especially important in relation to our attitudes in worship. Corporate worship is designed to unite rather than divide, so it must include elements with which different segments of the worshiping community can identify. As believers meet around the Lord's Table, we are united in eating the one bread and drinking from the one cup. The Eucharist is a powerful reminder of the price that Christ himself was prepared to pay for our reconciliation to himself and to one another. We are indeed made one body in Christ (1 Cor. 10:16–18).

The frequently used term *worship wars* is in reality an oxymoron, but it highlights the need to address cultural and generational preferences in an attitude of mutual understanding, or at least one of tolerance. Problems arising in the church in Corinth highlight the need for sensitivity regarding traditions and customs. Their issues may be foreign to our contexts, but the underlying principles apply.

For instance, Paul argues that women should worship with their heads covered (1 Cor. 11:1–16), which has nothing to do with women wearing hats in church. Rather, Paul is insisting that "liberated" women parading their freedom in culturally offensive ways show lack of consideration for others. N. T. Wright suggests that "perhaps some of the Corinthian women had been taking him [Paul] literally, so that when they prayed or prophesied aloud in church meetings (which Paul assumes they will do regularly; this tells us something about how to understand 14:34–35) they had decided to remove their normal head covering, perhaps also unbraiding their hair, to show that in the Messiah they were free from the normal social conventions by which men and women were distinguished."[24] Paul was aware that the actions of the women in uncovering their heads and unbraiding their hair were likely to be misconstrued, especially by visitors from the pagan world. Women who behaved in that manner were generally assumed to be prostitutes. N. T. Wright captures the spirit of the passage when he writes, "If the watching world discovered that the Christians were having meetings where women 'let their hair down' in this fashion, it could have the same effect on their reputation as it would in the modern West if someone looked into church and found the women all wearing bikinis."[25]

What are we to make of Paul's reasoning that a woman should cover her head as a symbol of subservience to her husband, which on the surface seems to be his argument? First, there is another way of interpreting this passage that is consistent with Paul's statement that "there is no longer male and female;

24. Wright, *1 Corinthians*, 140.
25. Ibid., 140–41.

for all of you are one in Christ Jesus" (Gal. 3:28). Wright notes that "in the Western world we don't like the implications of the differentiation he maintains in verse 3"—where the man has assumed superiority over the woman, just as the Messiah is "head" of the church in this sense. At least this is how it is frequently interpreted in the Western world. Against this view, Wright suggests,

> A good case can be made out for saying that in verse 3 he is referring not to "headship" in the sense of sovereignty, but to "headship" in the sense of "source," like the "source" or "head" of a river. In fact, in some of the key passages where he explains what he is saying (verses 8, 9 and 12a) he is referring explicitly to the creation story in Genesis 2, where woman was made from the side of man.
>
> The underlying point then seems to be that in worship it is important for both men and women to be their truly created selves, to honor God by being what they are and not blurring the lines by pretending to be something else.[26]

Although the cultural issues are different in the contemporary church, the underlying principle remains—namely, that the various groups in the church must be sensitive to one another's perspectives, interpretations, and preferences. This is especially important for worship in relation to tastes in music. Not every hymn or worship song will appeal to all. Sometimes musical styles may even be difficult to tolerate; for instance, older generations often say contemporary worship music is played so loud that they cannot hear the words. But it is important to provide times of worship that embrace all generations and musical tastes. Most people want to come to church to sing their favorite hymns and worship songs. Are they equally prepared to sing the favorites of other people?

It is legitimate to examine the biblical content of all that we sing, especially considering that our theology is shaped more by songs than by sermons. Much contemporary worship reflects both the strengths and the weaknesses of the culture it expresses. On the one hand, it is strong on relationships, addressing God directly rather than speaking about God. On the other hand, many contemporary songs are highly individualistic in nature, stressing "me" and "my" at the expense of a corporate understanding of worship. More traditional worship incorporates hymns that are rich in theological and biblical content. These two approaches must not divide into warring camps but must instead discover mutual enrichment, for the twin emphases of relationships and theologically rich content are needed in intergenerational worship.

Another issue on display in Corinth is one very much with us today—the division between rich and poor—which will undermine the very nature of

26. Ibid., 141.

worship if left unchallenged (1 Cor. 11:17–22). In addition to economic discrimination, we must also add racial and gender exclusion. Such issues assume greater significance when churches meet in homes and worship takes place in the context of a meal, as was the practice in the early church. N. T. Wright helpfully describes the New Testament social context: "Many rich people in the ancient world prided themselves on showing hospitality to those less well off, but they often did so in a way which let the others know they were inferior, and even made them feel ashamed. Sometimes they had a small main dining room for themselves and their closest friends, where excellent food and wine would be served, and another room, or a sequence of rooms, with food and drink of poorer quality."[27] Likewise, churches today must ensure that their fellowship is not undermined by events that emphasize social prejudice or economic inequality. They must ensure that there is equal access to all programs, so that poorer members are not excluded because they cannot afford the costs involved.

Courage to Confront

Throughout Paul's letters we find him addressing specific moral issues in which the churches are embroiled. He is determined to confront painful issues, recognizing their power to corrode and destroy if not exposed and dealt with in a discerning and forthright manner. He appeals to the church in Corinth to "make room in your hearts for us" (2 Cor. 7:2). Paul had undergone sufferings of all kinds on behalf of the churches. He lists these sufferings in chapter 11, concluding with the admission, "Besides other things, I am under daily pressure because of my anxiety for all the churches" (2 Cor. 11:28).

Paul has to be brutally frank in addressing specific issues to ensure that healthy relationships are maintained. He confronts sexual immorality in the form of incest (1 Cor. 5:1–13) and the failure to control sexual appetites (1 Cor. 6:12–20). Kenneth Chafin highlights the moral challenges facing the Corinthian church when he states, "The problem within the Corinthian church was how to resist the pressure of conforming to an immoral society. After all, they had only recently been a part of that world, and they brought into the church deeply ingrained habits of thought and action which stood in stark contrast with the ideals that God had for them in their new relationship with him."[28]

Paul also takes the church to task for allowing lawsuits between believers to be brought before pagan courts (1 Cor. 6:1–8). They must be prepared

27. Ibid., 146.
28. Chafin, *1, 2 Corinthians*, 67.

to settle their own differences, thereby demonstrating the strength of their relationships. It is better to accept injustice than to expose the fellowship to scandal and ridicule from society at large.

Summary

We have argued in the opening chapter that the ills of contemporary society, and the economic and moral challenges it faces, cannot be adequately addressed by political, economic, and social programs. As important as these may be, trying to implement them without strong relational networks in place will be like pouring water into the sand. Relationship building is crucial, and the church can play a significant role in this regard if it lives out the values of the gospel in the power of the Holy Spirit before a watching world. It cannot pretend to be an ideal society, for the church does not fully encapsulate the reign of God. It is always the becoming church, serving as a sign and servant of God's future kingdom. In our divided and competitive world, the church's role is to demonstrate the possibility of reconciliation and mutual respect.

Regrettably, the contemporary church more often mirrors the divisiveness and discourtesy so prevalent in society. The church must repent of succumbing to the standards of our culture and turn to the gospel for the renewal of *its* relationships if it is to demonstrate the gospel's transforming and reconciling power to the world.

Conclusion:

People change through the forging of relationships that provide support, encouragement, and mutual accountability, which enable individuals to discover their identity and ministry.

9

Mission and Ministry,
Then and Now

One of the greatest challenges in activating and equipping the members of the local church for ministry in the church and mission in the world is the consumer culture that the great majority of churches have generated and sustained over many centuries. The result of this departure from an understanding of the church as the body of Christ, in which every member has both a place and a function, is an overreliance on professional clergy. In this scenario, the clergy serve a largely passive congregation who show up to have their spiritual and social needs met.

In recent decades there has been an increasing emphasis on "every-member ministry," but this attitude is notoriously difficult to establish in congregations dominated by a consumer attitude. In such contexts a small segment of the membership typically steps forward to exercise ministries in accordance with their gifts and interests, and others may be persuaded to get involved in one or another area of ministry, but the vast majority of members remain largely passive. The 80/20 rule—that 80 percent of the work is done by 20 percent of the people—seems to apply.

Addressing Consumerist Inertia

In response to the challenges presented by congregational inertia, church leaders often resort to preaching series of sermons laying out the biblical principle of every-member ministry, and this is an important first step. Then seminars are introduced to provide further teaching on the various ways in which the Holy Spirit gifts individual members to play their part. These often include spiritual-gifts inventories that participants are invited to fill out. It is hoped that their answers to the long list of questions will help them identify their particular gifts.

The challenge persists for church leaders to match individuals to a specific ministry in the church. Such efforts will usually produce some positive results, with more members identifying their gifts and getting involved in appropriate areas of ministry. The problem, especially for larger churches, is that this process is very labor intensive, with many people falling through the cracks. Having identified their gifts, they remain disengaged and become disillusioned. Despite strenuous efforts, the majority of members remain stubbornly passive.

There are two underlying issues that need to be addressed, issues that we covered in chapters 6 and 8 but now need to relate specifically to the emergence of ministry and mission. First, the consumer-driven church has produced undiscipled church members on a vast scale, with the majority of them also, but only loosely, connected to other members of the body of Christ. Many wise commentators have noted that you do not first gather a church and then seek to make disciples out of the attendees. Rather, you first make disciples and from them build a church. Those who engage in ministry must first be authentic Christ-followers.

Second, ministry arises out of relationships, not out of seminars and gift-identification questionnaires. As we have seen, the churches of the New Testament were small and met in homes with a capacity of twenty to thirty-five persons, which enabled members to know each other intimately. Furthermore, within the household structure, many if not all members worked together throughout the week. They were aware therefore of one another's temperaments, interests, and skills, as well as the contribution each made to the dynamics of the team. When such relationships are nonexistent or are shallow and intermittent, it is an uphill battle to get those disconnected persons involved in any form of ministry.

The problem arises because we have taken the passive, consumer model of church for granted for far too long. This model of church is not one that can be built upon. It has to be dismantled, and the church brought into line with the New Testament norm of faith communities composed of disciples engaged in mutual ministry. In such environments, ministries and leadership arise spontaneously. At the same time, these faith communities require engaged and discerning leadership—hence Paul's focus on establishing elders in every church.

Simply moving people from being couch potatoes in front of their televisions to becoming "pew warmers" in front of the pulpit or altar does not represent significant progress. Within Western cultures we need to take steps to move from being a passive society to being a participatory one, and the church should be taking the lead in this regard. It is called to demonstrate an alternative society that tackles both loneliness and agressiveness. Fulfilling this call is especially important in societies experiencing high unemployment, increasing economic deprivation, and the breakdown of law and order and the ability to discern right from wrong. In response, churches need to work together and alongside other community groups, whether religious or secular, for community solidarity.

Paul's letters offer valuable insights into the emergence of local ministry. Even the small faith communities he addressed displayed a diversity of ministries. This diversity indicates the manifold ministries that the ascended Lord continues to exercise through each local church by the enabling of the Holy Spirit. The challenge is to achieve diversity without fragmentation. Exclusive focus on the diversity of gifts can result in churches being pulled in different directions by dominant individuals or pressure groups. As we examine this vitally important topic of ministry development, we will gain valuable insights from the letters of Paul.

Essential Dimensions of Ministry

The diversity of the gifts of the Spirit is impressive. There is no comprehensive list of these gifts to be found in the New Testament. The lists that are included provide examples rather than identify them in their totality. If we attempt to compile a comprehensive list out of those lists mentioned in various places in the New Testament, we arrive at a total of about twenty-six. It is difficult to bring these together into an integrated whole, or to decide which are the most significant in the life of a particular church at each phase of its development. What is needed is an overarching framework into which the gifts can be clustered to show how they complement and reinforce one another. This is where the five interlocking spheres of ministry that Paul describes in Ephesians 4:4–13 are of such significance.[1]

The passage in question has usually been interpreted in one of two restrictive ways. The first limits its purview to the first generation of the church, on the assumption that the apostolic role here referred to came to an end following

---

1. Alan Hirsch and Tim Catchim, *The Permanent Revolution,* provide the most comprehensive, scholarly, and practical exposition of this passage.

the deaths of the Twelve. The second allows for the continuance of all five spheres of ministry identified in Ephesians 4, but links these to leadership in the church to the marginalization of the total membership.

With regard to the former, we draw attention once again to the New Testament's use of the term *apostle* in both a narrow and a broader sense. Within the Gospels, it refers to the twelve apostles appointed by Christ as the foundation on which he will build his church. However, Paul uses the term in a much broader sense. When he identifies individuals by name as apostles of the church, none of them is included in the twelve original apostles chosen by Christ himself. For Paul, apostles are groundbreakers who establish churches and have an ongoing concern for them.

With regard to the latter, when the Ephesians 4 passage on the fivefold ministry is read in the broader context of the whole chapter, it is clear that Paul is speaking of the entire body of believers being involved in one or more spheres of ministry. God's grace is extended to every person in the body without exception. They are appointed by the ascended Christ and not simply selected by the leadership. The role of the leaders in each of the five spheres is to help individuals discern God's gifting and call and to set them in an appropriate context of supportive relationships.

First, during the Christendom era, with its static and institutional understanding of church, the focus was almost exclusively on the role of the pastor-teacher as providing leadership for existing churches. This emphasis was to the neglect of the role of the apostle, the prophet, and the evangelist. This restrictive view of leadership has contributed to the static image of the church. Insistence on the inclusion of the other three roles does not diminish the importance of the pastor (shepherd) and teacher. In the twenty-first century, as in the first century, these two closely related roles are essential for the well-being of any Christian community. The breakdown of the family and high work-related stress levels in our day call for the pastoral ministry of the church, to help members through difficult times.

Second, with the current widespread biblical illiteracy, the role of the teacher has never been more important. Western churches have so focused on a therapeutic and need-related "gospel" that church members have lost sight of the big story of God's unfolding plan of redemption revealed in the Scriptures from Genesis through Revelation. Furthermore, as a consequence of the absence of apostolic leadership, the vast majority of churches have become preoccupied with internal concerns to the neglect of their commission to engage in mission to the world.

When the pastor-teacher model of leadership becomes dominant, the congregation tends to become introverted and self-focused. The church's ministry is out of balance precisely because it has neglected the other three spheres of ministry identified in Ephesians 4. During the centuries in which Christendom prevailed in the Western world, the negative consequences of restricting ministry to pastor-teachers went largely unnoticed. The essential nature and urgency of the ministries of apostle, prophet, and evangelist were either marginalized or ignored because local churches had an established position within society. Though Christianity began as a dynamic movement, over time the church became largely a static institution. The entrepreneurial ministries of the church by default became the concern of parachurch ministries, operating either on the home front or as mission agencies pioneering overseas. By outsourcing its mission obligation, the church drove a wedge between ecclesiology and missiology, to their mutual impoverishment.

Now that the churches in the West find themselves in a post-Christendom context in which an increasing number of churches struggle to survive, or find that they no longer have the resources to meet their situation, the neglected ministries of apostle, prophet, and evangelist assume much greater significance. *Apostles*, in the Pauline understanding of that term, ensure that the church is no longer a static institution but that it is breaking new ground by birthing and nurturing new faith communities.

Each local church needs to identify those in its midst with an apostolic calling and passion and needs to commission them to launch new outreach ministries to take the gospel to segments of the local community that remain largely unreached and overlooked. Apostles may have a particular burden for a geographical area, whether near or far; alternatively, their calling may be to reach a particular lifestyle enclave.

Prophets are individuals who have learned to listen to God and to speak God's word—which may be a word of encouragement, guidance, or rebuke—into particular situations. In the absence of that sensitivity, the church can readily become subverted by the surrounding culture. It then becomes more a mirror of those prevailing values than a light of the gospel, exposing and challenging accepted norms that are contrary to the values inherent in the reign of God. The prophet agitates for the church to reorder its priorities accordingly.

In the majority of historic churches, the role of *evangelist* is ignored or, at best, marginalized in the life of the local church and the ministry structures of the denomination. Consequently, those called to evangelism must either connect with a parachurch agency or establish their own independent organizations. Within the early church, in contrast, we see clear evidence that evangelization was not a hiccup in the life of the church but was its very heartbeat.

Negative Consequences of Reliance on a Solo Pastor

Alan Hirsch contends that within churches emphasizing pulpit ministry, about 5 percent of the church is active in ministry. Churches emphasizing a wider contribution of persons leading public worship and range of elective programs fare little better, with about 10 percent of the church active in ministry. Hirsch says that in such churches most of the people "are in a receptive mode and basically receive the services offered. That is, they are basically *consumptive*. They come to 'get fed.' But is this a faithful image of the church? Is the church really meant to be a 'feeding trough' for otherwise capable middle-class people who are getting their careers on track?"[2] So firmly entrenched is this established pattern that it requires great skill and patience to guide a church through the transition process. This is not a challenge confined solely to traditional churches but one that both independent megachurches and new emerging churches also face, especially those whose main attraction is a high-profile celebrity preacher and performer.

The challenge facing the church today consists in the development and integration of each of the five areas of ministry described by Paul in his letter to the Ephesians. A solo pastor cannot be expected to fill each of these five roles. We have seen abundant evidence of the negative consequences of relying on a solo pastor to perform in areas for which God never equipped him or her.[3] The solo-pastor model leads to unrealistic expectations among church leaders and congregation members. Paul, the apostle who is typically on the move, could easily have become a loner in his mission calling. But Paul works with a team, within which he is mentoring young leaders. As we have seen, Paul frequently mentions his coworkers by name in his letters.

In churches that operate with a solo- or lead-pastor model, the weaknesses of the current pastor tend to be contrasted with the strengths of his or her predecessor. Some churches looking for a new pastor try to replicate the gifts of the predecessor; they want another gifted preacher or another shepherd to provide loving one-on-one pastoral care or another leader whose primary gift is evangelism.

A second consequence of the established norm of the solo pastor is an inevitable male gender bias. In response to such male dominance of the past, some denominations have increasingly emphasized the need for female leadership. But this new emphasis can result in the creation of the opposite problem—the feminizing of the church. We have argued that team leadership was the norm

---

2. Hirsch, *Forgotten Ways*, 43.
3. The latest available data indicates that "the majority of American congregations average about 100 persons in attendance on a typical weekend and [have] a paid staff of seldom more than one professional and a few part-time support staff" (Roozen, *Decade of Change*).

in the early churches and that the team included both men and women, some-times married couples.

A third consequence of this overreliance on one individual is the margin-alizing of other people with leadership potential. Leaders who feel insecure become controlling and suspicious of initiatives by individuals or groups. Spiritual gifts do not flourish in a hierarchical, controlling environment.

A fourth consequence is burnout or blowup arising from solo pastors' in-ability to meet all of the ministry expectations placed upon them. There is disturbing evidence of a high casualty rate among pastors.[4] Many have not only left the church they were serving but have abandoned pastoral ministry altogether, because they were so severely hurt in the church or churches they endeavored to serve. Others, while not physically leaving their pastoral min-istry, have sought emotional escape in illicit sexual affairs or pornography.

All Are Engaged in Ministry and Mission

Clearly, the severe strains on the traditional restrictive model could be alleviated by a return to the Pauline pattern of ministry, which was diverse in nature and polycentric in structure. Notice that the task of this fivefold ministry was "to equip the saints for the work of the ministry, for building up the body of Christ, until all of us come to the unity of the faith and of the knowledge of the Son of God, to maturity, to the measure of the full stature of Christ" (Eph. 4:12–13). Attaining this level of maturity entails the involvement of every member in one or another of the spheres of ministry. Contrary to the interpretation of many commentators, the Ephesians 4 model is not confined to leaders but is addressed to every member of the body of Christ. Paul introduces the topic by reminding the church members, "But each of us was given grace according to the measure of Christ's gift" (Eph. 4:7).

The purpose in identifying the five spheres of ministry is not leadership se-lection but member distribution, "to equip the saints for the work of ministry" (Eph. 4:12). This is not to deny that leadership needs to be exercised in each of these areas but rather to emphasize that when the fivefold pattern is operating effectively, it will provide both inspiration and a structure in which everyone can find his or her niche. Mature leadership in each of these spheres is essen-tial, both for the ongoing development of diversified ministry and for ensuring that every leader shares the broader vision that encompasses all five spheres.

4. See Vitello, "Taking a Break"; National Public Radio, *Talk of the Nation*, "Clergy Members Suffer from Burnout, Poor Health," August 3, 2010; and Croucher, "Stress and Burnout in Ministry."

Leaders do more than instruct and exhort; they also embody their own teaching and serve as inspirational models. This is what Paul has in mind when he writes, "Brothers and sisters, join in imitating me, and observe those who live according to the example you have in us" (Phil. 3:17; see also 1 Cor. 11:1). They are to look to Paul and to those who have followed in his steps and contrast them with those who claim to be teachers but are in reality enemies of Christ (Phil. 3:18). Paul further urges them to "keep on doing the things that you have learned and received and heard and seen in me, and the God of peace will be with you" (Phil. 4:9). They are to continue doing everything that contributes to the kind of life that God requires of followers.

Every leader must serve as a model of Christlike character, but no single individual can provide a model for leadership in every sphere. We cannot impart to others what God never gave to us in the first place; neither should a leader succumb to the demands to lead in areas beyond his or her sphere of calling and gifting. It is the lead pastor's responsibility to ensure that effective leadership is in place in each of the five spheres of Ephesians 4, but he or she should not attempt to meet such comprehensive leadership demands personally.

Furthermore, leaders are to be examples of humility, not persons seeking to inflate their own sense of self-importance at the expense of those who lead in the other four spheres of ministry (1 Cor. 4:6). Every leader operates out of the grace of God. All that we have to contribute comes from the Lord, so there can be no ground for boasting. To the spiritually proud Corinthians, Paul sent the young Timothy to appeal to them to imitate Paul. He is very explicit about the ministry entrusted to Timothy: "For this reason I sent you Timothy, who is my beloved and faithful child in the Lord, to remind you of my ways in Christ Jesus, as I teach them everywhere in every church" (1 Cor. 4:17).

Paul's exhortations are as relevant today as when he first issued them. The majority of catastrophic failures in ministry arise out of character flaws rather than incompetence. They are also a consequence of ministers holding themselves aloof, without the safeguards of fellow believers to hold them accountable. Furthermore, the prevailing academic model of training has tended to neglect spiritual formation and character building. This oversight has serious consequences for the church.

Diversity in Gifting and Calling

Having emphasized the norm of the fivefold ministry as identified in Ephesians 4, we now look briefly at the wide range of gifts mentioned in the New Testament and see how they are clustered in order to actualize each of the spheres of ministry. In the absence of an appreciation of those five spheres of ministry, a stress on diversity of gifts easily leads to fragmentation. Individuals also become confused as to where they fit in the scheme of things. Placing clusters of gifts under these overarching ministries helps to counteract any tendency of individuals to focus on their giftedness and need for recognition by placing them within a team context and giving them a more comprehensive vision.

There are lists of gifts provided in the New Testament (1 Cor. 12:8–10, 28–30; Rom. 12:6–8), but these lists differ. As we have already noted, there is no single comprehensive list of gifts to be found in the New Testament. Even when a composite list is made, that list in all likelihood is not complete, though the diversity of gifts found on it is impressive: wisdom, knowledge, faith, healing, miracles, deeds of power, prophecy, discernment of spirits, tongues, assistance, leadership, ministry, exhortation, generosity, compassion. These gifts are simply illustrative of the manifold ministries of the ascended Lord operating through the church. It is difficult to be precise regarding the nature of some gifts because we have so little information, and a number appear to overlap. Which gifts will manifest at any given time or place will be determined by the needs of that ministry or mission context.

Diversity in ministry and the engagement of the total membership also emphasizes the need to exercise discernment in differentiating an authentic work of the Spirit from that which is simply ego-driven. Paul cautions the Thessalonians: "Do not quench the Spirit. Do not despise the words of prophets, but test everything" (1 Thess. 5:19–21). While prophetic ministry is not to be quenched, it is to be tested. Such testing entails discerning the origin of the prophetic claims and checking their agreement with the teaching of the apostles (2 Thess. 2:2). Are there biblical antecedents to what is being prophesied? Some prophets today claim extrabiblical revelation and even reject the plain teaching of Scripture that contradicts their prophecy.

Paul cautions the Corinthians against false apostles who proclaim a different gospel and demonstrate a different spirit, being proud and self-seeking (2 Cor. 11:1–15). He considers the situation particularly dangerous in Corinth because of the influence of false apostles, who are endeavoring to change fundamental beliefs rooted in the gospel. Their attack on Paul is particularly vicious in that it accuses him of propagating his message for personal gain. N. T. Wright comments concerning the situation in Corinth, "He [Paul] seems to have been very concerned that nobody in Achaea should ever be able to accuse him of preaching the gospel in order to get rich. Or perhaps (this is precisely the sort of point where we are reduced to guesswork) he was determined that nobody in Achaea should imagine that they owned him, that by paying him for his services they would be able to control him, to make him do things their way, or to trim his message to their tastes."[5]

In the churches Paul addressed, "professional" ministers did not lead church meetings. Everyone participated according to the gifts each had been given. On the one hand, room was made for spontaneous contributions; yet on the other hand, worship was to be orderly. Its purpose was to build up the whole body, not to provide individuals with opportunities for exhibitionism. Worship both then and now is participatory. Each person who has a gift should be given opportunity to exercise it, but not in a competitive spirit or in such a manner as would create disorder. Preventing such misuse is more difficult in a large congregation or one in which individuals are not accountable to one another. When we gather to worship God, each of us needs to bring all of our gifts, insights, and experiences with God.

Concern to Advance the Gospel

A pressing question that arises from a careful reading of Paul's letters relates to whether he expected local churches to participate in the Great Commission by continuing to evangelize or whether he believed this mandate was restricted to the apostles. In defense of the second position, some biblical commentators have noted that there is no evangelistic exhortation to be found in any of the letters. But James Ware challenges this narrow view in his detailed study of Philippians 1:12–2:18. In his exposition of the passage, Ware shows "that Paul understood the Philippians' partnership for the gospel to involve not only their financial support, but also their own missionizing activity for the extension of the gospel, and that Paul reflects throughout Philippians 1:12–2:18 upon the spread of the gospel throughout the Christian community. Paul in Philippians is specifically concerned, not only with his own apostolic mission, but with the participation of the Philippians and others in the work of spreading the gospel."[6]

Churches that are birthed under apostolic leadership share from day one their leaders' passion for the advance of the gospel, which explains the absence of exhortation to evangelize, in that they were already engaged in that urgent task. As Ware notes, such leadership zeal for evangelization was not confined to the apostle Paul but is unmistakably evident in the ministry of his coworkers and other apostles.[7] For further evidence of a young church

5. Wright, 2 Corinthians, 117–18.
6. Ware, Paul and the Mission of the Church, 170.
7. Ibid., 177.

engaging from its first days in spreading abroad the gospel, we turn to Paul's letter to the Thessalonians. "For the word of the Lord has sounded forth from you not only in Macedonia and Achaia, but in every place your faith in God has become known, so that we have no need to speak about it" (1 Thess. 1:8).

In regard to his own continuing ministry, Paul asks the Colossians for their prayers, "that God will open to us a door for the word, that we may declare the mystery of Christ, for which I am in prison, so that I may reveal it clearly, as I should" (Col. 4:3–4). Writing to the church in Rome, he speaks of his desire to "reap some harvest among you as I have among the rest of the Gentiles" (Rom. 1:13).

Paul's call from Christ to take the gospel to the Gentiles does not mean that he has turned his back on his own people. He expresses his continuing nagging concern for his fellow Jews to receive Christ. "I have great sorrow and unceasing anguish in my heart. For I could wish that I myself were accursed and cut off from Christ for the sake of my own people, my kindred according to the flesh" (Rom. 9:2–3). Here he reveals the heart of the evangelist, which is reinforced by his further statement, "Brothers and sisters, my heart's desire and prayer to God for them is that they may be saved" (Rom. 10:1).

So we see that Paul the apostle is concerned for the spreading of the knowledge of Christ everywhere (see also 2 Cor. 2:14–17). The continuing advance of the gospel should be the concern of every Christ-follower, because the good news of Christ is too important and life changing to keep to ourselves. The presence of apostolic leadership in the local church safeguards this priority; such leaders demonstrate a constant restlessness to reach out to new people in the name of Christ.

Paul distinguishes his own calling from that of Apollos, the scholarly teacher. While Paul's role is to plant the seed of the gospel, the role of Apollos, to change the metaphor, is to build upon the foundation that Paul has laid (1 Cor. 3:5–13). Each has an assigned task, whether to plant or to water. But whatever the role each plays, it is God who makes it grow. So one ministry must not be set against the other.

A key issue facing apostolic leadership is the need to consolidate while continuing to advance. Momentum lost in the interest of prolonged periods for consolidation is extremely difficult to regain. As a wise builder, Paul is aware of this tension. In his planting and building he is concerned that the plant survives and grows in a healthy manner and that the building is securely built on a firm foundation. Furthermore, the one who plants and the one who waters must not be set against each other, for "they have a common purpose" (1 Cor. 3:8). Those who follow on the heels of the apostle must ensure that they build on the foundation already laid, and with quality materials (1 Cor. 3:10–14). Shoddy workmanship will be exposed on the Lord's return, if not before.

Though the ministry of both pioneers and consolidators is essential, they are not to be the focus of attention. They all serve as "God's fellow workers" (1 Cor. 3:9 NIV). Paul, although an apostle, is not taken with his own importance, but acknowledges that all has been achieved through the grace of God. It was especially important for the Corinthians to grasp this point, as it appears many in the church were in danger of treating human teachers as their foundation. The only legitimate foundation is Jesus Christ.

Church leaders in any age are in no position to compete for authority. If Paul describes himself and his coworkers as "servants of Christ and stewards of God's mysteries" (1 Cor. 4:1), today's church leaders can claim no more. Paul's point is further emphasized when we realize that the Greek word rendered "stewards" here literally refers to enslaved under-rowers in a galley ship. Even such as these could be entrusted with great responsibility to manage the treasure in a rich storehouse.

By contrast, some self-proclaimed apostles today hold to a very authoritarian and controlling understanding of apostolic ministry. They develop empires and networks. Here in the West, such ministry is influenced by a personality and celebrity culture that has been part of our secular life in politics, business, education, and medicine. In each field strong personalities gather around them disciples of their way of thinking and acting. We in the church are partners not only with everyone at work in the church today but also with those who have gone before and those who are yet to come. We honor our predecessors and successors as well as our contemporaries.

Ambassadors for Christ

The church cannot remain content with confining its communication to talking to itself. Unless its members are prepared to respond to the call of God and to go into the world, people will have no opportunity to hear the message (Rom. 10:14–17). The continuing advance of the gospel requires sustained, bold initiatives. Yet it also requires statesmanlike wisdom and tact. Paul captures this aspect of groundbreaking ministry when he describes those who communicate the gospel as "ambassadors for Christ" (2 Cor. 5:20).

Ambassadors are called to faithfully represent the culture and policies of their countries. They are not operating according to self-interest or personal agendas and opinions. They have a message to communicate faithfully. Their skill lies in reading the local situation well and responding with the right approach and timing.

In the lead-up to this passage, Paul makes clear his own motivation. He operates out of a reverential fear of the Lord (2 Cor. 5:1), who will hold him accountable. Yet it is not fear that dominates his sense of calling to communicate the gospel. Rather, it is the love of Christ that urges on Paul and his companions. Because the heart of their message is that Christ died for all, they can no longer live for themselves (2 Cor. 5:14–15). No matter how adverse the personal circumstances of the Christians in Philippi, they are encouraged to "shine like stars in the world . . . by holding fast to the word of life" (Phil. 2:15–16).

Consequences of the Absence of Apostolic Leadership

We have traced Paul's passion for the sustained advance of the gospel in some detail in order to draw attention to the vision and motivation lost by churches that fail to recognize the continuing strategic significance of apostolic ministry. The recapturing of apostolic vision is especially urgent for post-Christendom Western churches.

Apostolic leaders provide new churches with a model and establish a DNA among those believers from day one. Those in Thessalonica who began by imitating Paul and his associates themselves became an example to all the believers in Macedonia and in Achaia. Through the irrepressible joy given by the Holy Spirit, they refused to be intimidated into silence by the hostile community that surrounded them. By contrast, the church today must face the challenging question, to what extent does silence mark our churches, such that we can easily be ignored? Every church is to become a place from which the message is broadcast far and wide.

Longing for Lives to Be Transformed by the Gospel

In Paul's day, traveling teachers carried letters of commendation to authenticate their ministry and credentials, as N. T. Wright explains: "The practice of writing letters of recommendation was a way of making sure that people who showed up out of the blue, claiming to be servants of Jesus the Messiah, were actually genuine."[8] Chafin makes the same point in reference to the book of Philemon: "Such letters were especially important in the days of the early church. This was the only way fledgling congregations had of knowing whether a new prophet or teacher who appeared on the scene had the right credentials and could be trusted. The Book of Philemon was such a letter, and

---

8. Wright, *1 Corinthians*, 26–27.

frequently at the close of his epistles Paul had a habit of commending certain people, and in other cases warning against them."[9]

In response to those in Corinth who were challenging his apostolic credentials, Paul declares that the fruit of his ministry is evident in the transformed lives of those who have come to faith. They are his letters of commendation: "You yourselves are our letter, written on our hearts, to be known and read by all; and you show that you are a letter of Christ, prepared by us, written not with ink but with the Spirit of the living God, not on tablets of stone but on tablets of human hearts" (2 Cor. 3:2–3). This transformation came about as a result of being exposed to the glory of the Lord, a process Paul sees both himself and the Corinthians undergoing. "And all of us, with unveiled faces, seeing the glory of the Lord as though reflected in a mirror, are being transformed into the same image from one degree of glory to another; for this comes from the Lord, the Spirit" (2 Cor. 3:18). To receive divine glory in our earthly life anticipates our being like Christ in the next life (Rom. 8:29; 1 Cor. 15:51).

Paul's emphasis on the transformation of lives as an essential fruit of his ministry provides a necessary corrective to those who overemphasize numerical growth. If converts continue to live in conformity to the world's standards, then numerical growth has little spiritual significance. By contrast, Paul anguishes over his converts—that their lives might be transformed. The process of transformation will take time; they must come to "maturity."

Such transformation entails the renewing of their minds. So Paul exhorts the believers in Rome, "Do not be conformed to this world, but be transformed by the renewing of your minds, so that you may discern what is the will of God—what is good and acceptable and perfect" (Rom. 12:2). The renewal of the mind leads to the transformation of a person's life, as Paul emphasizes to the Ephesians: "You were taught to put away your former way of life, your old self, corrupt and deluded by its lusts, and to be renewed in the spirit of your minds, and to clothe yourselves with the new self, created according to the likeness of God in true righteousness and holiness" (Eph. 4:22–24).

How is this transformation to be realized? At the spiritual level, it will be brought about only by the action of the Holy Spirit in the lives of individuals and in the community of faith. At the structural level, preaching to a largely passive audience does not result in peoples' lives being transformed. Preaching and teaching may inform, inspire, and motivate, but there must be a corresponding response structure in place.

Transformation mainly takes place in small groups, which provide opportunity to apply teaching to real-life situations, as well as encouragement and

9. Chafin, *1, 2 Corinthians*, 216.

accountability. These groups offer the kind of structure we explored in the previous chapter. They are not a luxury for the spiritual elite in a congregation but a necessity for all. When we examined the structure of churches in New Testament times, we noted that these churches were small and that the members were well known to one another and all played an active part. No one remained a mere consumer.

Ministry cannot be divorced from discipleship. Within small groups, diverse expressions of ministry emerge as individuals in the group discover and are affirmed in their spiritual gifting. Within each fellowship and ministry context, some will emerge as leaders in their fields. This comes about not through an academic approach to ministry preparation but through establishing an apprenticeship model. Because groups are made up of people that relate to one another regularly—in the neighborhood, at work, or in shared interests—they strongly emphasize applying the truths of the gospel in daily life. This approach is in keeping with the very nature of the New Testament, which largely represents applied theology.

Spiritual formation consists of the integration of teaching and application through discernment given by the Holy Spirit. It is the result of the breaking down of the dichotomy of the sacred and the secular. Transformation takes place as individuals become involved in a church's mission in the wider community. Many people testify that their engagement in service projects in company with a group of Christians—for example, feeding the hungry, constructing homes for the homeless, working in orphanages—led to their appreciating the life-transforming impact of the gospel and to their personal commitment to Christ.

This essential process for churches must also be demonstrated in the seminary preparation of those who will lead congregations. The traditional academic models tend to be strong in the area of rational intelligence but weak in terms of relational intelligence. Consequently, many churches reflect the same relational weakness. Ministries emerge out of transformational relationships, and out of these ministries leadership comes to the fore.

Motivation for Ministry

There are many unworthy motivations for ministry. Some individuals become involved to strive for recognition and public acclaim. Others are driven by a desire for power over others within the fellowship or by personal, hidden agendas. Still others engage in ministry as a means of sexual entrapment.

Paul has to constantly make plain that his own motives are pure. For instance, he calls upon the Thessalonians to join in God's assessment of his motives as honest and devout. He lives under God's continuing scrutiny, which goes beyond merely observing his actions to testing his heart (1 Thess. 2:3–6). Paul does not make financial demands among those he ministers to but works hard to provide his own support (1 Thess. 2:9–10; 2 Thess. 3:8; 1 Cor. 4:12; 2 Cor. 11:9; Acts 20:34). He is motivated, not by his own accomplishments, but by the evidence of the power of the gospel in the lives of those who have come to Christ and grown in Christ through his own ministry. They are his pride and joy (1 Thess. 2:19–20).

Such approval, whether from God or the churches, is not a once-for-all matter. Paul cannot presume upon it because motivation can change over time and in response to fresh challenges. All who are engaged in any form of ministry, and especially those in leadership, must honestly face the following question: what determines my relationships with those among whom I minister—do I regard them as there for my benefit, or am I ministering with their needs constantly in view?

Training Members to Think and Act Missionally

It is a challenge to lead a congregation from being self-focused to appreciating that true worship leads to mission precisely because "God so loved the world that he gave his only Son, so that everyone who believes in him may not perish but may have eternal life" (John 3:16). From Genesis to Revelation, the reader is presented with the God of mission.[10] Mission is not a marginal activity or department of the church but its very heartbeat. As has often been quoted, "It is not the church of God that has a mission, but the God of mission who has a church." Francis DuBose clarifies the distinction even further: "What is needed is not so much a theology of mission but a missional theology. In other words, mission does not so much need to be justified theologically as theology needs to be understood missiologically."[11]

The church in the West has been so locked into the Christendom mind-set and structure that it struggles to reimagine the church in a post-Christendom environment in which it enjoys no special privileges and has to redefine itself in terms of its mission in the world. The capacity to use imagination and the nerve to take risks are in short supply in most of our churches. Yet creativity and imagination are crucial not only for the survival of the church but also for the revitalization of its world-transforming mission.

10. See Wright, *Mission of God.*
11. DuBose, *God Who Sends: A Fresh Quest for Biblical Mission* (Nashville: Broadman, 1983), 148–49, quoted in Van Gelder and Zscheile, *Missional Church in Perspective,* 44.

Sir Ken Robinson, who was knighted in the United Kingdom for his work in imagination and education, provides a critique of academic programs preparing people for industry and commerce, one that could well be applied to the training of pastors and other church leaders. "Employers are complaining that academic programmes from schools to universities simply don't teach what people now need to know and be able to do. They want people who can think intuitively, who are imaginative and innovative, who can communicate well, work in teams and are flexible, adaptable and self-confident. The traditional academic curriculum is simply not designed to produce such people."[12]

It is no wonder that the church struggles under leadership trained to meet the challenges and opportunities of yesterday rather than capitalize on the possibilities of today. A strong rationalistic bias emphasizes analysis and critique at the expense of imagination and creativity. As we noted in chapter 1, Sir Ken Robinson draws attention to the fact that during times of paradigm transition, when everything is changing around us, leaders must be able to engage their chaotic environment with discernment, imagination, and creativity. "Creativity is a basic human attribute that must be nurtured among all people, not just artists and scientists. The freedom to learn, to create, to take risks, to fail or to ask questions, to strive, to grow; this is the ethic upon which the United States was founded. Promoting creativity among all people of all occupations, economic classes and ethnic backgrounds is essential for the common good."[13]

During the past fifty years, we have seen tremendous advances in evangelical scholarship. The advance is evident in the quantity and quality of scholarly theological books published by evangelicals, the appointment of evangelicals to academic chairs in major universities, and the contributions evangelicals make in the Society for Biblical Literature and other professional associations. But in making these gains we seem to have lost something important along the way—namely, the evangelistic passion that was expressed and exemplified by the apostle Paul and that permeated the early church.

An older generation of evangelicals spoke about and demonstrated what they called "a passion for souls." Charles E. Fuller, one of the cofounders of the seminary in which I taught for twenty-five years, was propelled by this passion. The challenge facing seminaries is how to recapture this evangelistic passion without losing our zeal for scholarly excellence. If the church leaders we are training are not on fire with evangelistic passion, they are unlikely to ignite the churches they serve. Professor David Wenham provides a theological

12. Robinson, *Out of Our Minds*, 52.
13. Ibid., 195.

undergirding of this apostolic priority when he writes, "Given Jesus' own urgent sense of a new day of salvation dawning, it is only logical that he should have shared his ministry with others. There is no reason to doubt that the religion of Jesus was a 'missionary' or 'apostolic' religion from the start."[14] In our day, there is a growing realization that the church must learn to think and act as a missional movement instead of a static institution.[15]

Prepared for Self-Sacrifice

Especially during times of cultural upheaval and numerical church decline, both leaders and members of local churches must be prepared for self-sacrifice. No longer can those preparing for ministry in our seminaries assume they will be called to a church at the successful conclusion of their training. Instead of being *given* a church, they may have to *grow* one, which means there would be no group present at the outset that could pay their salary or provide a budget for the church. Most will have to undertake bivocational ministry until a faith community with sufficient resources has been established.

Paul provides a pioneering example of self-sacrifice. He has the right to support from those he has introduced to Christ and formed into faith communities, yet he sets aside those rights. He mentions three specific rights to the Corinthians: "the right to our food and drink," "the right to be accompanied by a believing wife," and the "right to refrain from working for a living" (1 Cor. 9:4–6). Although he and his coworkers have these rights, they are prepared to give them up for the sake of the gospel. Such a humble attitude of self-sacrifice challenges contemporary Christians who have become part of the entitlement generation. Guided by self-interest, these Christians lay down conditions before getting involved in ministry.

In the same letter, however, Paul reminds the Corinthians of their obligation to those who have set aside other sources of income in order to minister among them: "Who at any time pays the expenses for doing military service? Who plants a vineyard and does not eat any of its fruit? Or who tends a flock and does not get any of its milk?" (1 Cor. 9:7). Church leaders' willingness to forgo their rights must not be abused by churches.

14. Wenham, *Paul*, 166.

15. See Gibbs, *ChurchMorph*, which provides five chapters (chaps. 3–7), each of which identifies and evaluates one of these movements in the contemporary church: fresh expressions of church within traditional denominations; the growing number and significance of megachurches; urban engagement; resurgent monasticism; and expanding networks.

Urgency of the Need for Multiplying Ministry

New Testament churches were strongly encouraged to undertake mutual ministry, as we can see from the many "one another" passages. For a number of reasons, mutual ministry is especially needed today. To cite just one instance, the increased frequency of cohabitation and divorce has put additional strains on families, especially children. Providing counseling for dysfunctional and broken families has become extremely time consuming and perplexing and is not something a faith community can hope to accomplish alone.

A further complicating factor arises from cultural transitions from one generation to the next. Within many congregations, four generations are represented, each of which has been profoundly affected by life experiences. The *builder* generation was profoundly impacted by the Great Depression, the Second World War, the building of the giant industries, and women taking the place of their soldier husbands in war production. The *boomer* generation enjoyed the postwar affluence, with many moving to the suburbs and naively equating a rising standard of living with increased quality of life. The *Generations X and Y* were born into the information age, with access both to powerful search engines linking them to all they need to know and to instant communication through social-networking sites. Furthermore, today's young people are experiencing high unemployment, with many high school graduates unable to afford a four-year university or even a local community college because of economic cutbacks. The challenge facing local church leaders is to explain the distinguishing features of each of these generations, in order to help perplexed parents and grandparents understand the younger generation and their assumptions and challenges.

The social needs of the twenty-first century are no more severe than those of the first century. Paul recognized the urgent need to establish a climate within the newly established faith communities in which ministry among the members would emerge promptly and naturally. He expresses his joy for the Philippians' partnership in the gospel. They partnered with him in practical ways, by sending money for food and other needs while Paul was in jail on account of the gospel. These new believers were also proclaiming the gospel by their verbal testimony and their manner of life (Phil. 1:27; 2:16). Paul treated new believers not as dependents but as partners.

Ministry must not be confined to a professional team or to a spiritual elite. It should arise from within each local faith community. Leadership must be fostered intentionally in response to the Spirit calling and equipping individuals for diverse avenues of service. Their calling should not be restricted to serving the needs of existing members; in response to the mission of God, it should extend into the surrounding community and beyond.

Such ministry flows from relationships. Within every community of believers, each person begins to make his or her distinctive contribution as needs arise among the members and in response to the group's broader vision of ministry and mission in the community. As these ministries multiply, leadership emerges among persons who set a course and provide a vision that inspires others. By this process, churches move away from passive dependence on a professionally trained single pastor or pastoral team. "The de-centering of leadership from solo clergy to polycentric teams not only reflects a renewed emphasis on the variety of spiritual gifts within the community and the emergence of a more participatory culture in postmodernity, but it also invites a more thoroughly trinitarian imagination for the church as created in the Trinity's image."[16]

Even when Paul acknowledges the formal leaders of a church, such as elders, bishops, and deacons (as when he specifically mentions "bishops and deacons" in Phil. 1:1), he goes on to address the whole church in which each member shares in ministry. Gordon Fee comments on the opening verse of Philippians, "After being singled out in the address, they [bishops and deacons] are not hereafter mentioned or spoken to. They are simply reckoned as being within the community. When they are singled out, as here, the leaders are not 'over' the church but are addressed along with the rest."[17]

In emphasizing homegrown leadership, the contemporary church, following the example of the churches planted by Paul and the other first-century evangelists, has to address the issues of respect for and acceptance of the leaders that have emerged among the members. Paul requires the Thessalonians to respect the newly appointed homegrown leaders among them (1 Thess. 5:12–13). Envy can easily arise when one person within an intimate group is recognized as a leader. Because members in such groups live so closely together, it is all too easy for new leaders to ruffle feathers!

As leaders emerge, a number of factors need to be taken into consideration, including principally, the four Cs: *character*, *competence*, *charisma*, and *commitment*.[18] Of these qualities, the New Testament places the greatest emphasis on character. Without a godly character, trust is quickly eroded.

Stephen Covey emphasizes the need for trustworthiness by drawing attention to the high costs of the erosion of trust and the difficulty of reestablishing it.

---

16. Van Gelder and Zscheile, *Missional Church in Perspective*, 157.
17. Fee, *Philippians*, 42.
18. For a more comprehensive list of essential leadership traits, see Gibbs, *LeadershipNext*, chap. 6.

Compliance is no adequate substitute for trust. Covey uses the following illustration to highlight the importance of trust, which is an often hidden variable:

> One time I hired a guide to take me fly fishing in Montana. As I looked over the river, he said, "Tell me what you see." Basically I told him I saw a beautiful river with sun reflecting off the surface of the water. He asked, "Do you see any fish?" I replied that I did not. Then my guide handed me a pair of polarized sunglasses. "Put these on," he said. Suddenly everything looked dramatically different. As I looked at the river, I discovered I could see *through* the water. And I could see fish—a lot of fish! My excitement shot up. Suddenly I could sense enormous possibility that I had not seen before. In reality, those fish were there all along, but until I put on the glasses, they were hidden from my view.
>
> In the same way, for most people, trust is hidden from view. They have no idea how present and pervasive the impact of trust is in every relationship, in every organization, in every interaction, in every moment of life. But once they put on "trust glasses" and see what's going on under the surface, it immediately impacts their ability to increase their effectiveness in every dimension of life.[19]

Paul reminds the Thessalonians, "You know what kind of persons we proved to be among you for your sake" (1 Thess. 1:5). He could also call upon them to bear witness, along with God, to "how pure, upright, and blameless our conduct was toward you believers" (1 Thess. 2:10). Trust depends on character. Is this person consistent and aboveboard? Is this leader motivated by self-interest or by concern for those he or she is leading? These questions are pertinent today, given the prevalence of outwardly successful pastors and leaders later exposed as sexually immoral or financially corrupt. Their exposure brings devastating consequences for themselves and their congregations and drags the whole church into disrepute.

Incompetence and lack of commitment can also undermine trust. Covey provides the balance: "Trust is a function of two things: character and *competence*. Character includes your integrity, your motive, your intent with people. Competence includes your capabilities, your skills, your results, your track record. And both are vital."[20] Leaders who provide visionary leadership only to suddenly disappear from the scene leave their churches in a state of disarray and feeling abandoned. Although Paul is frequently on the move in his apostolic ministry, he assures the churches that he continues to have them in his heart (2 Cor. 7:3; Phil. 1:7–8). He appreciates that trust rests on accountability.

19. Covey, *Speed of Trust*, 19–20.
20. Ibid., 30.

Throughout this chapter we have emphasized the priority of generating leadership that embodies the mission élan of the apostle Paul and translates into a passion shared by congregations. Ministry and mission are the calling of the whole people of God. Every person plays a part according to his or her calling, passion, and gifting.

Summary and Conclusions

The opening chapter suggested that the social, economic, and spiritual crisis facing Western societies cannot be adequately addressed by central government. Whether that government is run by the Left or by the Right makes no difference; neither grapples adequately with the complex problems of a dysfunctional society marked by individualism and rampant consumerism. The prophetic tradition, evident in the Hebrew prophets and the message of Jesus taken up by the early church, contains elements of protest and vision and the challenge to move from highlighting the problems to becoming part of the solution.

Whether from the political Left or Right, the radical voices of protest raised by people taking to the streets or "tweeting" online provide powerful evidence of the depth of frustration and anger felt by people of all ages and sections of society. The outstanding question remains, however: having expressed their anger in identifying the problems, how can they become part of the solution? It is this transition that moves protest toward prophecy.

Issues of powerlessness have to be addressed so that the church's vision is shaped, translated, and owned from the ground level up, by the formation of communities made up of people who know and care about one another. This book represents the viewpoint that churches, working alongside other locally grounded groups, have the potential to make a significant contribution to the realization of such communities. The strategy proposed here does not call for reinstating the old Constantinian model from below but recognizes that most Western societies are pluralistic and that the church must work alongside other faith-based groups and whoever shares the vision of replacing an individualistic and consumerist society with one that develops networks of relationships.

This book has focused on urban environments because the early church was predominantly an urban movement. We compared and contrasted the Greco-Roman world of Paul's day with the urban reality of the twenty-first century in order to appreciate the similarities and differences between Paul's pioneering work of establishing faith communities around the Eastern Mediterranean and the challenges facing urban pioneers today. His context was pre-Christendom and preindustrial, while ours is post-Christendom and increasingly postindustrial, but awash with information and interconnected by digital technology. Contemporary mission communities need the skills to exegete the city and come to terms with the complex nature of urban societies.

We noted that the early church was a dynamic movement that birthed reproducible household churches and contrasted this with the largely static historic denominations and new independent congregations of our time. If the churches are to establish networks of faith communities as a significant part of the revitalizing of local communities, they have to find ways to translate Paul's strategy into urban contexts. What can we learn from the apostle about connecting and providing resources for churches as they engage in mission and ministry?

As Western societies undergo significant transition from Christian to post-Christian, churches will need abundant resources to deepen their understanding of the gospel and to promote obedience in every sphere of life. As their core beliefs are relentlessly challenged, churches will need to know how to defend them and to appreciate afresh their significance and the consequences of surrendering them.

The next two chapters examined the significance of relationship building in creating healthy and robust communities of faith in which disciples are formed. Finally, we addressed the importance of every member sharing in the ministry of his or her faith community. The involvement, commitment, and creativity of churches would provide models of community challenging both the individualism and the consumerism of Western societies.

In addition to supporting one another, such faith communities carry gospel values into the surrounding neighborhoods. Hopefully such a sustained missional engagement will make a significant contribution in bringing about a transformative impact as "salt" and "light." As each faith community gives birth to other faith communities, a network is formed that provides a context for identifying and developing leaders to serve not only in the church but also in the wider community.

In the forgoing chapters, we have covered a wide range of topics precisely because Paul's letters are extensive in their concerns and insights. The following distillation of that teaching attempts to identify the necessary elements of a transformative church. These elements are evident in Paul's letters to the young churches, from which much older churches have much to learn.

So here are six defining characteristics of a congregation making up a faithful local church as indicated by Paul's letters. The list is applicable to churches in every age.

1. *Relational*: churches that are not just a gathering of individuals, but a community of people who love and support one another and hold one another accountable;

2. *Reproducible*: churches that demonstrate the necessary vision, motivation, resources, and freedom to give birth to new faith communities;

3. *Incarnational*: churches that manifest a variety of expressions appropriate to their context and calling;

4. *Faithful*: churches that are committed wholeheartedly to the mission of Paul in seeking to translate the message of Jesus from its original Jewish (in our case "ecclesial") context to the contemporary world;

5. *Resourceful*: churches that rely upon the empowerment and gifting of the risen Lord made available through the Holy Spirit, who indwells every member individually and each church corporately;

6. *Hopeful*: churches that are filled with assurance grounded in Christ's resurrection and oriented toward his personal return to earth.

Conclusion:

Local congregations must endeavor to
engage their total membership in ministry to
one another and in mission to the world.

May the Lord, who is the head of the church and the lord of all creation, grant that these elements will increasingly characterize the church as anticipatory signs of God's coming reign on earth!

Bibliography

Anderson, Ray S. *An Emergent Theology for Emerging Churches*. Downers Grove, IL: InterVarsity, 2006.

Archbishop's Council on Mission and Public Affairs. *Mission-Shaped Church: Church Planting and Fresh Expressions of Church in a Changing Context*. London: Church House, 2004.

Bailey, Kenneth E. *Paul through Mediterranean Eyes*. Downers Grove, IL: IVP Academic, 2011.

Beale, G. K. *1–2 Thessalonians*. Downers Grove, IL: IVP Academic, 2003.

Blond, Phillip. *Radical Republic: How Left and Right Have Broken the System and How We Can Fix It*. New York: W. W. Norton & Company, 2012.

———. *Red Tory: How Left and Right Have Broken Britain and How We Can Fix It*. London: Faber and Faber, 2010.

Brooks, David. "The Broken Society." *New York Times*, March 19, 2010, New York edition, A25.

Bruce, F. F. *The Book of Acts*. Grand Rapids: Eerdmans, 1954.

Chafin, Kenneth L. *1, 2 Corinthians*. Nashville: Thomas Nelson, 1985.

Covey, Stephen M. R. *The Speed of Trust*. With Rebecca R. Merrill. New York: Free Press, 2006.

Crouch, Andy. *Culture Making: Recovering Our Creative Calling*. Downers Grove, IL: InterVarsity, 2008.

Croucher, Rowland. "Stress and Burnout in Ministry." http://www.churchlink.com.au/churchlink /forum/r_croucher/stress_burnout.html (accessed December 10, 2012).

Davis, Lindsey. *Ode to a Banker*. New York: Time Warner Books, 2001.

Deiros, P. A. "Apostolicity, Contemporary." In *Global Dictionary of Theology*, edited by William A. Dyrness and Veli-Matti Kärkkäinen, 60–61. Downers Grove, IL: IVP Academic, 2008.

DeYoung, Kevin, and Greg Gilbert. *What Is the Mission of the Church?* Wheaton, IL: Crossway, 2011.

Drucker, Peter. *Adventures of a Bystander*. 1978. Reprint, New York, NY: HarperCollins, 1990.

Fee, Gordon D. *Philippians*. Downers Grove, IL: IVP Academic, 1999.

Ferguson, Everett. *Backgrounds of Early Christianity*. 3rd ed. Grand Rapids: Eerdmans, 2003.

Frost, Michael, and Alan Hirsch. *The Shaping of Things to Come: Innovation and Mission for the 21st-Century Church*. Peabody, MA: Hendrickson; Erina, Australia: Strand Publishing, 2003.

Fryling, Robert A. *The Leadership Ellipse*. Downers Grove, IL: InterVarsity, 2010.

Garner, Martin. *A Call for Apostles Today*. Cambridge, UK: Grove Books Limited, 2007.

Gehring, Roger W. *House Church and Mission: The Importance of Household Structure in Early Christianity*. Peabody, MA: Hendrickson, 2004.

Gibbs, Eddie. *ChurchMorph: How Megatrends Are Reshaping Christian Communities*. Grand Rapids: Baker Academic, 2009.

———. *ChurchNext: Quantum Changes in How We Do Ministry*. Downers Grove, IL: InterVarsity, 2000.

———. *I Believe in Church Growth*. Grand Rapids: Eerdmans; London: Hodder and Stoughton, 1981.

———. *LeadershipNext: Changing Leaders in a Changing Culture*. Downers Grove, IL: InterVarsity, 2005.

Grant, Michael. *The Ancient Mediterranean*. New York: Charles Scribner's Sons, 1969.

Guder, Darrell L. *The Continuing Conversion of the Church*. Grand Rapids: Eerdmans, 2000.

———, ed. *Missional Church: A Vision for the Sending of the Church in North America*. Grand Rapids: Eerdmans, 1998.

Hansen, G. Walter. *Galatians*. Downers Grove, IL: IVP Academic, 1994.

Hirsch, Alan. *The Forgotten Ways: Reactivating the Missional Church*. Grand Rapids: Brazos; Erina, Australia: Strand Publishing, 2006.

Hirsch, Alan, and Tim Catchim. *The Permanent Revolution: Apostolic Imagination and Practice for the 21st-Century Church*. San Francisco: Jossey-Bass, 2012.

Hirsch, Alan, and Lance Ford. *Right Here, Right Now: Everyday Mission for Everyday People*. Grand Rapids: Baker Books, 2011.

Hirsch, Alan, and Debra Hirsch. *Untamed: Reactivating a Missional Form of Discipleship*. Grand Rapids: Baker Books, 2010.

Hunter, James Davison. *To Change the World: The Irony, Tragedy, and Possibility of Christianity in the Late Modern World*. New York: Oxford University Press, 2010.

Jongkind, Dirk. "Corinth in the First Century AD: The Search for Another Class." *Tyndale Bulletin* 52, no. 1 (2001): 139–48.

Kreider, Alan, and Eleanor Kreider. *Worship and Mission after Christendom*. Milton Keynes, UK: Paternoster, 2009.

Küng, Hans. *The Church*. New York: Burns and Oates, 1968.

Kynaston, David. *Austerity Britain, 1945–51*. London: Bloomsbury, 2007.

———. *Family Britain, 1951–57*. New York: Walker & Co., 2009.

Leithart, Peter J. *Against Christianity*. Moscow, ID: Canon, 2003.

———. *Defending Constantine: The Twilight of an Empire and the Dawn of Christendom*. Downers Grove, IL: IVP Academic, 2010.

Ling, Roger. "The Arts of Living." In *Oxford History of the Classical World*, edited by John Boardman, Jasper Griffin, and Oswyn Murray, 718–47. New York: Oxford University Press, 1986.

Maggay, Melba P. "The Message of Galatians." In *The Bible for Everyday Life*, edited by George Carey, 245–47. Grand Rapids: Eerdmans, 1988.

Matthews, John. "Roman Life and Society." In *Oxford History to the Classical World*, edited by John Boardman, Jasper Griffin, and Oswyn Murray, 748–70. New York: Oxford University Press, 1986.

McGavran, Donald A. *Understanding Church Growth*. Grand Rapids: Eerdmans, 1970.

McKechnie, Paul. *The First Christian Centuries: Perspectives on the Early Church*. Downers Grove, IL: IVP Academic, 2001.

McLaren, Brian. Foreword to *An Emergent Theology for Emerging Churches* by Ray S. Anderson. Downers Grove, IL: InterVarsity, 2006.

Meeks, Wayne A. *The First Urban Christians*. New York: Yale University Press, 1983.

Meggitt, Justin J. *Paul, Poverty and Survival*. Edinburgh: T&T Clark, 1998.

Mellor, Ronald, and Marni McGee. *The Ancient Roman World*. New York: Oxford University Press, 2004.

Mouw, Richard J. *Uncommon Decency: Christian Civility in an Uncivil World*. Rev. ed. Downers Grove, IL: InterVarsity, 2010.

Murray, Oswyn. "Life and Society in Classical Greece." In *Oxford History to the Classical World*, edited by John Boardman, Jasper Griffin, and Oswyn Murray, 204–33. New York: Oxford University Press, 1986.

Newbigin, Lesslie. *Lesslie Newbigin, Missionary Theologian: A Reader*. Compiled and introduced by Paul Weston. Grand Rapids: Eerdmans; London: SPCK, 2006.

Pagitt, Doug. *Church in the Inventive Age*. Minneapolis: Sparkhouse, 2010.

Patzia, Arthur G. *The Emergence of the Church: Context, Growth, Leadership and Worship*. Downers Grove, IL: IVP Academic, 2001.

Peterson, David G. *The Acts of the Apostles*. Grand Rapids: Eerdmans, 2009.

Purcell, Nicholas. "The Arts of Government." In *Oxford History to the Classical World*, edited by John Boardman, Jasper Griffin, and Oswyn Murray, 560–91. New York: Oxford University Press, 1986.

Rackham, Richard B. *The Acts of the Apostles*. London: Methuen, 1901.

Robinson, Ken. *Out of Our Minds: Learning to Be Creative*. Chichester, UK: Capstone, 2001.

———. "Schools Kill Our Creativity." TED talk, February 2006. www.ted.com/talks/ken _robinson_says_schools_kill_creativity.html.

Roozen, David A. *A Decade of Change in American Congregations, 2000–2010*. Hartford, CT: Hartford Institute of Religion Research, 2011. http://faithcommunitiestoday.org/decade-change.

Roxburgh, Alan J., and Fred Romanuk. *The Missional Leader: Equipping Your Church to Reach a Changing World*. San Francisco: Jossey-Bass, 2006.

Stark, Rodney. *The Rise of Christianity: How the Obscure, Marginal, Jesus Movement Became the Dominant Religious Force in the Western World*. San Francisco: HarperCollins, 1996.

———. *The Victory of Reason: How Christianity Led to Freedom, Capitalism, and Western Success*. New York: Random House, 2006.

Stockton, David. "The Founding of the Empire." In *Oxford History to the Classical World*, edited by John Boardman, Jasper Griffin, and Oswyn Murray, 531–59. New York: Oxford University Press, 1986.

Stott, John R. W. *The Message of Ephesians*. Downers Grove, IL: InterVarsity, 1984.

———. *The Message of 1 & 2 Thessalonians*. Downers Grove, IL: InterVarsity, 1991.

———. *The Message of Galatians*. Downers Grove, IL: InterVarsity, 1968.

Tickle, Phyllis. *The Great Emergence: How Christianity Is Changing and Why*. Grand Rapids: Baker Books, 2008.

Van Gelder, Craig, and Dwight J. Zscheile. *The Missional Church in Perspective: Mapping Trends and Shaping the Conversation.* Grand Rapids: Baker Academic, 2011.

Vitello, Paul. "Taking a Break from the Lord's Work." *New York Times,* August 1, 2010, New York edition.

Ware, James P. *Paul and the Mission of the Church: Philippians in Ancient Jewish Context.* Grand Rapids: Baker Academic, 2011.

Wenham, David. *Paul: Follower of Jesus or Founder of Christianity?* Grand Rapids: Eerdmans, 1995.

Wright, Christopher J. H. *The Mission of God.* Downers Grove, IL: IVP Academic, 2006.

Wright, N. T. *After You Believe: Why Christian Character Matters.* New York: HarperOne, 2010.

———. *Paul for Everyone: 1 Corinthians.* Louisville: Westminster John Knox, 2004.

———. *Paul for Everyone: 2 Corinthians.* Louisville: Westminster John Knox, 2004.

Index

257